More Praise for *The Time Cure*

"*The Time Cure* offers a major innovative contribution to the treatment of post-traumatic stress disorder. Professor Zimbardo combines his unparalleled psychological knowledge and insight with the Swords' vast clinical experience to provide an important new way forward to a more positive and fulfilling life for those who have suffered the ravages of war, sexual assault, and other horrific experiences. The authors present compelling empirical evidence as well as evocative and engaging case studies demonstrating the miraculous power of shifting time perspective from a negative past into a positive future to create comfort and relief. Even when everything else has failed, this treatment modeling can supply hope and healing for those who deserve it most. This book should be read by all those who have suffered from these conditions and all those seeking to treat them in an ethical, effective, responsible and compassionate manner."
— **Rose McDermott,** professor of Political Science, Brown University

"*The Time Cure* is a magnificent offering to the PTSD literature. It is destined to become a classic and no serious researcher or clinical professional in the field of psychological post-trauma should be without a copy on their bookshelves. With the burgeoning number of war veterans with PTSD as well as traumatized individuals from other walks of life, this timely book can be generalized to a wide variety of settings and situations. The essential truth behind its effectiveness and impact — that is, how we suffer depends on the extent to which we perceive, handle, and embrace the past, present, and future — guarantees a high receptivity and impact among PTSD sufferers. Dr. Philip Zimbardo is one of psychology's finest and needs no introduction; Dr. Sword and Rosemary Sword are outstanding clinicians and founders of a PTSD temporal therapy movement in Hawaii that has the solid support of the veteran population, international organizations, and the mental health community at large."
— **Harold Hall, Ph.D., ABPP, APN,** editor, *Terrorism: Strategies for Intervention*; director, Pacific Institute for the Study of Conflict and Aggression

"*The Time Cure* is filled with touching stories, exciting transformations and helpful information. The Swords and Dr. Zimbardo have done a stupendous job helping people in distress. I will definitely recommend *The Time Cure* to my colleagues and patients."

—**Mel Borins, M.D.** and author, St. Joseph's Health Centre, Toronto, Canada; Fellow, College of Family Physicians of Canada; associate professor, Department of Family and Community Medicine, University of Toronto

"*The Time Cure* offers an alternative to the most widely prescribed therapies for PTSD that, due to their revisiting of painful past experiences, often drive clients away before long-lasting healing can begin. Unable to return to therapy and tormented by their symptoms, veterans and other sufferers live in a trauma-centered personal hell that impacts every aspect of their lives and the lives of those around them. Time Perspective Therapy utilizes cognitive tools that empower users to refocus thoughts into more productive pathways that lead out of the negative past into a more hopeful, goal-directed future. Those using TPT are enthusiastic and excited about continuing their treatment due to the positive outcomes they experience. This promising new methodology could revolutionize the manner in which PTSD is treated."

—**Don Kopf, Ph.D.,** psychologist, Positive Potential Counseling & Consulting, Honolulu, Hawaii

the time cure

the time cure

overcoming PTSD with the new psychology of time perspective therapy

philip g. zimbardo
richard m. sword
rosemary k. m. sword

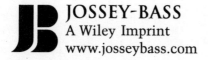

JOSSEY-BASS
A Wiley Imprint
www.josseybass.com

Published by Jossey-Bass
A Wiley Imprint
One Montgomery Street, Suite 1200, San Francisco, CA 94104-4594—www.josseybass.com

Jossey-Bass books and products are available through most bookstores. To contact Jossey-Bass directly call our Customer Care Department within the U.S. at 800-956-7739, outside the U.S. at 317-572-3986, or fax 317-572-4002.

Wiley publishes in a variety of print and electronic formats and by print-on-demand. Some material included with standard print versions of this book may not be included in e-books or in print-on-demand. If this book refers to media such as a CD or DVD that is not included in the version you purchased, you may download this material at http://booksupport.wiley.com. For more information about Wiley products, visit www.wiley.com.

Library of Congress Cataloging-in-Publication Data
Zimbardo, Philip G.
    The time cure: overcoming PTSD with the new psychology of time perspective therapy / Philip G. Zimbardo, Richard M. Sword, Rosemary K.M. Sword. – 1st ed.
        p.; cm.
    Includes bibliographical references and index.
    ISBN 978-1-118-20567-9 (cloth); ISBN 978-1-118-28529-9 (ebk.);
ISBN 978-1-118-28229-8 (ebk.); ISBN 978-1-118-28292-2 (ebk.)
I. Sword, Richard M., 1947- II. Sword, Rosemary K. M., 1955- III. Title.
1. Post-traumatic stress disorder – Treatment. 2. Time perspective – Psychological aspects.
    RC552.P67
    616.85′21 – dc23

                                                                                2012030112

Printed in the United States of America
FIRST EDITION
HB Printing   10 9 8 7 6 5 4 3 2 1

contents

dedicated to my son, adam, in part for making me a
grandfather through his newly minted children—philip (aka
panda) and victoria (aka hopper)—who will carry on the
zimbardo legacy into the hopefully bright future
—**phil zimbardo**

for our families, our clients, and you, the reader
—**rick and rose sword**

introduction

Some years ago a young man I'll call James came to see me in my Stanford University office for help with his shyness. In the course of our conversation about the origins of his awkwardness around people, he told me that almost everyone he met reminded him of someone who had hurt him or rejected him in the past, so he could not risk being open to them. And then he related a very interesting image: his life, he said, was organized around the eighty slides that he had arrayed in what he called his "Kodak Carousel mental slide projector." Once the slide show started, the images were projected into his current consciousness in a predictable and reliable sequence. So his present sense was the slide on his mind's screen, his past sense was the slide he just viewed, and his future sense was determined by the slide or slides coming up next. My first thought was that this seemed like a reasonable metaphor for memory.

What he told me next, however, was quite unsettling: James's slide tray was filled with slides of *negative experiences only*—rejections, failures, missed opportunities, mistakes, miscalculations, bad deals, and more. His present sense, then, was always of a past negative event; his past sense was also of a negative event; and his anticipated future slide was always a predictable negative event from his past! Worse, his mental slide show was out of his conscious control—it could be turned on at any time by a triggering experience; so repeatedly viewing all of these horrific images of his past negative experiences, so vividly projected, further burned them into his brain.

I thought hard about a treatment plan, and arrived at a solution that seemed to fit his particular imagery. I informed James that Kodak had just developed a 120-slide carousel, which meant that he would now be able to add *40 new slides* to his old show. I encouraged him to explore his memory to find any events that were positive: successes, good birthdays, friends, favorite foods, movies, books . . . and for each positive image he was able to recall, we created a new, vividly bright slide and inserted it randomly into his mental carousel. Although the negatives still dominated the set, there was now some occasional relief. He could see that his life had many good people, experiences, successes, and more that were balanced against the bad.

We gradually replaced more and more of the bad slides with good ones from recent positive experiences. Over a period of months, this impromptu treatment program began working to provide James with a more balanced, nuanced conception of his life over time and of his ability to shape his current life. It also had a profound impact on me, encouraging me to think more deeply about the nature of our temporal orientation and the real impact that our individual concepts of past, present, and future have on our lives.

In the early 1970s I began to investigate aspects of time perspective in earnest. This fascinating two-plus-decade journey (which you can read about in Chapter Two) led to the development of Temporal Theory and, in 1999, to the Zimbardo Time Perspective Inventory, or ZTPI: a valid, reliable, and easy-to-administer measure of individual differences in time perspective.

By 2008 the ZTPI was being used by researchers around the world. The time had come to really go public — beyond academic publication for psychologists to trade book publication for the general public. *The Time Paradox,*[1] coauthored with John Boyd, was the exciting culmination of much theoretical speculation and proposed new research projects. I thought this was the end of my professional journey with time perspectives, but it was not — I had yet to meet Richard and Rosemary Sword.

◦ the Swords' work with PTSD and time perspectives

I was filled with joy when my first public presentation of our book was scheduled for a workshop at the Hawaii Psychological Association in Honolulu in 2008. At the end of my presentation, I was satisfied with how the session went and was looking forward to getting my reward—sunning on the beach in Waikiki. As I was packing up my gear, however, one of the participants came up to me nearly breathless with excitement over something I had said. Actually, it turned out his excitement was about *everything* I had said.

He told me that his name was Richard Sword, and that he was a therapist from Maui. For years, he said, he and his wife and colleague, Rose, had been working *along the very same lines I suggested in The Time Paradox* with war veterans who had suffered from debilitating PTSD for years—some for over seventy years, since World War II—and having good results. He said that he envisioned using my ideas as a therapeutic strategy for curing that terrible affliction. I politely gave him my card and invited him to stay in touch. Although I was busy, I said, I would be alert for his e-mails if marked URGENT on the subject line. I assumed he was like many others who get enthused by my dramatic talks but then fade from sight. I could not have been more wrong.

It turned out that our guy, Rick, was a man of his word, and his words were filled with an intoxicating blend of optimism and wisdom. He had an uncommonly intense dedication to helping American veterans of many wars overcome their suffering. He would not be satisfied just ameliorating their suffering and trauma, he said—he wanted to manage their PTSD to enable them to return to fulfilling, meaningful lives. It was not enough for him to change their negative existence to a zero state of no bad focus. He would not be satisfied until these courageous vets could return to the positive state they had enjoyed before their service and sacrifice for their nation. That was Sword's definition of a complete "cure" for PTSD in vets.

I have to admit, I first thought he was a bit of a wild-eyed visionary. I knew that PTSD had never been overcome by any therapeutic treatment;

at best, it might be made somewhat more bearable. But I remained an open-minded skeptic, eager to be proven wrong (a view of what it meant to be a good scientist that had been drummed into me from my graduate training in the Yale University Psychology Department). We communicated a great deal via e-mail, ideas flowing back and forth.

Now, following the model of Temporal Theory, Rick and Rose began to put into practice a new form of time metaphor therapy treatment with their clients in Maui. I was encouraged, but was hardly a true believer. Their time metaphor therapy revolved around getting clients to reconceptualize their problems using visualizations in which they would become "unstuck" from the traumatic past and move smoothly into a more positive present and future. The Swords put all of this in the context of the importance of time in our lives, and the importance of balancing our past, present, and future time perspectives. Their notion of being able to shift flexibly from one time zone to another — depending on circumstances, current needs, and realities — seemed to be taking ZTPI into a new and exciting dimension of practical use. Still, ever the scientist, I was still skeptical of this simple therapeutic approach.

○ time perspective therapy in action

After I returned home from the conference I began receiving letter after letter from the Swords' vets, describing to me the amazing changes they were experiencing from their treatment. They were euphoric, able for the first time in years to enjoy their wife, family, friends, former activities, going shopping, and more. They were no longer stuck in that horrible past that had gripped them for so long. They were starting to plan vacations and meet people they had been ignoring for years. They told me that their flashbacks had stopped and their smiling had resumed. And they were very eager to share their transformational experience with other vets who were still suffering from the agonies of PTSD.

Such astounding testimonials are rare for any kind of psychological treatment, and especially so when they come after only a few months of treatment. Yet my research training insisted on hard evidence to bolster these personal accounts. I encouraged the Swords and associates to gather pre- and post-treatment metrics on a variety of standard assessments of PTSD with a sufficiently large sample of time perspective therapy–treated vets. They did, and the data supported what the vets had told me: the measurable impact of time perspective therapy is highly statistically significant across a battery of standardized measures. It works!

And not only does it work but also *it can be shown to have an enduring positive effect for years—at least three years (the current follow-up duration).* Most of the initial salutary effects stayed in place for the majority of these time perspective therapy–treated veterans over this extended time period. Presumably these effects will remain longer and ideally permanently when measured subsequently, perhaps complemented by some "booster shots" occasionally if there is backsliding.

Meanwhile, the testimonials kept coming. At the 2009 American Psychological Association convention in Toronto, I wrapped up my presentation on time perspectives by talking about the Swords and their groundbreaking work with veterans. As I scanned the audience, I saw someone waving at me—a woman in a wheelchair. She looked excited and clearly wanted to tell me something. After I finished my talk she came to the podium and told me enthusiastically that she was a veteran previously suffering from PTSD who had undergone time perspective therapy with the Swords. She said it had helped her tremendously and that she was moving on with her life. Imagine my surprise—here, in Toronto, was a veteran to verify what I had just been sharing with this room full of thousands of mental health professionals!

Now we had a decision to make: Should we tell the world about this new form of therapy immediately, to give hope to those who have stopped hoping for improvement? Should we give guidance to therapists to add this type of therapy to their protocols for treating not only PTSD in vets but also all other time-synced traumas and abuses? Or is it better to wait until we conduct a formal clinical trial with hundreds of participants that will test our time perspective therapy against several of the most used current treatments, with random assignments and systemic assessments?

Ordinarily I would have lobbied my colleagues for that latter option. However, such an ambitious project requires a multimillion-dollar grant. These are hard to obtain and time consuming—a year in the getting and at least another few years in the doing. So we opted to apply for a major military grant to put our treatment plan into a testable practice setting in the military, and to go forth with writing this book. We are currently waiting for what we hope is good news from the military. But while we wait and hope, we have forged ahead and written the book you now hold in your hands.

The book you are about to enjoy and learn much from is unique. Its goal is simple: to provide an exposition of Temporal Theory, which I developed, and then to elaborate on how the Swords transformed these ideas into the most effective of any current practical treatments for relieving the suffering associated with PTSD. You will find the treatment plan clearly laid out, as well as much supporting evidence in vivid, memorable case studies and solid quantitative data.

Time perspective therapy is demonstrably effective, its impact is relatively quick—a few months or less—and it is cost effective. It does not require expensive MDs, or even PhDs, to administer. Masters-level practitioners can effectively use it, as can practical nurses or intelligent and committed caregivers.

Behind all of these words, ideas, plans, and agendas is the driving passion of these two healers, Rick and Rose, whose life mission is to use their training and talents to relieve suffering and work tirelessly to improve the quality of daily life of every client with whom they work. Their all-embracing arms reach out not only to veterans but also to many others who come to them for help—survivors of both physical and sexual abuse, of cardiac illnesses, of traumatic natural disasters, and more. It has been my pleasure to be touched by their passionate wisdom and endlessly optimistic view of what is best in human nature.

We hope that what you read here will help you or your loved ones move forward to a more positive life, and that you will share what you have learned on this journey with others you care about. The very act of your doing so reaffirms, strengthens, and expands the human connection.

Philip Zimbardo
San Francisco, California
June 2012

preface

For nearly three decades, Richard Sword has worked as a psychologist on the Hawaiian island of Maui, specializing in post-traumatic stress disorder, or PTSD. Seven years ago his wife, Rosemary, joined the practice. Most folks think of Hawaii as paradise, but every day we work with veterans who are still coping with the effects of horrific war experiences; with ordinary men and women suffering from the traumas of family abuse, rape, traffic accidents, and job-related incidents; as well as with disaster workers traumatized by the terrible suffering they must deal with.

For years our practice thrived using cognitive behavioral therapy (CBT), positive psychology, and *ho'oponopono*—the Hawaiian form of psychology based on making things right through forgiveness. It has always been our vision to build on these traditions, trying our best to find a simple, even more effective way to assist people suffering from mental distress. We were particularly inspired by the Japanese American veterans of the famed 442nd Regimental Combat Team that fought in World War II, whose unique philosophy provided them with an effective path through the labyrinth of PTSD, despite the terrible things they had seen, that differed from that of the other vets we'd treated.

The difference was simple: other American veterans would tend to talk about the bad things in the war and how it affected them, and they simply could not leave these horrific images behind and move on. The

Japanese American veterans, by contrast, would talk about the good things that happened in the war, the funny things, how they enjoyed each other, and how they're working for a better future. They would focus on the positive of the past to create a positive future. And that's what we essentially learned from them: *we look to the past to learn vital lessons; but when we want a better life for ourselves and our children, we must focus on the future.*

Since our first encounter with Philip Zimbardo at that workshop in Honolulu, the Z Team, a cadre of researchers, clinicians, media experts, and students, has worked tirelessly, collecting data and continually assessing treatment effectiveness.

We have applied Zimbardo's Temporal Theory to our own practice, creating what we now call time perspective therapy (TPT). To date, we've treated nearly 400 clients. Of these, 275 are war veterans suffering from PTSD, the vast majority awarded service-connected post-traumatic stress disorder disability ratings from the Veterans Administration. Our nonveteran PTSD clients also benefit from time perspective therapy. A number of our clients were kind enough to share their stories, which you will read in this book. To protect their privacy, their names and certain details have been changed.

Although TPT grew out of CBT and positive psychology, it is qualitatively different from other therapies currently used to treat PTSD. TPT most notably differs in the language it uses and the lens through which it views PTSD.

TPT uses specific terms that are based in ordinary language. We found that our clients had automatic responses to the usual psychological terms, such as *anxiety* and *depression*, that upset them and seemed to keep them from moving on. So, in TPT, we use specific time perspective terminology, referring to past thoughts and experiences as being either *positive* or *negative*. This may not sound like much of a difference, but the impact on the client's engagement with therapy can be immediate. For instance, we've found that speaking of being "stuck in the past negative" (something you'll learn about later in this book) is easy to understand and relate to. It feels much less charged to talk about than anxiety and depression, and easier to find ways to resolve.

The second big difference—and it is a big one—is that TPT views PTSD as a mental *injury* rather than a mental *illness*. PTSD is caused by trauma, which injures your thought process, much as the trauma of a car accident might do physical harm to your body. Again, it may seem like a small thing; but for PTSD sufferers it is huge. Living with a mental illness can feel oppressive, incomprehensible, and hopeless. Living with a mental injury offers hope of healing.

Over the last few years we have held TPT workshops in Hawaii for mental health specialists, students, and interested laypeople. Larry Borins, an independent psychotherapist in Toronto who teaches mindfulness-based cognitive therapy and CBT (he works in an outpatient mental health organization), has attended two such workshops. He had the following to say about the difference between mindfulness-based approaches and TPT:

> One of the practices in mindfulness is labeling and identifying thoughts; recognizing that thoughts are not facts but products of the mind. Sometimes thoughts are rational and sometimes they are not. One way to get clients to wake up and become more aware is to help them learn to separate thoughts from facts. When people are in depression or anxiety their thoughts are confused, which causes them to question who they are as persons. Using mindfulness is one way to step out of the autopilot and reactivity. Another way is to change your perspective through TPT. I see TPT as being an easy and effective tool to realizing one's relationship to the situation and present moment.
>
> I just treated another patient using TPT and she had a remarkable recovery. I didn't even use mindfulness—I just used TPT and it was so cool! She took right to it . . .
>
> TPT is a perfect complement for cognitive behavioral therapy (CBT) and mindfulness-based therapy.

Time perspective therapy is a simple, effective, and very successful tool to help even those most negatively affected by traumatic events to develop the balanced time perspective that can allow them to lift their foot from the muck and mire of the past and step firmly into a more positive future. At the end of each chapter in Part One, you will find suggestions for how you can begin to explore the simple techniques you read about in *The Time Cure* and apply them to your own life experience.

Reading this book, however, is not a substitute for therapy, but rather a guide in a journey to self-discovery. If you are currently in therapy and are intrigued by what you read, please share this information with your therapist.

Time perspective therapy truly is for everyone. It has changed our lives, and those of so many others. We hope it aids you, too, to *holo mua* — to move forward on your journey in a positive way. *Aloha.*

Richard and Rosemary Sword
Maui, Hawaii
June 2012

Note: A free, downloadable guide for therapists using time perspective therapy is available. To access this PDF guide, go to our publisher's Web site: www.josseybass.com/go/timecure.

part 1

PTSD and time perspective therapy

1

how PTSD sufferers get stuck in time

At age forty-five, Kara's life was full. She and her husband, Bud, had been married for twenty years. They'd decided early on that they would forego having children to focus on their relationship and have fun together, and they had done just that. They loved Alaska's outdoor life — riding motorcycles, deep sea fishing, camping, and hunting. Kara's job with the highways division of the State of Alaska Department of Transportation was fine too. She drove a pickup truck and hauled a light board signaling traffic to change lanes for the highway work crews. It was a good job, and it let her have the life she wanted — until one day a young woman driving a large pickup truck came speeding down the road and smashed into Kara's truck, catapulting it into the air where it flipped over, came crashing down, and landed on its roof with a scream of broken glass and metal on asphalt. Kara's coworkers dropped everything and rushed to help.

They found her trapped inside, hanging upside down, suspended by her seat belt, injured but alive. For Kara, everything was happening at once. She was in shock. She knew that her head, neck, shoulder, and back had been injured. She wanted to get out. And she was desperate to know what had happened to the driver of the vehicle that hit her. Her coworkers, concerned for their friend's life, told her not to worry about the other driver and not to move until the paramedics arrived.

But Kara could smell gas and feared that her truck might explode. Frantic, she tried to release her seat belt. It was jammed. And even if they had tried to, her coworkers would not have been able to help her out of the truck — it had been so flattened by the impact that there was no way for them to get to her. With the clarity that comes with shock, Kara saw that if she could get loose she could find a way out. So she reached into her pocket, found her pocket knife, and cut through the seat belt, falling abruptly and landing on her already injured head, neck, and shoulder.

Kara crawled out of her truck and tried to head toward the other pickup. Despite her many injuries, and even though her coworkers were physically restraining her, she was extremely anxious about the other driver and managed to force her way through the crowd, only to witness the young woman's last moments of life. Strewn all over the back of the cab were signs of family life — an infant car seat, a diaper bag, and baby clothes. But there was no infant, and a search failed to turn up anything. Kara later discovered that the woman who hit her was the mother of a toddler, who thankfully had not been in the vehicle at the time of the crash. But Kara was devastated to discover that the young mother had also been pregnant.

The accident changed Kara's life. She had sustained injuries to her skull, neck, spine, shoulder, abdomen, and knees, and underwent a series of operations and procedures to repair the damage. Physically, she was slowly improving; but the psychological damage was severe and more enduring. She began psychotherapy, including psychiatric and psychological treatment.

Four months into Kara's psychotherapy, Kara's psychologist was worried. Psychological testing confirmed extreme trauma, extreme depression, extreme anxiety, and panic attacks. Kara had severe post-traumatic stress disorder. And now it was the dead of the brutal Alaskan winter. With almost no hours of sunshine, it seemed impossible that

Kara would ever be able to conceive of a world without darkness, both external and internal. Her psychologist thought that a change of scenery to a warmer, sunnier climate might at least help—a lot of Alaskans escaped the winter by flying to Hawaii. Kara's workers' comp adjuster agreed. The psychologist did her homework, and discovered that on the island of Maui a psychologist named Richard Sword was practicing a new therapy that appeared to offer tremendous results for people like Kara.

Kara and Bud spent their first day in Maui settling into an ocean-side condo, and then got to work. During a get-acquainted session with Rick and his wife, Rosemary, also a psychotherapist, Bud told them how his wife had changed. Before the accident, he said, Kara had been an affectionate companion and an active and adventuresome woman—a social, positive person, quick with a smile and a joke. She was attractive, was proud of her appearance, and took great care of herself. But the woman who had returned from the accident was very different.

This new Kara was a depressed, paranoid stranger who didn't care what she looked like, didn't want to be touched, didn't know what fun was, and didn't seem to care about people—or about anything, for that matter. Plus, Bud was doubtful about this Maui doctor. How could Rick help his wife when others had not been able to?

The Swords explained that they would be working with a new therapy based on understanding how the way we feel about the past, present, and future influences the way we conceive of what is possible in our lives. It seemed to be especially helpful with PTSD—even with battered World War II veterans in their upper eighties and nineties who had been suffering for nearly seventy years from debilitating symptoms of PTSD due to the horrors they had lived through. This new treatment was succeeding where all other interventions had failed, making a significant improvement in their mental state and quality of life.

Bud and Kara agreed to give it a shot. "We've got nothing to lose but time," Bud said. In fact, as they learned, there was much to gain through time perspective therapy.

o PTSD basics

Post-traumatic stress disorder, commonly called PTSD, is an anxiety
disorder that begins with a trauma—a horrific one-time event, like
Kara's accident; continuing trauma, such as ongoing physical or verbal
abuse; or a terrible event in which you have participated, such as war.
You can even have PTSD as the result of being a caregiver or aid
worker—an emergency room doctor or nurse, or a volunteer worker in
a disaster like the earthquake in Haiti or Hurricane Katrina.

Whatever triggered your PTSD, that horrifying, frightening event
overwhelms your ability to cope with daily life and may lead to all sorts
of symptoms, including distrust, hyper-vigilance (always waiting for
the hammer to fall), and hyper-irritability. Hollywood often portrays
PTSD as nightmares, flashbacks, and being lost in past experiences to the
point of becoming dysfunctional in the present. As one of the Swords'
clients puts it, "If it wasn't for my flashbacks, I wouldn't have any memory at all."

All of this and more can be true. But these symptoms are only a
fraction of the turmoil that is going on inside sufferers. Inside they are
reliving the event over and over again, reexperiencing the very same
emotions; they infuse those fears and emotions into each moment, col-
oring past, present, and future with the same dark ink of fear.

the official definition: DSM-IV-TR criteria for PTSD

PTSD—once called "shell shock" or "battle fatigue" and ignored or
dismissed as something that would disappear with time—is now recognized by the American Psychiatric Association as a real disorder. And it
is no longer necessary to be a direct victim to be considered as having
been exposed to trauma:

> As long as one is confronted with a situation that involves threat to
> the physical integrity of one's self or others and one experiences
> the emotions of fear, horror, or helplessness, then the experience
> counts as exposure to a PTSD-qualifying stressor.[1]

In 2000 the American Psychiatric Association revised its criteria for this disorder in the fourth edition of the *Diagnostic and Statistical Manual of Mental Disorders,* commonly called DSM-IV-TR:

Diagnostic criteria for PTSD include a history of exposure to a traumatic event meeting two criteria and symptoms from each of three symptom clusters: intrusive recollections, avoidant/numbing symptoms, and hyper-arousal symptoms. A fifth criterion concerns duration of symptoms and a sixth assesses [current] functioning.

Criterion A: stressor
The person has been exposed to a traumatic event in which both of the following have been present:

1. The person has experienced, witnessed, or been confronted with an event or events that involve actual or threatened death or serious injury, or a threat to the physical integrity of oneself or others.
2. The person's response involved intense fear, helplessness, or horror. Note: in children, it may be expressed instead by disorganized or agitated behavior.

Criterion B: intrusive recollection
The traumatic event is persistently re-experienced in at least **one** of the following ways:

1. Recurrent and intrusive distressing recollections of the event, including images, thoughts, or perceptions. Note: in young children, repetitive play may occur in which themes or aspects of the trauma are expressed.
2. Recurrent distressing dreams of the event. Note: in children, there may be frightening dreams without recognizable content.
3. Acting or feeling as if the traumatic event were recurring (includes a sense of reliving the experience, illusions, hallucinations, and dissociative flashback episodes, including those that occur upon awakening or when intoxicated). Note: in children, trauma-specific reenactment may occur.
4. Intense psychological distress at exposure to internal or external cues that symbolize or resemble an aspect of the traumatic event.

5. Physiologic reactivity upon exposure to internal or external cues that symbolize or resemble an aspect of the traumatic event.

Criterion C: avoidant/numbing

Persistent avoidance of stimuli associated with the trauma and numbing of general responsiveness (not present before the trauma), as indicated by at least **three** of the following:

1. Efforts to avoid thoughts, feelings, or conversations associated with the trauma
2. Efforts to avoid activities, places, or people that arouse recollections of the trauma
3. Inability to recall an important aspect of the trauma
4. Markedly diminished interest or participation in significant activities
5. Feeling of detachment or estrangement from others
6. Restricted range of affect (e.g., unable to have loving feelings)
7. Sense of foreshortened future (e.g., does not expect to have a career, marriage, children, or a normal life span)

Criterion D: hyper-arousal

Persistent symptoms of increasing arousal (not present before the trauma), indicated by at least **two** of the following:

1. Difficulty falling or staying asleep
2. Irritability or outbursts of anger
3. Difficulty concentrating
4. Hyper-vigilance
5. Exaggerated startle response

Criterion E: duration

Duration of the disturbance (symptoms in B, C, and D) is more than one month.

Criterion F: functional significance

The disturbance causes clinically significant distress or impairment in social, occupational, or other important areas of functioning.[2]

stuck in time

The term *post-trauma* says it all: the trauma is in the past, but sufferers are unable to leave it behind and move on. They relive the event over and over — in nightmares that make sleep impossible, in flashbacks that have them time traveling back to a horrible past moment, and in recurrent negative thoughts that they cannot stop. This waking nightmare leaves them stuck in time, always running from the trauma and never able to escape. As one of Rick's clients said, "You leave the war, but the war doesn't leave you."

It's not surprising, then, that they are desperate to avoid anything in their present life that might remind them of the past trauma. This avoidance of people, events, places, noises, smells, and even the possibility that they might have to talk about the traumatic event often causes PTSD sufferers to become socially isolated.

They are always on guard because the traumatic event has set the subconscious regulatory forces within the brain — the adrenaline rush of the fight-or-flight response — to permanent ON. The OFF switch is effectively burned out, leaving them perpetually revved up and on edge. They have a hard time unwinding, going to sleep, being still, and recharging. Even the PAUSE switch, needed for reflection, is jammed. This naturally leads to fatigue and exhaustion. They can't think straight. They watch their lives collapse around them like a house of cards.

Their normal coping skills are shot, replaced with irritability, withdrawal, and alienation. Irrationally, they are drawn back again and again to their traumatic past experiences, which are as vivid and real as they were the day they happened — whether that was last week or sixty years ago. Sufferers eventually become addicted to their own adrenaline and excitability. The PTSD state becomes natural, and their anxious, irritable PTSD personality becomes the one they and others accept as real.

psychological responses to catastrophe

Psychological responses to natural and human-caused disasters have been theorized to occur in stages, as victims experience shock, feel intense emotion, and struggle to reorganize their lives.[3] Survivors typically pass through five stages[4]:

1. **Psychic numbness.** Immediately after the event, victims experience *psychic numbness,* including shock and confusion, and for moments to days they cannot fully comprehend what has happened. Severe, sudden, and violent disasters violate our basic expectations about how the world is supposed to function. For some, the unimaginable becomes a forced new experienced event.

2. **Automatic action.** During a phase of *automatic action,* victims have little awareness of their own experiences and later show poor recall of many details about what occurred.

3. **Communal effort.** In the *communal effort* stage, the sufferer and his or her support network pool their resources and collaborate, proud of their accomplishments but also weary and aware that they are using up precious energy reserves.

4. **Letdown.** Next, survivors may experience a *letdown.* Depleted of energy, they understand and feel the tragedy's impact. Public interest and attention fade, and survivors feel abandoned, even though the state of emergency may continue.

5. **Recovery.** An extended period of *recovery* follows as survivors adapt to changes created by the disaster.

These stages don't necessarily apply to everyone who experiences a trauma, but they do summarize commonalities across a range of individual experiences. In this sense, they help us understand what survivors may have experienced and what forms of assistance they may need. They also reflect the kinds of profound changes that contribute to PTSD.[5]

○ this is your brain on trauma

The brain is the most complex organ in the universe. In his book *Incognito, the Secret Lives of the Brain,* neuroscientist David Eagleman says:

> Your brain is built of cells called neurons and glia—hundreds of billions of them. Each one of these cells is as complicated as a city ... each cell sends electrical impulses to other cells... The cells are connected to one another in a network of such staggering complexity that it bankrupts human language and necessitates new strains of mathematics... Given the billions of neurons, this means there are as many connections in a single cubic centimeter of brain tissue as there are stars in the Milky Way galaxy.[6]

That's a lot of connections! When we realize the enormous complexity and diversity of the brain, it becomes easier to understand why such all-encompassing problems as PTSD are so difficult to weed out of one's brain, and subsequently to contain in one's psyche.

When traumatic events happen to us, we enter into a kind of altered state in which our normal thinking processes do not function and another operating system takes over. This is great if you suddenly find yourself in a situation in which you must run into a burning building to save someone or risk your life to save team members under fire—your ordinary mind would tell you it's crazy to do such a thing. That altered state is also a necessity if you are struggling to save your own life, whether you have been thrown from a horse, have been beaten by an abusive spouse, or are simply trying to get through each day in a severely dysfunctional family.

But the same system of brain chemistry that allows us to be heroes or survive extreme situations also imprints the traumatic event deeply within our memory, emotions, consciousness, and subconscious. In fact, neuroscience tells us that the brain stores these disturbing memories not just in one place but in multiple diverse locations, both in the thinking areas of the frontal cortex and in the emotional regions of the amygdala of the hippocampus.

The brain stores and encodes different types of memories, some of which are long-lived and some of which are easily replaced, using different chemicals. For example, the details of what you ate for lunch yesterday may be written in pencil—easily erased and replaced with the details of tonight's dinner—or its aroma may be saved for future remembrance. The name of a person you just met, or the place where you put your car keys yesterday, may be written in the disappearing ink of your short-term memory. But like that tattoo you wish you had never gotten, and that is now embedded forever just under your skin, a traumatic moment is written in permanent ink that will always be part of your long-term memory.

This complex encoding means that traumatic memories, such as those that generate PTSD, are multidimensional, insidious, and difficult to ferret out and come to terms with. The memories assault sufferers in an overwhelming experience that steals their future and leaves them feeling out of control, stuck in a horrible past and fatalistic present. Here, for example, is how Kara's brain stored the traumatic experiences of her traffic accident:

- **Sight.** The gruesome visual images she saw were encoded and stored in her *visual cortex,* in the rear part of the brain.
- **Sound.** The grinding screech of metal and cries of pain and shock she heard were stored in her *temporal lobes,* the sides of the brain above the ears.
- **Smell.** The vivid smells of the event—hot pavement, burning oil, and blood—were stored in the *olfactory cortex,* the part of the brain that lies just behind the eyes.
- **Touch.** The physical pain she experienced was stored in *muscle memory* throughout her body, affecting the pain and emotional centers of her brain.
- **Thought and memory.** The horrible memories of the other woman's suffering, combined with troubling worries about

the woman's toddler and unborn infant, were recorded in the *prefrontal cortex,* where thought occurs, as well as in the *limbic system,* where emotions are stored, that encircles the middle of Kara's brain. She literally carried the trauma with her everywhere, like worn-out, overstuffed luggage.

Figure 1.1 indicates the different parts of the brain that are affected by a PTSD experience.

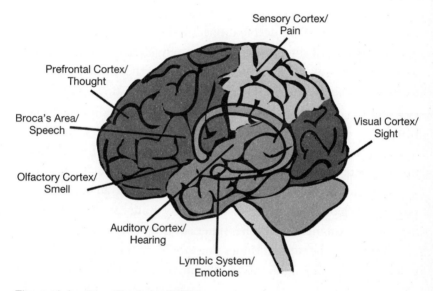

Figure 1.1   Your Brain on PTSD
This and other illustrations are based on illustrations by Noah Milich.

◉ when PTSD goes untreated

The experience of PTSD is not the same for everyone. Just as one can be minimally or extremely depressed or anxious, one can suffer from minimal or extreme PTSD. Think, for example, of the range of intensities you have seen in the color blue. In this example, the intensity spectrum of PTSD might range from powder blue (minimal PTSD) to deep cobalt (extreme PTSD).

A person who suffers from minimal PTSD will probably get better over time. For instance, perhaps you've been in a frightening motor vehicle accident in which you didn't suffer physical injury but others did. In time your car is repaired, so you aren't reminded of the accident every time you look at the car. And with a little more time, you can drive by the site of the accident without constantly thinking of the "what ifs": What if I had left home five minutes earlier? What if I had taken a different route to work? What if that hedge had been properly trimmed? With time, you can bleach the pale blue away.

But if you have been brutally physically assaulted and raped, for example, you may be so deeply dipped in the darkest blue of memory that no amount of time will ever completely bleach it away. It might fade a bit, but it's always there; and in some cases, the blue deepens to extreme depression. Almost immediately you start adjusting your thoughts and routines around these dark emotions. And these adjustments cost you dearly. You've kept it a secret, so you don't want to talk about it, much less see anybody. You don't feel good about yourself, so why go to the trouble of trying to look presentable? Because you don't want to see anybody and you don't care about how you look, why go to the gym or take that walk or get out of bed at all? Clearly, Kara ceased caring about her outer appearance because her inner landscape was so tumultuous.

Eventually, the normal things you would do for or with others—going to work, cooking dinner, being interested in what they did that day—become chores that eventually turn into resentment, which causes you to feel irritable and angry toward them. Simple things both at work and at home that would never have bothered you before the trauma—the sound of a pencil tapping on a table, a coworker who throws papers on your desk, finding a parking place in a crowded parking lot, riding the elevator to the office—are now monolithic obstructions that must be dealt with before you can mentally curl up in the fetal position and go over and over the what ifs again and again.

They may seem closed off and uncaring, but deep down inside people with PTSD know they need help. Sometimes getting help seems like one more chore that's just too overwhelming to contemplate. Often they don't get help because they are afraid of being judged, compartmentalized, and deemed mentally ill. And for the rest, fatalism and cynicism step in and say, "Why bother? Nothing's going to change no matter what you do or what they say."

People with untreated severe PTSD can sink into the deepest, darkest depth of depression with no apparent way out. They don't dare look up, afraid they might find their ugly trauma looking back down at them.

PTSD is mental *injury*, not mental illness

We believe that PTSD should be thought of as a mental injury rather than a mental illness, and research supports this view. Studies show that traumatic experiences can alter the overall structure of the brain,[7] as well as its chemical levels (in particular neurosteroids, which may figure in the body's response to stress),[8] creating and contributing to PTSD.[9]

A study by Alexander Neumeister of Yale University School of Medicine found that veterans diagnosed with PTSD and also suffering a co-morbidity (for example, one or more psychiatric diagnoses, such as depression, anxiety, childhood trauma, or suicidal ideation), had brain images on functional magnetic resonance imaging (fMRI) and positron emission tomography (PET) scans that differed from those of individuals only suffering from PTSD. In summary, "PTSD, depression and substance abuse can all be seen as a physical, chemical injury to the brain that occurs when the brain is exposed to trauma."[10]

The overexcited psychological and physiological state of people suffering from PTSD can, of course, be reduced through medication. And recent research indicates that adding cognitive behavioral therapy to a drug therapy regimen improves the overall results in comparison to control groups.[11] This research makes it clear that the drugs alone are not the best way to go.

This fits perfectly with our philosophy and experience in treating PTSD with time perspective therapy: it is far more effective to teach people to reduce their stress naturally by learning to take control of their own physiology and balancing their own time perspective. When medication helps, it's the meds—not the sufferer—that get the credit for any improvement. When something *you* do makes a difference in the quality of your life, then you can take some of the credit for improvement.

o how PTSD affects others

Very often, people with PTSD agree to therapy because their family and friends are worried about them—they are in danger of losing their job, or they get into fights, or they are abusing drugs or alcohol, or their rage is making it very hard for anyone else around them to have a peaceful existence. It is family or friends who typically encourage and persuade sufferers to try a treatment that they were not likely to initiate on their own. This is a common and very sad state of affairs for everyone involved with someone suffering from PTSD.

Imagine the PTSD sufferer as a single drop of water polluted by trauma and all its symptoms: depression, anxiety, avoidance, isolation, fear, anger, and all the rest. This tear-shaped drop splashes into a clear, calm freshwater pond—the person's circle of family and friends—causing ripples that spread out, disturbing the peace of the water and distributing the poison of the trauma throughout the pond. PTSD sufferers don't mean to make waves; it just happens—over and over again. And the effects they cause in their social circles can be enormous and destructive. No wonder they so often choose to simply withdraw into themselves. No wonder their circle of friends often eventually withdraws from their contaminating impact.

Yet when PTSD sufferers isolate themselves in this way, they remove themselves from normal activities and social situations—and that also can affect loved ones negatively. This may mean that children can't talk to their parents or bring friends home, that spouses feel shoved aside and see their own social circle narrow, or that coworkers grow intolerant of colleagues who are rude when they are at work or just don't show up half the time.

People with severe PTSD frequently lose their ability to handle even simple tasks and situations. They can't focus on what is going on around them because they can only see the trauma being replayed over and over in their mind. They are hostages, compulsively bound to the memory of that traumatic moment in time. In this state they might revert to irritability and anger, taking it out on those closest to them. Extreme sufferers may take the show on the road, raging at the waitress or grocery store clerk, their coworkers, or other drivers they perceive to be cutting them off.

This ripple effect can become a tidal wave of negative, destructive emotions. Friends, family, and coworkers quickly learn to get out of the way. They adapt their behavior and grow sensitive antennae, always on the alert for trouble. The family avoids the sufferer at the first hint of anger. They learn when not to ask for help with his or her homework or for a hand getting the vase out of the upper cabinet. Friends might eventually stop calling because the PTSD sufferer doesn't want to do anything, is "too busy," never shows up, or acts unpredictably. The person behind the counter shrugs and thinks, *What a jerk!* Coworkers stay clear of the "loose cannon." Other drivers on the road may even respond by following the seemingly aggressive driver home and beating him or her up. PTSD affects not only the sufferer but also, to some degree, everyone in his or her world—for the worse.

○ why PTSD has been so hard to treat

The National Institute of Mental Health estimates that 7.5 million adult Americans currently suffer from PTSD. It is "the most common mental health disorder" among veterans of the conflicts in Iraq and Afghanistan,[12] but it is a problem for veterans of all wars.

Because so many military personnel are men, PTSD tends to be associated with husbands and sons who go off to war and return to their home and family as "zombies" or loose cannons, seeming changed forever by their experiences. But as we have seen in this chapter, women also suffer from PTSD. According to the National Center for PTSD,

> Findings from a large national mental health study show that a little more than half of all women will experience at least one traumatic event in their life... The most common trauma for women is sexual assault or child sexual abuse. About 1 in 3 women will experience a sexual assault in their lifetime. Women are also more likely to be neglected or abused in childhood, to experience domestic violence, or to have a loved one suddenly die.[13]

For various reasons, an enormous number of adult Americans—both men and women—are currently suffering from PTSD. And until now psychology has had a very difficult time helping people with PTSD do anything more than learn to cope with their symptoms or medicate the worst of the pain. The following therapies are currently used to treat PTSD:

cognitive behavioral therapy

Cognitive behavioral therapy (CBT), a blend of behavioral therapy and cognitive therapy, focuses on the here and now. To date, it has been the therapy with the most success in overcoming trauma. A talk-based therapy, CBT aims to problem-solve around intense abnormal emotions, behaviors, and thoughts through a methodical, goal-oriented approach. Used in both individual and group therapy, the techniques often include keeping a journal of events and related feelings, thoughts, and behaviors, and implementing different reactions and behaviors.

cognitive processing therapy, prolonged exposure therapy, and virtual reality therapy

Cognitive processing therapy, prolonged exposure therapy, and a new modality called virtual reality therapy are currently employed by the Veterans Administration to treat veterans suffering from PTSD. In all three processes, the veteran relives past military traumas in an attempt to extinguish the negative emotions associated with his or her traumatic military experience.

Sadly, many veterans who have undergone prolonged exposure therapy and cognitive processing therapy have become psychological casualties. Only one veteran who was a client of the Swords shared that these therapies were positive experiences that helped him feel better about himself and his future. The rest of our veteran clients (like Alex, whose story is told in this chapter) reported that these therapies made them regress in gains they had been making through the time perspective therapy process. They reported an increase in nightmares, flashbacks, social isolation, and anger, as well as suicidal and homicidal thoughts. A number of veterans reported that these processes made them so angry that they returned to their earlier coping skills of hostility and violence.[14]

alexs perspective: a desert storm vet 's experience with cognitive processing therapy and prolonged exposure therapy

Operation Desert Storm, also called the Gulf War, was waged from August 1990 to February 1991. As wars go, it was relatively quick. But for vets like Alex, it never ended.

Over the course of four years, Alex thought he had been making good progress coping with his chronic and severe PTSD. In hopes of making even more progress, he underwent cognitive processing therapy (CPT) and prolonged exposure therapy (PE). In September 2010, after he completed CPT and had tried PE, he wrote this statement to the Veterans Administration:

> I thought [CPT] would be a good step forward, but it wasn't. The can of worms that was tucked away for so long, way back on the top shelf, that I had somewhat managed to control was ripped wide open and the floodgate of emotions and imagery overwhelmed me once again. I suffer a constant barrage of flashbacks and dreams—more so with watching the news footage and death tolls of the Iraq and Afghan Wars. Feeling the guilt and remorse eating at me, knowing all of this should have been prevented if we had just finished the job the first time when we were there in 1991. The CPT process put me back into a state of mind parallel to my original experiences. My mind tells me one thing, but the emotional onset overrules all thought processes.
>
> After CPT, I was asked to partake in Prolonged Exposure Therapy which I was very reluctant to attempt. But after completion of the third session it proved to be a complete disaster. My mental state leaving each session and then having to go deal with the day-to-day grind of my job and home life proved to be just overwhelming. I am in a constant state of rage; everything sends me into an uncontrollable spiral taking out my anger and frustrations on whoever is in front of me at the time. I find myself not

being able to be the bigger man [Alex is 6'7" tall] and walk away from situations and confrontations. I've reverted back to old habits of self-medicating with alcohol to lessen the sting of the pain and images that haunt me once again—day and night. This is not setting well with my wife; she's seen the results of my alcoholism post Desert Storm to 1991. It wasn't a pleasant road I took my wife and family down. She told me point blank this time around she refuses to travel it again, and if I continue I'll do it alone.

I continue to receive phone calls from my superiors verbally reprimanding me for customer complaints of me being too rigid and stern, unwilling to give, too military; customers threatening to pull out of the business if I don't back down. Knowing that I will be replaced way before they lose a customer. My job entails driving ... but since CPT and PE, driving puts me in imminent danger. My wife refuses to ride with me if I'm driving and hates it when I am the passenger. But I just don't care. I'm tired of struggling to be everything for everybody and if I can't live up to everyone's standards to include the ones I set for myself—why bother... This process is definitely not Veteran friendly.

For vets like Alex, CPT and PE were like psychological water boarding.[15]

drug therapy

For the past several decades, drug therapy has been a common approach to the treatment of anxiety, depression, trauma, and other behavioral disorders. We agree with Youngstown State University professor Stephen Ray Flora, whose fields of expertise are applied behavioral analysis, behavioral intervention techniques, and human learning, who assessed that "when behavior is out of balance, the body, including the brain, gets out of balance."[16] When the behavior comes back into balance, then the body and brain return to balance. But Flora states unequivocally, "There are no drug 'cures' for behavioral problems."[17] Drugs have provided some help, but they're certainly not a panacea. In addition, numerous studies have found that adding pharmacologic treatments to CBT did not enhance the overall end result.[18] Meds may, at best, keep the experience from getting worse, but they do not make it any better.

The assumption is that the medications will break up the non-functional pattern of thought, allowing the individual's mental health to return naturally; but this is an overly optimistic assumption. Drugs do not get to the root of the problem. They are a temporary solution that alters behavior, *but drugs do not address the cause.* Predictably, the behavior often returns when the drugs wear off, leaving the PTSD sufferer feeling like nothing will ever change, or simply wanting to use the drugs to mask the pain. Also, when drug therapy does not work, that further promotes a fatalistic perspective that nothing can alter the deeper suffering being experienced.

does critical incident stress debriefing work to head off PTSD before it begins?

Critical Incident Stress Debriefing (CISD), first developed by Jeffrey Mitchell,[19] is sometimes mandated as a treatment for first responders and victims in a number of organizations, including some police and fire departments. The point of this early intervention strategy is to clear the trauma from the brain soon after the incident, defusing PTSD before it has a chance to get ingrained. It seems to make sense, and many believe that it does. Yet despite CISD's popularity, the question of whether it actually works is still hotly debated.

CISD is based on Freudian therapeutic catharsis, whereby a client works in conjunction with a trained psychotherapist in a safe environment. Therapeutic catharsis is careful, controlled, and geared to the client's readiness. When the therapist believes the timing is best for encouraging the client to open up emotionally, psychological catharsis can be very healing. CISD, in contrast, is forced on a group of strangers as soon after the common traumatic event as possible. In addition, listening to the traumas of others adds to the PTSD sufferer's already bleak worldview, further embedding the negative emotional experiences in his or her amygdala.

Although CISD is intended to head off PTSD before it begins, at least seven studies and a meta-analysis reveal that it either does nothing at all or can make PTSD symptoms worse.[20] According to a recent report, psychological debriefing—the most widely used method—has undergone increasing empirical scrutiny, and the results have been disappointing. Although the majority of debriefed survivors describe the experience as helpful, there is no convincing evidence that debriefing reduces the incidence of PTSD, and some controlled studies suggest that it may impede natural recovery from trauma. Most studies show that individuals who receive debriefing fare no better than those who do not receive debriefing.[21]

○ why reliving trauma only goes so far

Research indicates the importance of stories or *narratives* in working through catastrophic experiences. To learn from and make sense of catastrophic loss, our brain naturally formulates an account that describes what happened and why. We are especially likely to develop narratives when an event is surprising or unpleasant,[22] or when it violates our basic expectations.[23] Narratives help us find meaning in loss, which in turn facilitates healing. Given this, you might wonder why traditional psychology — which regularly uses life narratives — has had such a difficult time dealing with PTSD.

Perhaps the reason is overreliance on these stories.

In general, these methods aim to fight fire with fire: they return again and again to the terrible things that happened in the past to try to desensitize the sufferer. For instance, a cognitive processing therapy psychotherapist might ask Kara to speak and write about her trauma numerous times, and then again from various perspectives. First she might write a description of the trauma, and then she would describe what was happening to her physically during the trauma. Then Kara might write about her emotional state during the trauma, how she felt physically right after the trauma, how she felt emotionally right after the trauma . . .

In traditional PTSD therapy, clients must relive the trauma over and over again. Although this may be an effective treatment for some, the Swords have found that it is more often detrimental to many of their clients. Reliving trauma — which the PTSD sufferer already does every moment of every day, awake or asleep — is painful. *It hurts.* And we all want to avoid pain. To go back in time is painful, yet the present and future seem hopeless. It is not surprising that outcomes from traditional PTSD therapy have been partial at best.

o time perspective therapy transforms past, present, and future

Time perspective therapy takes a different approach entirely. It begins by respecting the trauma for what it can teach us rather than dwelling on how it harmed us. This idea, a positive reframing of the event, reflects the ancient Japanese tradition embodied by the veterans of the 442nd Regimental Combat Team. This famous regiment was composed mainly of Japanese Americans and Japanese Hawaiians — many of whom had been classified as enemy aliens, despite the fact that they were U.S. citizens.

Thousands of Japanese Americans living in the continental United States were forced by their own U.S. government to leave their homes, their schools, and their businesses and live in internment camps. Mothers, fathers, sisters, brothers, cousins, aunts, and uncles lived in these camps for the duration of World War II. Yet many young Japanese American men volunteered to fight for the U.S. Army in the war. These men were true patriots. They not only served with distinction but also became "the most decorated unit in U.S. military history for its size and length of service. There were over 18,000 individual decorations for bravery, 9,500 Purple Hearts, and seven Presidential Distinguished Unit Citations."[24] Many of the members of this group, known simply as the 442nd, who survived the terrible battlefields of World War II were afflicted with undiagnosed PTSD; yet, unlike many other war veterans, they were able to come out and continue their positive, "go for broke" spirit in civilian life.

Rick and Rose were honored to meet many of these men, and to know some as clients. And they were intrigued. Why, they wondered, were these men able to remain so positive when the other American veterans would tend to talk about the bad things in the war and how they affected them? The vets of the 442nd would reminisce about the good things that happened to them during the war, the funny moments, and how they enjoyed each other, and they would talk about how they are working for a better future. Their focus on the positive aspects of the past helped them create a positive future. "We look to the past to learn," they told Rick, "but we focus on creating a better future for ourselves and our children."

This nugget of truth was the genesis of what would become a new kind of therapy—one that would fit well within the framework of Philip Zimbardo's work in Temporal Theory. Time perspective therapy understands that we each have a *unique time perspective* based on our personal experiences, and this perspective is the lens through which we view our lives. But our experiences do not need to lock us into a particular way of seeing the world and our place in it—particularly when that way of seeing things is destructive to ourselves and to those we love. No matter what our experiences have been, *we always have a choice.* By changing our time perspective, we can change our lives. For PTSD sufferers, this means gaining the real and lasting ability to move beyond the terrible past and live in a healthy balance of past, present, and future.

The realization that we always have the choice to change how we view the times of our lives is essential to this orientation. Over the course of this exciting new therapy, PTSD sufferers move away from a narrow focus on the traumatic past and a cynical present denial about the possibility of ever achieving a hopeful future, instead journeying toward a balanced time perspective in which it seems possible once again to live a full and promising life.

This concept is reflected in ordinary language that time perspective therapists use. Most people suffering from PTSD have already been labeled as anxious, depressed, or even mentally ill. When they hear these words, and identify with them, the possibility of ever emerging from such a state feels very distant. Reframing their "illness" as an "injury," and recasting their depression and anxiety as a "negative past" that they can replace with a "positive present" and "brighter future"—and ultimately with a balanced time perspective—may seem overly simplistic, especially to those of us trained in psychotherapy. But to PTSD sufferers, the idea of having a forward-leaning framework in which to understand and work on their issues most often comes as an enormous relief and a welcome ray of light in the darkness.

○ seeking balance

The goal of time perspective therapy is to establish a balanced time perspective of past, present, and future. The therapist helps the PTSD sufferer move from mental distress—from a time perspective that is seriously tipped toward the negative past—to a time perspective in which a brighter future can be imagined and enabled. To understand this view, take a look at Figure 1.2.

The illustration at the top of Figure 1.2 shows a time perspective typical of someone suffering from PTSD: the negatives of the past—all that junk we carry around with us—far outweigh hopes for a better future. In fact, the future seems to be full of nothing but questions without satisfactory answers. And the balance point of the present is so far removed from the past that it leaves very little room for any kind of future at all. This is the starting point for most people with PTSD when they begin time perspective therapy (TPT).

As TPT progresses, however, the overflowing junk heap of our past begins to get sorted out. We still carry around some bad memories, but they have become more manageable, smaller, and less burdensome "baggage" rather than an overflowing dumpster of despair. In response to this lighter load, the balance point of the present is able to move closer to the center. Now the future has room to exist, and we are able to create some positive hopes and plans to balance out the negative past.

MENTAL DISTRESS

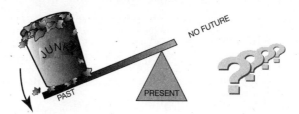

TIME PERSPECTIVE THERAPY IN PROGRESS

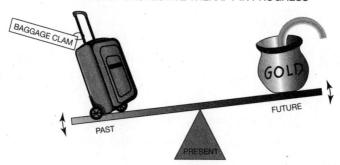

BALANCED TIME PERSPECTIVE

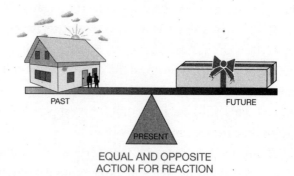

EQUAL AND OPPOSITE
ACTION FOR REACTION

Figure 1.2   A Question of Balance?

As we move forward into a more balanced time perspective, we learn to live in the present. The junk of the past has been removed, allowing us to retrieve the more positive memories. And there is now plenty of room in the future not only to plan and dream but also to realize some of those dreams down the line. This seesaw of time balances perfectly when the present acts as the balance point. Living in the present allows us to realize that we can make plans for the future and make peace with our past.

Now we can once again connect to ourselves as well as to our family, our culture, and our legacy. From the present we gain the energy to explore our universe, to seek what is novel and stimulating. From the future we gain the distant vision to soar to new realms of experience, to become whatever we can imagine. In that temporal balance we uncover not only the ideal treatment for PTSD but also a code for the fullest appreciation of our lives and the new guide to realizing our fullest potential — for all of us.

The positive effects of time perspective therapy are real. Not only has TPT been shown to work but also *its benefits last over the long term.*

In this book you will learn about Kara's experiences with TPT, and will read the stories of other men and women who have recovered from PTSD. In the next chapter, you will learn about the revolutionary psychological structure that gives TPT its power: Zimbardo's Time Paradox, a new psychology of time. You will also get a chance to discover your own time perspective by taking the Zimbardo Time Perspective Inventory, an invaluable psychological tool in treating PTSD and other issues.

o to sum up

- Post-traumatic stress disorder, or PTSD, is an anxiety disorder that begins with a trauma and overwhelms the individual's ability to cope with daily life. An estimated 7.5 million adult

American men and women currently suffer from PTSD. It is a
problem for veterans of all wars.

- PTSD sufferers are "stuck in time," reliving the trauma over and
  over, unable to leave it in the past and move on.
- With PTSD, the traumatic event is imprinted and stored in
  many different parts of the brain, which is one reason why it
  is so difficult to treat.
- It is much more helpful to view and treat PTSD as mental injury
  rather than mental illness, and research supports this view.
- PTSD doesn't only affect the sufferer; it can negatively affect the
  sufferer's family, friends, coworkers, and entire social network.
- To date, cognitive behavioral therapy (CBT) has been the therapy with the most success in overcoming trauma. This therapy
  focuses on the here and now. Drugs have provided some help,
  but not enough. They are a temporary solution that alters behavior, but they do not address the cause.
- Although all therapies are time based, time perspective therapy
  takes a different approach. It begins by respecting the trauma,
  and seeks to create a balance of past, present, and future that
  allows the PTSD sufferer to leave the past in the past and move
  toward a more hopeful future. TPT works in the context of Zimbardo's Time Paradox, a new psychology of time.

now it's your turn: past negative to past positive

Find a comfortable position in a safe place, and allow yourself five uninterrupted minutes to replace some of your bad or negative memories with good ones.

Close your eyes. Breathe slowly, deeply, and rhythmically. Allow your body to relax deeper and deeper with each breath.

Once you've completed four of these relaxing breaths, imagine going back in time to the first good memory that comes to mind. This memory may be from yesterday, last week, last year, or as far back as your childhood. Recall as much as you can about this experience: who was there, the time of day, where you were, a particular smell or aroma associated with the event, and so on.

Now move on to the next good memory that comes to mind. And then the next.

You may find this difficult to accomplish at first, especially if you have undergone severe trauma. And it may not happen in the first five minutes of your first attempt. But we've found that once you've remembered one good memory, the next is usually easier.

Just as James learned to replace some of his bad slides with good ones in the "Kodak Carousel" of his mind (see the Introduction to read this story), you can begin to draw on your own happy memories to sustain you during tough times.

2

a new psychology
of time

Before the accident that changed her life, Kara enjoyed the pleasures of the present moment fueled by enjoyable memories of the past. She and her husband, Bud, enjoyed fishing, hunting, motorcycle riding . . . activities they frequently and spontaneously participated in together. Like most of us, she had lived through her share of bad times and heartaches; but she had overcome them and was intent on focusing on the positive aspects of her past. The future, like the present, looked bright, but didn't require a lot of planning. And then the accident slammed her into a dark, painful reality that seemed to have no exit.

During the worst of Kara's PTSD, Kara was stuck in a time loop of compulsive thoughts about the accident, her injuries, and the young mother who had died — she felt literally haunted by the woman. When she wasn't fixated on the accident and its results, she dwelled on her feelings of survivor's guilt and how drastically her life had changed for the worse. These obsessive ideations wiped out all of the positive memories and experiences she had built up through the years. Kara felt that she no longer deserved to have fun of any kind.

Kara's past was filled with terror and guilt, her present was pain and hopelessness, and her future had ceased to exist. Rather than living in a balance of past memories, present actions, and future plans, Kara experienced a time perspective that had contracted to a narrow range, allowing for little hope and little change.

As was the case for Kara, our personal sense of time is one of the most powerful influences on our thoughts, feelings, and actions. No matter what time it is in our part of the world, in our head we live in a mix of three subjective psychological time zones: the past (what was), the present (what is), and the future (what will be). Each of these time zones is colored and further divided by our cultural biases; our spiritual beliefs; and a myriad of hopes and dreams, memories, and life experiences. Inevitably, each of us has a slightly different mix of temporal biases in our psychological makeup. And to a much greater extent than you may realize, we make our daily decisions, both conscious and unconscious, from the perspective of the individual time zone in which each of us lives.

When Temporal Theory is applied to helping PTSD sufferers recover from their emotional wounds, the effects on their lives and those of members of their family and social circle are profound and enduring.

brief history of temporal theory

Philip Zimbardo first began to investigate aspects of time perspectives in the early 1970s. Curiously, his first research was designed to change an individual's time perspective from future oriented to present oriented using hypnosis. In these experiments, Stanford students who were premeasured as "hypnotizable" and who were likely to be future oriented (not surprisingly, most Stanford students think seriously and continually about their future) were given a posthypnotic suggestion to alter their time zone. They were instructed that their past and future were distant and remote, and that the present would begin to fill their mind and would continue to expand during the session together. Their comparison group was told merely to think about time in their lives, while under hypnosis or not. These students were then put in a variety of test situations to determine if internalizing this new time focus had changed their time perspective.

Indeed, it did. The students in the "expanded present condition" immediately began to act more childlike—laughing more, joking more, wanting to play, getting totally immersed in making nothing out of a clay blob, and losing track of time. These measurable changes were significantly different from the behavior of their peers, who were not living for the moment in an expanded present condition.

Had their perception of time changed in any enduring way? Were they now more present oriented than they had been? Such basic questions could not be answered because there was not a measure of differences in time perspective with which to assess such transformations. Phil searched the literature for such metrics, but came away disillusioned. None of the available measures was reliable enough—they did not consistently generate the same scores; nor were they valid enough, that is, shown to be related to other measurable time-related tests and indicators.

Phil embarked on a long journey to develop a new scale to measure individual differences in time perspective that would be valid, reliable, and easy to administer and score. After much trial and error, he and his research team decided to create a new scale that would give precise scores on various dimensions of past, present, and future time orientations. A factor-analyzed scale was created and tested in the field to prove that it had significant links to more than a dozen other standard psychological scales and could predict various behavioral outcomes in new experiments.

Thus was born the Zimbardo Time Perspective Inventory (ZTPI) in 1999, after an elephant-like gestation, with Phil's graduate student assistant John Boyd serving as midwife. The team then went into high gear, using the ZTPI as a metric in many correlational and experimental investigations. Everything they did worked.

Soon Phil began getting feedback from colleagues and graduate students around the world. They were all getting robust effects

from using the ZTPI in a host of different studies, from physical conservation of energy to school and work performance, from smoking
cessation and drug addiction to much more. Today a dozen such young
researchers have created a cross-cultural research team to promote
the ZTPI as a research tool by standardizing its use, and by establishing what modifications are necessary for different national and cultural
settings.

○ temporal theory in a nutshell

We can reduce the complexity of our lives to a simple equation:

all actions taken + all actions not taken = our current experience

Some actions we take work out as planned, and we can take pride
in them ("I studied hard for that test and got an A"); there are other
actions, not in our best interest, that lead to bad outcomes, and for
which we are sorry ("It was a mistake to stay up drinking until 3:00 a.m.
the night before my job interview"). The actions we do *not* take also
have split consequences. Some we were right to reject, and we reflect on
how wise we were ("I'm so glad I didn't go out with Bill and that I went
out with Harry instead because Harry's the love of my life"); others we
later realize we should have taken, which leads to regret and resentment
("If only I had bought that hot technology stock when it was offered to
me years ago, I'd be set for life now").

At the very heart of this decision matrix are the largely unconscious
decisions that spring from our subjective psychological sense of time:
our *time perspective*. This arises from the daily flow of our personal
experiences, which we automatically view through the lens of our own
time perspective. And depending on which lens we wear, our actions —
and our expectations of them and reasons for taking or not taking
them — will be very different.

phil's perspective: growing up in the past and present tense

Phil writes,

I grew up in a poor Sicilian immigrant family living in New York's South Bronx ghetto in the 1930s. Despite the poverty, almost everyone took pleasure in the present, enjoying good food, good wine, good conversation, friends, singing, dancing, making music, romance, and nature. They also loved to tell stories and to sing about the glorious past—but I couldn't help but notice that there was no place for tomorrow. No one planned ahead, no one made reservations for anything requiring one, no one had an agenda or a to-do list. Today and yesterday were vivid realities, whereas tomorrow was uncertain.

With poverty, life is not all wine and roses; but for some it is an endlessly bitter brew that leads to cynicism about ever being able to improve it by one's own actions. There was always the old aunt who was totally fatalistic, saying, "Nothing will change, our lives are controlled by cruel fate." But living out a hedonistic or fatalistic present, or being stuck in reliving the negative past, for better or for worse, leaves out the one thing that is essential to progress in life, to success in school and business, to achieving goals, to transforming reality: a vibrant sense of the future. Why work hard for a better tomorrow? There was just no reason.

Ultimately, my family's philosophy was summed up in the common Sicilian saying "Che sarà sarà, whatever will be, will be." We would just wait for better times.

I found my family's attitude maddening. Education, hard work, achieving set goals, planning short-term and long-term goals ... these were clearly essential for survival. With that driving force of a focus on the future always in high gear, I was able to succeed in school and ultimately in a career. What did I sacrifice for that achievement? The joys and pleasures of the present. Play. Fun. Fooling around. Being a kid. Just doing nothing but being.

I was always acutely aware of this dialectic in my life, and in my brain: Future Work versus Present Play. Over the years I wondered how common such a trade-off is, and what a more balanced time focus might be.

Psychological time became an obsession for Phil early on. As a mature psychologist, he wondered if such vague human conceptions could be studied, measured, and instilled in people. Eventually he learned that this was indeed possible, and discovered just how central a role our perceptions about time play in our lives:

> Recently, I learned an interesting fact: there is no future tense verb in Sicilian dialect! Now it all made sense: How can any planning go on if there is no "what will be" or "what could be" to balance against "what is" and "what was"?

o the six main time perspectives in a nutshell

Each of the three primary subjective time zones—past, present, and future—is divided into two parts. This gives us six main time perspectives:

1. **Past positive** people focus on the "good old days." They may keep scrapbooks, collect photos, and look forward to celebrating traditional holidays.
2. **Past negative** people focus on all the things that went wrong in the past: "It doesn't matter what I do, my life will never change."
3. **Present hedonistic** people live in the moment—seeking pleasure, novelty, and sensation, and avoiding pain.
4. **Present fatalistic** people feel that decisions are moot because predetermined fate plays the guiding role in life: "What will be, will be."
5. **Future**-oriented people plan for the future and trust that their decisions will work out.
6. **Transcendental-future**-oriented people have faith that a better time is coming after death, and plan for this afterlife during their current lifetime.

As shown in Figure 2.1, *past-oriented* people make decisions based on negative or positive memories of similar situations. *Present-oriented* people take immediate action based on pleasure or avoidance, without thought for consequences. *Future-oriented* people make decisions based on a reasoned assessment of the future consequences, engaging in cost-versus-benefits reasoning.

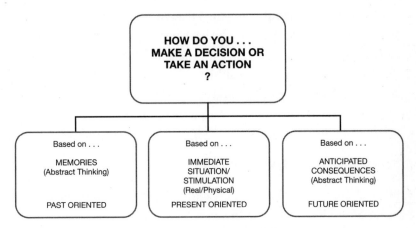

Figure 2.1   **Conceptual Time Perspective Model**

That's Temporal Theory—the theory of time perspectives—in a nutshell. Yes, it's simple; perhaps even obvious. But the consequences of understanding time perspectives and using that understanding are great. With that goal in mind, let's take a deeper look at how individuals with each time perspective see the world.

o biased toward the past

Good and bad things happen to everyone, but not everyone sees the world in the same way or gives equal weight to experiences. Put simply, some of us naturally see the world through rose-colored glasses (past positive), whereas others see the world through a darker lens (past negative). We have found that people who primarily focus on the past value the old more than the new; the familiar over the novel; and the cautious, conservative approach over the daring, more liberal or risky one.

past positive: remember the "good old days"

People with a past positive point of view see constant reminders of what used to be good and wonderful, a treasure trove of beloved mementoes, of life as it could and should be. They judge, evaluate, and react to everything in the present moment through memories of happy past experiences. In general, people who have positive feelings about the past tend to be less anxious than those with negative feelings about the past. They also tend to be happier, healthier, and more successful — regardless of whether or not their rose-colored glasses saw events as they objectively occurred.

past negative: life always lets you down

Phil's old aunt, who viewed her world through dark prisms of the past, is a good example of the past negative bias. People who see through this lens judge, evaluate, and react to everything in the present moment through memories of unhappy past experiences. They live in a museum of horrors ornamented by their failures, regrets, illnesses, gullibility, and deceptions. When they inevitably experience a tragedy or personal trauma, they cannot let it go and move on. They tend to replay

Table 2.1   **Past Positive Versus Past Negative Decision Making**

Past Positive	Past Negative
I'm going to ask her out — she reminds me of my favorite cousin.	My ex used to love that movie too — I can't be with her any more.
Law was a good field for my dad, so I'm going to be an attorney too.	My father was abusive, so I'm better off without a man in my life.
Sure, why not? Most things work out for me.	I always make mistakes — I should probably leave this alone.
I've had so many good things in my life — I'm really fortunate.	The older I get, the more things I see that I've missed out on.
You have my blessing — not everyone in that family was bad, just Grandpa's business partner.	No, you cannot marry into that family — they were responsible for sinking Grandpa's business.

that mental video over and over, keeping it fresh and current no matter how many years have passed. PTSD sufferers often tend to have a high past negative score.

People with a bias toward the past live in a déjà vu world in which each new "this" reminds them of an old "that." But there's quite a difference between a past negative and a past positive orientation, as shown in Table 2.1.

o biased toward the present

People who live in the present are far less—or not at all—influenced by either past experiences or future considerations. They focus only on the immediate present—what's happening *now*. They make decisions based on the inner forces and outer pressures in their immediate stimulus situation: internal hormonal signals, feelings, smells, sounds, the attractive qualities of the object of desire, and what others are urging them to do. Remember the old parental question, "If all of your friends were jumping off a bridge, would you do that too?" For people with a bias toward the present, the answer is likely to be "Yes."

PTSD sufferers often score high in a bias toward the present, both as hedonists and fatalists. This leads to the risky behaviors that are so often linked to PTSD.

present hedonism: live for today!

Present hedonists are pleasure-seekers, and delayed gratification is not part of their psychological vocabulary. You've heard their mottos: "Do it now!" "Carpe diem!" "Let the good times roll!" "You only live once!" For them, a bird in the hand is always better than two in the bush; and devouring one delicious treat now rules over waiting for two later on.

When considering whether to have one more drink before driving home after the party, or to hook up with a new acquaintance for some casual sex, they make decisions in the *now*. Even though the same behavior in the past may have landed them in jail, or with an unwanted pregnancy, or in an accident, they do not take that information into consideration. They do not seem to learn from experience or worry about tomorrow. They want what they want when they want it, and that's it.

Present hedonism in moderation — selected present hedonism — is a good thing. But too much of a good thing can cause us to feel like our lives are stuck on an out-of-control roller coaster. Because present hedonists actively seek pleasure, it's not surprising that they tend to be happier and more creative than their fatalist counterparts.

present fatalism: what will be, will be

The other way to live in the present is quite different: to believe that all of one's decisions are determined by fate, by external forces, or by religiously determined destiny. Present fatalists do not see the need to spend time planning and plotting and considering behavioral options because their decision is already fated. What will be, will be. They relinquish all decisional control to God or the universe, believing the outcomes of each decisional dilemma are already predetermined.

Present fatalists share a present focus with hedonists, but they could not be more different. Whereas present fatalists feel their lives follow a fated plan over which they have little or no control, present hedonists desperately seek to overcontrol by indulging in immediate pleasure, frequently to avoid pain, without regard for the consequences. Both of these types of people focus on neither the past nor the future, but simply persist in their present situation. This orientation is understandable among folks who have lived in poverty for an extended time, and whose efforts at improving their lot have failed to make anything better. It is also understandable for those who have or believe they have an incurable illness, or whose religion dictates that a higher spiritual force is making their decisions for them. PTSD sufferers often relinquish control in this way.

People with a bias toward the present live in the now. The past doesn't exist, and the future doesn't matter (see Table 2.2).

Table 2.2   **Present Hedonistic Versus Present Fatalistic Decision Making**

Present Hedonistic	Present Fatalistic
Sure, why not? Live fast, die young—that's my motto.	Sure, why not? If it's gonna happen, it's gonna happen.
College? No. Too much work, not enough partying.	Why should I even bother going to college? If God wants me to be rich, I'll be rich.
I love writing, art, music, anything where I get to be creative.	I'm waiting for inspiration. I know it will strike sooner or later.
Sure, I shoplifted that ring—it was so pretty I just had to have it!	Sure, I shoplifted that ring—if I get caught, that's just my fate.
I love being spontaneous—you never know what will happen when you leave the door open.	Why make big plans? Fate always lends a hand.
I never make to-do lists! That would just cramp my style.	I never make to-do lists! Something always comes along.

a third path: the expanded or holistic present

There is a third attitude toward the present that is very different from both present fatalism and present hedonism. The expanded or holistic present is the absolute present, a concept central to Buddhism and meditation, and is very different from the Western linear view of time. The absolute present contains both past and future. The present is neither a slave to the past nor a means to the future. Daily meditation gives the practitioner the experience of being in the present moment, unfiltered through the lenses of past or future.

By opening your mind fully to the present moment, you give up longing and desire for future possibilities and surrender past regrets and obligations. This form of present attention or mindfulness can fill your entire being, replacing your sense of past and future with a sense of everything being one and the same. With this perspective, the past, the present, the future, the physical, the mental, and the spiritual elements in life are not separate but closely interconnected within you. The holistic present reflects neither the pleasure-seeking of present hedonism nor the cynicism and resignation of present fatalism.

Sanskrit, India's classical language, captures that unique attitude toward time in this ancient saying:

Yesterday is already a dream
And tomorrow but a vision
But today well lived makes every yesterday a dream of happiness
And every tomorrow a vision of hope.

Although the holistic present is not common in Western thinking, many Western philosophers and theologians have written about it as something of an idea. The present contains the reconstruction of time that has passed and the construction of virtual time that will soon be present. The past and future are abstractions, mental constructions that are subject to distortion; wishful thinking; and the psychological disorders of depression, anxiety, and worry.

The expanded or holistic present is a healthy perspective to have![1]

o biased toward the future

No one is born thinking about how to plan for the future. A number of conditions — including living in a temperate zone (where it's necessary to anticipate seasonal change), living in a stable family or society, being Protestant or Jewish, and becoming educated — can create future-oriented people. In general, future-oriented people do very well. They are less aggressive, are less depressed, have more energy, take care of their health, have good impulse control, and have more self-esteem.

Americans in general are concerned with planning for the future. But PTSD sufferers, locked into negative memories, have generally lost the ability to even conceive of a hopeful future and must journey toward this time perspective to create balance.

future: plan for tomorrow

Future-oriented people pay minimal attention to past experiences, and they brush off the clamor of the present to "act now." Instead, they pull out their mental calculator to figure out the possible future consequences of current actions. If they find that the anticipated costs are higher than the imagined gains, then it is a NO GO—the perceived risks trump the action in question. But if the imagined gains dominate over the imagined costs, then it is a GO DO.

Future-oriented people live in a world of contingencies, probabilities, and abstract mental representations of a virtual world on their horizon. They are not tempted by immediate gratification that could backfire later—like unprotected sex that could result in a sexually transmitted disease, an unplanned pregnancy, or a ruined reputation. They are not easily persuaded by salespeople hustling questionable products or services; yet they are able take a well-reasoned chance on a new idea.

Not surprisingly, the future orientation lends itself to problem solving and creating alternative strategies for reaching a goal. Future-oriented people finish what they start and get the job done. And they understand that although anything can happen, they can take steps to plan for a healthy, successful life. But they can also get *too* caught up in planning for the future. They may multitask like crazy, complaining that "there's not enough time" or sacrificing their family life for material success that will support their family financially.

time perspectives and behavior worldwide

Time perspective differences are global. The following selected research findings on time perspectives and behavior were found using the ZTPI and detailed in *The Time Paradox*[2]:

- College grades in introductory psychology courses were found to be highest for future-oriented, lowest for present fatalistic, and low-average for present hedonistic students.
- Future-oriented people tend to live longer because their dominant trait is conscientiousness, which has been shown to add several years of life over those who are low in this characteristic.

- Present-oriented college students (both female and male) at Cornell University and Stanford University are significantly more likely to drink alcohol to excess and engage in risky driving than are their future-oriented peers.
- Hospitalized heroin addicts, when compared to hospitalized nonaddicted controls, scored significantly higher on measures of present hedonism and fatalism, and lower on measures of future orientation.
- Among two samples of U.S. high school students, a present orientation was positively correlated with high-risk, high-arousal behaviors. This is in contrast to the negative correlations found with future-oriented high school students on risky driving, receiving DUIs, racing, not wearing seat belts, watching R-rated and X-rated movies, having sex, biking, and taking risks skateboarding.
- Present-oriented college students were most creative when making art within an experimentally induced process focus, but least creative with a focus on their product. This contrasts with future-oriented students, who excelled in art high in technical merit when they focused on their product.
- In Rome, future-oriented women were found to be more likely than present-oriented women to go to a free breast cancer checkup clinic.
- Future-oriented people in Brazil and Mexico were found to be more likely than their present-focused peers to engage in water and energy conservation and to have pro-environment attitudes.
- Students who scored high on past negative measures were found to be less likely to get constructive social support when under stress than those who were present or future oriented.
- Future-oriented Canadians were found to be more likely than others to make health responsibility and nutrition high priorities.
- British citizens who were homeless were more likely to have scored, high on past negative and present fatalistic measures.

transcendental future: look ahead — far, far ahead

As we have seen, future-oriented people are ambitious and motivated by goals. They operate totally within the realm of their lifetime and make decisions based on a relatively short or very long spans of time — focusing on next week, the quarterly return, or next season, or considering their legacy for the next generation. But for those with a transcendental future orientation, the ideal vision involves leading a good life in expectation of rewards they will not reap in their lifetime or their children's lifetime.[3]

religious beliefs   One type of transcendental future orientation grows out of religious or spiritual beliefs. (Of members of the major world religions, Christians and Muslims score higher on transcendental future orientation measures, whereas Jews and Buddhists score lower.)[4] For these believers, the real future begins after the death of the mortal body and extends to eternity: divine rewards, being reunited with loved ones who have passed on, eternal life, reincarnation into a better life, and so on. This motivates what is often considered to be irrational behavior, such as becoming a suicide bomber or self-immolation in the name of a cause; but expectations of future reward can also enable people to withstand terrible struggles and tribulations in this world, with the understanding that their reward is waiting for them in the next life.

secular beliefs   You don't have to be religious to have a transcendental future orientation: you may make decisions based on the needs of future generations. The Long Now Foundation, for example, has created the ten-thousand-year clock, promoting *very* long-term thinking about the future. Some seek to protect the future just because they feel "it's the right thing to do." The sustainability movement, for example, seeks to protect the world's natural resources in perpetuity. But this viewpoint is not new. The Great Law of Peace of the Iroquois, a confederacy of Native American Indian Tribes, says: "In every deliberation, we must consider the impact on the seventh generation ... even if it requires having skin as thick as the bark of a pine."[5]

People with a bias toward the future consider the experiences of past and present in their future plans. Table 2.3 contains examples of thought differences between future-oriented and transcendental-future-oriented people.

Table 2.3   Future-Oriented Versus Transcendental-Future-Oriented Decision Making

Future Oriented	Transcendental Future Oriented
I have to meet tomorrow's deadline.	The only thing that is important is eternity.
If I play my cards right, I can be successful in this life.	Whatever else happens, I'll get my reward in heaven.
I'm willing to forgo eating dessert tonight because I want to enjoy Thanksgiving tomorrow.	It doesn't really matter if I'm not well fed today—God will provide in the next life.
I can think of several ways to approach that problem! Let me work out the different scenarios.	The best way to approach this problem is the one that has the most benefit in the long term.

the zimbardo time perspective inventory

These interesting conjectures about differences in time perspective make sense. But the exciting part of Temporal Theory is that we have been able to make precise measures of each time factor, arriving at an individualized way to index how any one person differs from another in regard to each of the time perspectives just discussed. The Zimbardo Time Perspective Inventory, or ZTPI, was developed through the use of focus groups, interviews with many different people, surveys of thousands of students and older people, and repeated refinements.[6] This measuring tool captures these elusive qualities of mind in a way that has proven to be both reliable (the same results recur over subsequent tests) and valid (it predicts a range of other traits and behaviors).

The scale was initially limited only to future versus present factors because it was assumed that Americans (especially American students) were not very past oriented, and that the most interesting contrasts were between those who were highly future oriented and those who were present hedonistic. But when the team began to interview older people, that assumption proved to be both shortsighted and wrong.[7]

Finding Yourself on the ZTPI

The ZTPI consists of fifty-six simple statements that are a mixed blend of five time factors: future, past positive, past negative, present hedonism, and present fatalism. (A separate scale was developed to measure transcendental future orientation, to keep the ZTPI to a manageable length.) Everyone can find themselves on the ZTPI, and we hope you will. You can take the ZTPI right now (see below) to get an idea of your scores in the different time perspectives. You can also take the ZTPI (www.thetimeparadox.com/surveys/) and the Transcendental-future Time Perspective Inventory (TTPI) (www.thetimeparadox.com/surveys/ttpi/) online, where they will be scored for you automatically.

When you have finished answering the questions, follow the scoring rules. You will have a set of five scores that represent the degree to which each time factor operates in your makeup. Although we tend to talk as if there are distinct, broadly drawn temporal orientations, your overall time perspective is actually a matter of the extent to which you share in aspects from each of the five time factors. When you compare your numerical score to the average for each time factor, the result is a sense of how high or low you are on each of them. In this way you can determine how your life experiences have contributed to your unique ZTPI profile. The power of this measuring tool is evident in that it has been translated into more than thirty languages worldwide and that dozens of researchers from many nations have found significant effects using it in a host of research projects.[8]

Read each item and, as honestly as you can, answer the question: How characteristic or true is this of me? Check the appropriate box under the scale at the right. Please answer *all* of the following questions.

	1	2	3	4	5
	Very Untrue		Neutral		Very True
1. I believe that getting together with one's friends to party is one of life's important pleasures.	1	2	3	4	5
2. Familiar childhood sights, sounds, and smells often bring back a flood of wonderful memories.	1	2	3	4	5
3. Fate determines much in my life.	1	2	3	4	5
4. I often think of what I should have done differently in my life.	1	2	3	4	5
5. My decisions are mostly influenced by people and things around me.	1	2	3	4	5
6. I believe that a person's day should be planned ahead each morning.	1	2	3	4	5
7. It gives me pleasure to think of my past.	1	2	3	4	5
8. I do things impulsively.	1	2	3	4	5
9. If things don't get done on time, I don't worry about it.	1	2	3	4	5
10. When I want to achieve something, I set goals and consider specific means for reaching those goals.	1	2	3	4	5
11. On balance, there is much more good to recall than bad in my past.	1	2	3	4	5
12. When listening to my favorite music, I often lose all track of time.	1	2	3	4	5

	1	2	3	4	5
	Very Untrue		Neutral		Very True
13. Meeting tomorrow's deadlines and doing other necessary work come before tonight's play.	1	2	3	4	5
14. Since whatever will be will be, it doesn't really matter what I do.	1	2	3	4	5
15. I enjoy stories about how things used to be in the "good old times."	1	2	3	4	5
16. Painful past experiences keep being replayed in my mind.	1	2	3	4	5
17. I try to live my life as fully as possible, one day at a time.	1	2	3	4	5
18. It upsets me to be late for appointments.	1	2	3	4	5
19. Ideally, I would live each day as if it were my last.	1	2	3	4	5
20. Happy memories of good times spring readily to mind.	1	2	3	4	5
21. I meet my obligations to friends and authorities on time.	1	2	3	4	5
22. I've taken my share of abuse and rejection in the past.	1	2	3	4	5
23. I make decisions on the spur of the moment.	1	2	3	4	5
24. I take each day as it is rather than try to plan it out.	1	2	3	4	5
25. The past has too many unpleasant memories that I prefer not to think about.	1	2	3	4	5

	1	2	3	4	5
	Very Untrue		Neutral		Very True
26. It is important to put excitement in my life.	1	2	3	4	5
27. I've made mistakes in the past that I wish I could undo.	1	2	3	4	5
28. I feel that it's more important to enjoy what you're doing than to get work done on time.	1	2	3	4	5
29. I get nostalgic about my childhood.	1	2	3	4	5
30. Before making a decision, I weigh the costs against the benefits.	1	2	3	4	5
31. Taking risks keeps my life from becoming boring.	1	2	3	4	5
32. It is more important for me to enjoy life's journey than to focus only on the destination.	1	2	3	4	5
33. Things rarely work out as I expected.	1	2	3	4	5
34. It's hard for me to forget unpleasant images of my youth.	1	2	3	4	5
35. It takes joy out of the process and flow of my activities if I have to think about goals, outcomes, and products.	1	2	3	4	5
36. Even when I am enjoying the present, I am drawn back to comparisons with similar past experiences.	1	2	3	4	5

	1	2	3	4	5
	Very Untrue		Neutral		Very True
37. You can't really plan for the future because things change so much.	1	2	3	4	5
38. My life path is controlled by forces I cannot influence.	1	2	3	4	5
39. It doesn't make sense to worry about the future, since there is nothing that I can do about it anyway.	1	2	3	4	5
40. I complete projects on time by making steady progress.	1	2	3	4	5
41. I find myself tuning out when family members talk about the way things used to be.	1	2	3	4	5
42. I take risks to put excitement in my life.	1	2	3	4	5
43. I make lists of things to do.	1	2	3	4	5
44. I often follow my heart more than my head.	1	2	3	4	5
45. I am able to resist temptations when I know that there is work to be done.	1	2	3	4	5
46. I find myself getting swept up in the excitement of the moment.	1	2	3	4	5
47. Life today is too complicated; I would prefer the simpler life of the past.	1	2	3	4	5
48. I prefer friends who are spontaneous rather than predictable.	1	2	3	4	5

	1	2	3	4	5
	Very Untrue		Neutral		Very True
49. I like family rituals and traditions that are regularly repeated.	1	2	3	4	5
50. I think about the bad things that have happened to me in the past.	1	2	3	4	5
51. I keep working at difficult, uninteresting tasks if they will help me get ahead.	1	2	3	4	5
52. Spending what I earn on pleasures today is better than saving for tomorrow's security.	1	2	3	4	5
53. Often luck pays off better than hard work.	1	2	3	4	5
54. I think about the good things that I have missed out on in my life.	1	2	3	4	5
55. I like my close relationships to be passionate.	1	2	3	4	5
56. There will always be time to catch up on my work.	1	2	3	4	5

scoring key

Scoring Instructions

Before scoring the ZTPI, you have to reverse the answers for questions 9, 24, 25, 41, and 56. This means a

1 becomes a 5
2 becomes a 4
3 remains a 3
4 becomes a 2
5 becomes a 1

After reversing these answers, add your scores for the questions that comprise each factor. After adding your scores for each factor, divide the total score by the number of questions that comprise each factor. This results in an average score for each of the five factors.

the past negative time perspective

Add your scores on questions 4, 5, 16, 22, 27, 33, 34, 36, 50, and 54. Then divide this number by 10.

Question	Score
4. I often think of what I should have done differently in my life.	
5. My decisions are mostly influenced by people and things around me.	
16. Painful past experiences keep being replayed in my mind.	
22. I've taken my share of abuse and rejection in the past.	
27. I've made mistakes in the past that I wish I could undo.	
33. Things rarely work out as I expected.	
34. It's hard for me to forget unpleasant images of my youth.	
36. Even when I am enjoying the present, I am drawn back to comparisons with similar past experiences.	
50. I think about the bad things that have happened to me in the past.	
54. I think about the good things that I have missed out on in my life.	
Total Score:	

the present hedonistic time perspective

Add your scores on questions 1, 8, 12, 17, 19, 23, 26, 28, 31, 32, 42, 44, 46, 48, and 55. Then divide this number by 15.

Question	Score
1. I believe that getting together with one's friends to party is one of life's important pleasures.	
8. I do things impulsively.	
12. When listening to my favorite music, I often lose all track of time.	

Question	Score
17. I try to live my life as fully as possible, one day at a time.	
19. Ideally, I would live each day as if it were my last.	
23. I make decisions on the spur of the moment.	
26. It is important to put excitement in my life.	
28. I feel that it's more important to enjoy what you're doing than to get work done on time.	
31. Taking risks keeps my life from becoming boring.	
32. It is more important for me to enjoy life's journey than to focus only on the destination.	
42. I take risks to put excitement in my life.	
44. I often follow my heart more than my head.	
46. I find myself getting swept up in the excitement of the moment.	
48. I prefer friends who are spontaneous rather than predictable.	
55. I like my close relationships to be passionate.	
Total Score:	

the future time perspective

Add your scores on questions 6, 9 (reversed), 10, 13, 18, 21, 24 (reversed), 30, 40, 43, 45, 51, and 56 (reversed). Then divide this number by 13.

Question	Score
6. I believe that a person's day should be planned ahead each morning.	
9. If things don't get done on time, I don't worry about it.	
10. When I want to achieve something, I set goals and consider specific means for reaching those goals.	
13. Meeting tomorrow's deadlines and doing other necessary work come before tonight's play.	

Question	Score
18. It upsets me to be late for appointments.	
21. I meet my obligations to friends and authorities on time.	
24. I take each day as it is rather than try to plan it out.	
30. Before making a decision, I weigh the costs against the benefits.	
40. I complete projects on time by making steady progress.	
43. I make lists of things to do.	
45. I am able to resist temptations when I know that there is work to be done.	
51. I keep working at difficult, uninteresting tasks if they will help me get ahead.	
56. There will always be time to catch up on my work.	
Total Score:	

the past positive time perspective

Add your scores on questions 2, 7, 11, 15, 20, 25 (reversed), 29, 41 (reversed), and 49. Then divide this number by 9.

Question	Score
2. Familiar childhood sights, sounds, and smells often bring back a flood of wonderful memories.	
7. It gives me pleasure to think of my past.	
11. On balance, there is much more good to recall than bad in my past.	
15. I enjoy stories about how things used to be in the "good old times."	
20. Happy memories of good times spring readily to mind.	
25. The past has too many unpleasant memories that I prefer not to think about.	
29. I get nostalgic about my childhood.	
41. I find myself tuning out when family members talk about the way things used to be.	
49. I like family rituals and traditions that are regularly repeated.	
Total Score:	

the present fatalistic time perspective

Add your scores on questions 3, 14, 35, 37, 38, 39, 47, 52, and 53. Then divide this number by 9.

Question	Score
3. Fate determines much in my life.	
14. Since whatever will be will be, it doesn't really matter what I do.	
35. It takes joy out of the process and flow of my activities if I have to think about goals, outcomes, and products.	
37. You can't really plan for the future because things change so much.	
38. My life path is controlled by forces I cannot influence.	
39. It doesn't make sense to worry about the future, since there is nothing that I can do about it anyway.	
47. Life today is too complicated; I would prefer the simpler life of the past.	
52. Spending what I earn on pleasures today is better than saving for tomorrow's security.	
53. Often luck pays off better than hard work.	
Total Score:	

interpreting your scores

Once you've taken the ZTPI or TTPI and scored it, you may wonder what it all means. Figure 2.2 is a graph that we made by combining time perspective scores from a large sample of respondents. It shows average and "ideal" scores for each time perspective.

Average Scores (50 Percent): The *average score* for each time perspective lines up with 50 percent on the graph. For example, for the past negative time perspective, the average score is 3.0. For the past positive it is 3.7.[9]

Ideal Scores (Dots): The dots represent *our idea of ideal time scores*—they are not associated with the data in any way. We have included these ideals so that you can have an indication of how to improve your time perspective.

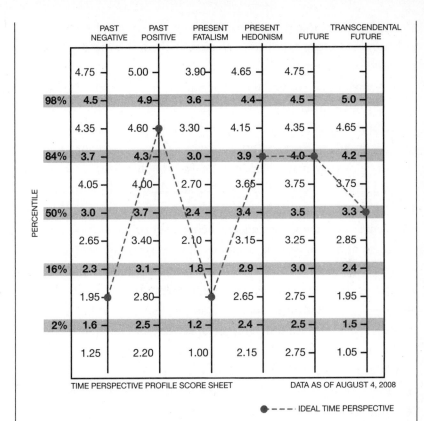

Figure 2.2   Average and "Ideal" ZTPI and TTPI Scores

To Compare Your Scores to the "Ideal": Plot your scores on the image, then connect the dots, as we have done here. How does your time perspective compare?[10]

o   developing a balanced time perspective

Our individual attitudes toward time are largely learned, and we generally relate to time unconsciously and subjectively. Each of us, in fact, has a time perspective that is largely *biased*—we overuse one of the time zones while underusing the others, even when they might be more appropriate in a given situation for a particular decision. We have found, however, that as we become more conscious of our temporal orientations we can take action to change them, journeying toward a balanced time perspective.

We divide the continual flow of our experiences into time frames that help give order, coherence, and meaning to events. These time frames may reflect cyclical and repetitive patterns, such as the changing seasons, holidays, your monthly menstrual cycle, or your children's birthdays; or they may reflect unique and singular linear events, such as the death of a parent, the day of an accident, or the start of a war. You use time perspectives in encoding, storing, and recalling your experiences; in sensing, feeling, and being; in shaping your expectations and goals; and in imagining scenarios of what is and what might be.

In our work we have consistently found that time perspectives play a fundamental role in the way people live. People tend to develop and overuse a particular time zone, for example, focusing on the future, the present, or the past. Although one perspective is not inherently "better," we see some striking features.

Future-oriented people tend to be more successful professionally and academically, to eat well, to exercise regularly, and to schedule preventive doctor's exams. People who are predominantly present oriented tend to be willing to help others, but appear less willing or able to help themselves. In general, present-oriented people are more likely to engage in risky sexual behavior, to gamble, or to use drugs and alcohol than are future-oriented people. They are also less likely to exercise, eat well, and engage in preventive health practices, such as brushing their teeth and getting regular health exams.

Consequently, future-oriented people are the most likely to be successful but the least likely to help others in need. Ironically, the people who are best able to help are the least likely to do so. In contrast, present-oriented people are less likely to be successful, but are more likely to help others. Again ironically, individuals who are most likely to help others may be those least likely to help themselves.

The situation is more complicated with past-oriented people. Divergent attitudes toward the past—negative or positive—play dramatic roles in daily decisions because they become binding frames of reference that are carried in the minds of those with positive or negative past views. Past positive people are friendly, are family oriented, and are likely to be Good Samaritans to help others in need, but primarily familiar others. Past negative people are so locked up in their orbit of self-torment that they are often unable to act in service to others or to their family and community.

If these characteristics sound like what you know so far of PTSD, you are right. People from any time perspective can be knocked into past negative or present hedonistic orientations by trauma. To understand how drastically time perspectives can change in the lives of those with PTSD, let's revisit Kara's experience:

- Before the accident, Kara's time perspective was heavy on *present hedonism* with a healthy dose of *past positive.*
- Like most of us, she had lived through her share of past negatives, but she had overcome them and was intent on focusing on the positive aspects of her past. Her *future,* like her present, looked bright, but didn't require a lot of planning.
- During the worst of Kara's PTSD, her time perspective included extreme *past negative* and *present fatalistic* orientations. Her obsessive thoughts replaced any past positives she had built up through the years, and her *future* ceased to exist.

After two months of intensive therapy (three times a week) with the Swords, Kara's time perspective had come full circle. She was still in some physical pain from her injuries, but she had regained her desire to enjoy her life and was indeed thankful to have a life. Her most recent ZTPI scores indicate a significant rise in *present hedonism* and a return to a *past positive* outlook, as well as an increase in a *future* positive orientation. She is moving toward a balanced time perspective. (Note: In our time perspective clinical work, we discovered that just as our past time perspective is split between positive and negative, so is the future time perspective; hence we refer to future positive and future negative or future fatalistic.)

In the next chapter, we'll see how Richard and Rosemary Sword's work with traumatized war veterans fits into Zimbardo's Temporal Theory to reveal an exciting new way to help PTSD sufferers move forward to a brighter future.

o to sum up

- The three subjective psychological time zones in which we live are the past (what was), the present (what is), and the future (what will be). Each of these time zones is further divided by cultural biases; spiritual beliefs; and countless hopes, dreams, memories, and experiences.
- *Past-oriented* people make decisions based on negative or positive memories of similar situations. *Present-oriented* people take immediate action based on pleasure or avoidance, without thought for consequences. *Future-oriented* people make decisions based on a reasoned assessment of the future consequences.
- There are six main time perspectives that shape how people see the world:
    1. **Past positive** people focus on the "good old days." They may keep scrapbooks, collect photos, and look forward to celebrating traditional holidays.
    2. **Past negative** people focus on all the things that went wrong in the past: "It doesn't matter what I do, my life will never change."
    3. **Present hedonistic** people live in the moment—seeking pleasure, knowledge, and sensation, and avoiding pain.
    4. **Present fatalistic** people feel that decisions are moot because predetermined fate plays the guiding role in life: "What will be, will be."
    5. **Future**-oriented people plan for the future and trust that their decisions will work out.

6. **Transcendental-future** – oriented people have faith that a better time is coming after death, and plan for this during their lives.

The Zimbardo Time Perspective Inventory allows precise measures of each time factor, arriving at an individualized way to index how any one person differs from another concerning each of the temporal perspectives.

now it's your turn: selected present hedonism

Allow yourself five uninterrupted minutes to relax in a safe place. Close your eyes. Breathe slowly, deeply, and rhythmically. Allow your body to relax deeper and deeper with each breath.

Once you've completed four of these relaxing breaths, think of something you enjoy doing. If you've been through trauma and have been unable to enjoy yourself, you may have to go back to a time before the trauma and remember what used to bring you joy.

Now make a commitment to yourself to follow through with this selected present hedonistic activity as soon as possible. There is no time like the present!

If you now have a disability and can no longer do what you used to enjoy, then now is the time to discover new things that will bring you joy. These can be simple things, such as sitting in the sun, visiting a flower shop, listening to music, playing a board game with your family, watching a comedy, sharing a meal with your favorite people, crocheting, reading a good book, enjoying nature, petting a furry animal … the possibilities are yours to discover.

3

time perspective therapy

"That first TPT [time perspective therapy] session was a long one," Kara said, "because Dr. Sword wanted to know about us as a couple." She continued,

> Bud did all the talking. He said we were a fun-loving couple and liked doing things together... Then Dr. Sword asked what I was like now. I was kind of shocked when Bud told him I was like a stranger—depressed and paranoid and didn't give a rat's ass about how I looked. Then it got kind of humiliating because he said I didn't want to be touched anymore; I didn't seem to know what fun was and didn't care about anything. Listening to Bud talk about how I used to be and about how I was—that was one of the hardest things I have ever done. I just sat there and cried. What had become of Kara? Where was she? And would Bud and me ever get her back?

PTSD sufferers like Kara get stuck in time: *The past is behind me,* they think, *and it was horrifying. The future is rushing toward me—and all I can see is more of the horrors of the past repeating forever.* In other words, the future—which hasn't yet happened—has already turned into a bad memory. *If I can't move backward because it's too frightening, and I can't move forward because nothing good can possibly happen,* they think, *then I certainly can't make a plan or even take an action. It doesn't matter what I do. The safest place for me is to stay stuck right here.*

Most traditional therapy models take PTSD sufferers back into the horror in the hope of desensitizing them to the trauma, or to plant the meaning of the present firmly in the experiences of the past. This may mean dwelling in the past for anywhere from a few hours, to a few weeks or months, to literally years, looking at painful experiences and reliving them from a number of perspectives. As we have seen, this can feel like torture and seems to be only partially effective.

Time perspective therapy takes a very different route toward emotional and psychological recovery. We say, "Where you are going is more important than where you have been. *Your past is not your potential—your future is your potential.*" We begin by airing out the trauma, giving it the respect it deserves; but we do not dwell there. Instead, we go even further back, gathering positive strengths from the person's past—finding the person he or she was before the trauma. Then we come back to the present, helping our client discover ways to enjoy each day as it comes. Finally, we proceed full tilt toward a balanced time perspective and a brighter future.

how long does TPT take to work?

All clients want to know how long it will take before they feel better. This is a natural question! Some of our PTSD clients have carried this burden for seventy years. For others it has been a few years, or maybe just a matter of months—but nothing they have tried so far has been much help, and they feel pretty hopeless.

It sometimes happens that a self-realized, determined client can grasp the basics of Temporal Theory, understand how TPT works, and learn how to balance his or her time perspective in one session. Yes, it has happened. On a few occasions we have met one time with clients who were highly motivated; they got it, and moved on. We have bumped into them outside the office and found that they are still doing well. Unfortunately, this is rarely the case for clients suffering from chronic and severe PTSD.

In practice, we have found that it generally takes from four to eight sessions for clients to gain a working knowledge of Temporal Theory and to be able to apply these concepts in their lives. However, it can also take more sessions and a longer time, depending on the severity of the client's PTSD and his or her resistance to change.

o TPT basics

The primary goal of TPT is the same regardless of what brought the client to therapy—achieving a balanced time perspective. But there are many different ways to proceed. The journey may be shorter or longer, and it can be personalized to suit both therapist and client.

Time perspective therapy is an evolution of cognitive behavioral therapy (CBT), a goal-oriented talk therapy. Like CBT, TPT maintains a positive, respectful therapeutic alliance between client and therapist. As with all therapeutic relationships, trust between therapist and client is essential. PTSD clients *must* trust the therapist—after all, they are about to divulge very sensitive, painful, and scary material about themselves to someone they probably just met. The client wants to feel listened to and understood, not judged. So establishing a relationship of trust is imperative.

In the TPT process, we work with clients to . . .

- Understand time perspectives and how they frame the way we see ourselves and our possibilities.
- Respect the trauma. We acknowledge that this was an important event and should not be downplayed.
- Recognize that PTSD sufferers are mentally injured, not mentally ill.
- Learn self-soothing behaviors, including breathing exercises and visualizations.
- Boost past positives. For PTSD in particular, we want to eventually eclipse the past negatives.

- Encourage healthy present hedonism. We promote selected activities that are enjoyable but not irresponsible or life threatening.
- Encourage pro-social behavior, bringing the PTSD sufferer back into healthy human relationships through social interaction in a relaxed group setting. Family members and significant others are also invited to attend therapy sessions if possible.
- Help them make, and act on, both short- and long-range plans for a positive future—a brighter future.

We work closely with each client—following up and checking in throughout the therapy process. If the person has completed therapy, we find the opportunity to check in when we see him or her out and about—at community activities, at social functions, or shopping. We frequently have the opportunity to follow up when the former client brings in a family member, friend, or coworker for therapy.

The following steps outline the TPT process and further explain the bullet points just mentioned.

step 1: understanding time perspectives

Understanding time perspectives and how they determine the way we see our lives and our possibilities in life is the key to success in TPT, so this is the place we start with every client. This simple concept is an eye-opening and easy-to-comprehend new way for clients to understand their behavior.

We explain that one can either be stuck in one or two time perspectives (such as past negative and present fatalistic) at the expense of the others (past positive, present hedonistic, and future positive), or be balanced in all three major time zones. An overall balanced time perspective usually results in greater emotional well-being, so this is our goal for them in therapy. In our experience it is more helpful for clients to learn, understand, and talk about their time perspective than their clinical symptoms. Speaking of being stuck in the past negative feels much less charged—and easier to understand and resolve—than talking about anxiety and depression. We take their problems out of the psychiatric realm of mental illness and into the everyday realm of personal problems that need fixing.

Next we explain that the Zimbardo Time Perspective Inventory (ZTPI) is a psychological instrument devised by Philip Zimbardo and John Boyd to assess a person's time perspective, and that we can use it to discover the client's own time perspective. Further, we explain that when one learns to understand one's own time perspective and the time perspectives of others, one's quality of life increases and level of emotional distress drops significantly.

For PTSD clients, the negative past is everything. Their vivid, recurring memories and nightmares make the past more real than *anything* that is happening now—and more real than the future. Given this, we concentrate on helping them move into the more hopeful time perspectives: past positive, selected present hedonism, and future positive. We focus on setting goals, making specific plans to achieve those goals, following through with these plans, and involving the important people in their lives to help them complete those plans.

A stockbroker with whom Richard Sword was recently working understood this concept in financial terms. He said, "Sure, I get it. The only way to overcome past losses is future gain!" A person who enjoys fishing might say that when you are not getting what you want, you cut bait and move your boat on to better fishing grounds. No matter what metaphor you use, with PTSD, working to enjoy the present and achieve a positive future represents the power pair that can overcome the negative past.

time perspective signatures for PTSD, anxiety, or depression

People with PTSD suffer from the triple whammy of trauma, depression, and anxiety; they also share, to some degree, a specific time perspective signature. It bears mention that people may suffer from depression without having experienced trauma or anxiety; others may suffer from anxiety without having experienced trauma or depression. However, we have found in our work that people suffering from PTSD, anxiety, or depression have a similar time perspective signature. Here's what the scores on their ZTPI look like:

- High past negative
- Low past positive
- High or low present hedonism
- High present fatalism
- Low future

step 2: returning to the past

The first session, then, is concerned with establishing rapport. The therapist explains the components of PTSD, Temporal Theory (TT), and the basics of TPT. During the explanation of TT and TPT, many clients have an "Ah ha!" moment. They see that their trauma has knocked them off balance and caused them to face backward, toward the past. They usually experience a glimmer of hope when they discover that our ultimate goal in TPT is to gently turn them around so they can face forward and begin their journey toward the future. First, however, we must return to the past to unlock its grip on current functioning: we need to hear the client's story.

Whatever the time perspective (TP) therapist's method or the client's resolve, we start with what brought the client in for therapy in the first place—the trauma that knocked him or her off balance. Once clients feel comfortable with the TP therapist, they begin to share their story. Depending on both the severity of the trauma and the severity of the clients' PTSD symptoms, it's not unusual for their backstory to take up the remainder of the first session. If clients experienced extreme trauma that involved injury to others, their story may require several sessions to relate completely.

Some clients, on the other hand, make the story short—perhaps because they feel that they and their loved ones have suffered long enough, or because moving quickly onward is simply their nature, or because they are so uncomfortable or emotionally raw that they do not want to dwell on the trauma. These clients will generally provide the TP therapist with the CliffsNotes version of their past, including their trauma.

Retelling the trauma can, understandably, be terribly upsetting for clients. Toward the end of the session, therefore, the therapist gives them easy, practical tools — a simple breathing technique to help them calm themselves and focus, relaxation and visualization CDs or videos, and the like — to help them cope with the myriad feelings and emotions that have been stirred up in the session. Repeating the breathing technique throughout the day helps it become a habitual practice that clients can use to remain calm and cope with anxiety.

rose's perspective: the river of time

Rosemary Sword writes,

> We often share a video with our clients called *The River of Time* (www.thetimecure.com), which is based on TPT and contains a straightforward breathing technique for relaxation. We have found that this simple metaphor makes sense to people suffering from PTSD.
>
> Like a river making its way toward the sea, our lives travel in their own channel—sometimes rushing, sometimes meandering as we make our way to our final destination. And just as a river picks up and carries all manner of things—gravel and fish, a sparkling penny, lost shoes and timeworn love letters, old cans of paint thoughtlessly tossed into the waterway—we carry our life experiences: natural milestones (learning to walk and talk); happy moments (falling in love, the birth of a child); and the tragedies and traumas (war, accidents, rape). All of these experiences—everyday and extraordinary, the wonderful and the painful—make us who we are.
>
> Sometimes a boulder may be thrown into the stream, damming it off or forcing us to work around it. But as we gain distance, we notice that these seemingly immovable objects are in the past, and the future is free of obstruction. Looking back, these immense obstructions become smaller and smaller. We know they're still there, but we move on.

Even when our river of time has been polluted almost to extinction by toxic trauma, there is hope: for just as a once-polluted river may later run clear again, we too can be cleansed by the passage of time and the help of others.

We sometimes talk about what we term the *cycle of distress* (shown in Figure 3.1), putting it in the framework of TT. The cycle of distress starts with either past trauma or negative (present) thinking. These negative thoughts are projected into the future in the form of a fear of recurrence or an additional traumatic event, and then returns to the present in the form of a future negative time perspective. From there it automatically transfers into the past negative time perspective, which in turn reinforces the negative past where one is stuck ... and returns to the present to keep the cycle of distress going endlessly. This cyclical negativity is emotionally and spiritually draining for the person creating it, who is forced to experience it again and again.

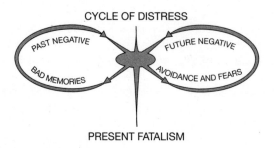

Figure 3.1   **Cycle of Distress**

step 3: psychological testing

Early in therapy, the client is given a series of psychological tests. These include a trauma severity indicator (we use the Post-trauma Checklist for civilians [PCL-C] or the Post-trauma Checklist for military [PCL-M]); a depression test (the Burns Depression Checklist [BDC]); an anxiety test (the Burns Anxiety Inventory [BAI]); and the ZTPI. These tests are scored by the therapist and discussed with the client during the next session. The ZTPI in particular gives us the information we need to work within the context of time perspective therapy.

understanding the ZTPI graph: emotional distress and emotional well-being

You have probably already taken the ZTPI, included in Chapter Two, and compared your own time perspective scores to the ideal scores plotted on our graph. Let's look at the graph again in terms of what it says about emotional distress and emotional well-being (see Figure 3.2).

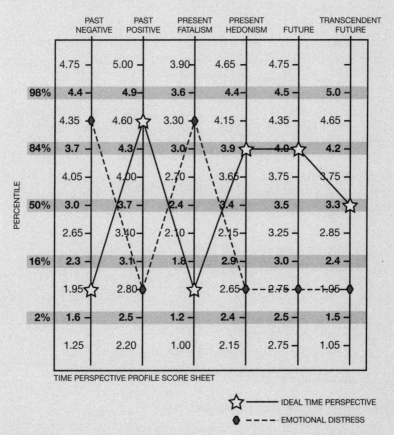

Figure 3.2 Emotional Distress Versus Ideal Time Perspective

As a reminder, this graph shows two time perspective signatures: emotional distress (shown by the stop signs) and emotional well-being, which is the ideal time perspective (shown by the stars). It's easy to read: just find the six time perspectives listed at the top of the graph, then look at where the star or stop sign falls on each vertical line (a continuum of each time perspective from low to high).

The percentiles on the left represent the percentages of the population (the people in Phil's original study). In other words, the 50th percentile (50 percent) represents the average score of the population for each particular time perspective scale (past negative, past positive, and so forth). It's just like grades in school. The numerals within each vertical time perspective scale are called "raw scores"—these are the results of the population in the original ZTPI study. For the past negative time perspective scale, this is a low of 1.25 to a high of 4.75. Where you plot your score indicates where you are in that particular time perspective scale—for example, low, medium or high.

The difference between feeling emotional distress and perceiving emotional well-being is like that between night and day. Whereas one may feel shrouded in darkness and despair, the other may bask in the warm light of hope.

emotional distress

The stop signs in this graph describe a person whose time perspective encompasses the following scores:

- **High past negative:** "I am bothered by the past."
- **Low past positive:** "Nothing is good about the past."
- **High present fatalism:** "Nothing can change my fate, so I give up."
- **Low present hedonism:** "Nothing is good about my life right now."
- **Low future:** "I avoid the future and fear it."
- **Low transcendental future:** "When I die, that's it."

This time perspective signature describes many people with PTSD. They dwell on and magnify bad past experiences and minimize any good past experiences. They believe that there is no conceivable way to change their view of the past or their experience of the present and future. In fact, the future looks like a repeat of the bad experiences of the past. Their sense of fatalism feeds and perpetuates their feelings of depression, anxiety, and trauma.

emotional well-being

The stars in the graph represent the time perspective signature of an individual who enjoys an inner sense of well-being:

- **Low past negative:** "The stuff that happened in my past wasn't so bad."
- **High past positive:** "I enjoy thinking about the past."
- **Low present fatalism:** "I can make things better if I try."
- **High (selected) present hedonism:** "I love life; I enjoy my significant others."
- **High-medium future:** "The best is yet to come."
- **Moderate transcendental future:** "There is an afterlife, and it's good."

People with this time perspective signature are living in balance. Rather than focus on the bad experiences in their past, they relish the positive experiences. They feel that hard work pays off, and they enjoy what they are doing right now. The future looks brighter, and they also consider and may even look forward to an afterlife. Whereas those with the negative stop signs spiral downward over time, those with the star pattern may spiral upward with positives begetting more positives.

step 4: discussing the present

In a follow-up session, we can usually begin to discuss clients' symptoms (nightmares, flashbacks, intrusive recollections or thoughts, avoidance, isolation, anger and irritability, hyper-vigilance or paranoia, sleep deprivation, and so on). Understanding how their trauma and the ensuing depression and anxiety affect every aspect of their lives, as well as the lives of those close to them, is an eye-opening and sometimes upsetting experience. We always help them understand that they are mentally injured, not mentally ill.

We've found that the best way to help PTSD sufferers overcome their past traumas is to encourage them to envision a better future. This is accomplished by setting goals and figuring out specific means by which these goals can be achieved. In turn, this encourages feelings of a sustainable and secure future. Then we engage them in a visualized narrative, a time metaphor that contrasts the current negatives being experienced with imagined positives that could be possible for them.

First, we ask them to imagine that they have one foot stuck in the quicksand of the past, and the other resting on the mud of the fatalistic present. The fatalistic view is reasonable given that nothing has worked to help them out of the quicksand. In this state of imbalance they are emotionally immobilized.

To make a start, *all they need to do is lift that one foot out of the muck and mire of the past and put it on the solid ground of the future.*

Then they need to bring the other foot out of the mud of present fatalism and rest it on the more solid ground of present hedonism. Now they are beginning to get a firm footing.

When they can feel the ground becoming more solid beneath them, we ask them to take a small step into the future by making a simple plan.

As they find that each step forward is still bringing them to ever more solid ground, they can begin to see a real future ahead.

This imagery seems to be especially useful for our clients who are veterans, and whose traumas have been particularly brutal. We also can work at stepping on the really secure ground of past positives, where all the good things in their past are still ready to be appreciated once again.

Most of our nonmilitary clients suffer from situational or circumstantial trauma, such as motor vehicle accidents; work accidents; rape; and depression and anxiety (usually from loss, such as the death of a loved one, the loss of a job, investment loss, or health crises). We have found that understanding their personality before they experienced situational trauma is vitally important. We consider how the traumatic situation has changed their thoughts, feelings, and behavior, as well as how it has affected various aspects of their lives. Although their lives may have changed forever, we suggest that the person they were before the trauma continues to live within them but has been overshadowed by the trauma. We build on these past positives in helping them create a brighter future.

Clients' PTSD symptoms mean that their relationships also suffer. Each relationship is examined and discussed individually. We begin with a review of the relationship before the trauma, and the client shares pre-trauma thoughts, feelings, and emotions about the other person. Then we move into the current status of the relationship, which frequently evokes feelings of guilt and negligence and can be very painful for the client to recount. Most of our clients with chronic and severe PTSD are so caught up in their depression and anxiety that there is no room for anyone or anything else but the black hole in which they have found themselves post-trauma. But we haven't met with one PTSD client who hasn't wanted to improve his or her PTSD-battered relationships.

At this point, we often schedule a session with the client's significant other or close family members in order to familiarize them with PTSD and its effects on others. These sessions are similar to the client's first TPT session, with brief explanations of how PTSD, TT, and TPT work. The client is given the option to attend these sessions or not. Sometimes the client sits in on the first portion of the session, and then asks to be excused because it is too painful to hear loved ones describe his or her PTSD symptoms and behavior.

If the client is comfortable talking about his or her issues in front of family members, then the family members are welcome to sit in on future TPT sessions with the client to assist in the client's healing process.

Here's how one of our Iraq War veterans, a young man named Everest (whose story is detailed in the next chapter), describes his early experiences with TPT:

> That first session is a blur. I know I hinted at some of my stressors and some of the things that trigger my flashbacks. But I wasn't comfortable talking about my "crazy" thoughts—about thinking of ways to take out people who pissed me off or ways to commit suicide . . . those things came

out later. We set up weekly appointments with Dr. Sword for therapy as well as a series of two appointments with Rose. She would interview me, document my traumatic experiences in Iraq and start on a report Dr. Sword was going to submit to the Veterans Administration. I left there with the feeling these people wanted to help me.

My first interview session was a three-hour emotional marathon . . . I told Rose about what happened in Iraq. While she was typing what I said, I felt something wet on my cheek—and I was crying. It was such a relief to cry—to know I could cry—to know I could feel . . .

In my next session with Dr. Sword, he explained about PTSD being a mental wound, not a mental illness or disease. This made me feel better somehow. Apparently, I'd already taken the first steps towards healing by talking about my traumatic Iraq experiences. We talked about goals and I told him one of my major objectives was to get off medications. He suggested another goal should be to have some hope for the future. I thought that was a nice idea but the future looked pretty bleak to me.

I had a second marathon session with Rose but it wasn't as emotional as the first. Since my previous session, I had looked up PTSD symptoms on the Internet. It didn't surprise me when she asked questions about my sleep patterns, did I avoid people and certain situations or places, what made me angry, how I was doing at work, how I related to family members. Then she asked if I minded my parents meeting with her or Dr. Sword so they could be informed about PTSD. She said although I was the client, they were also concerned about how my family was handling things. I told her it was okay with me so she set it up for the next week.

In my third session with Dr. Sword, he gave me psych tests and explained how I suffered from severe to extreme trauma, depression, and anxiety. This was no surprise. He brought up Type A behavior because of my anger issues. I was familiar with it through my college studies and I knew exactly what he was talking about. We immediately went to work modifying my behavior, starting with slowing down my breathing; I would do this whenever I started to feel angry or frustrated. I would slow down my movements, relax my muscles, lower the tone, timbre, and volume of my voice and think things through instead of reacting or overreacting in a military style the way I did in

Iraq. These are simple things that are hard to do when you're starting to spin out of control. But that day I made a vow to myself to be more conscious of my behavior. I wasn't in the military anymore.

My mom met with Rose while my father and sister met with Dr. Sword. After their meeting, my mom told me she learned a lot about PTSD and how it affects everyone in the family. This made me feel guilty. I guess it showed because my mom hugged me and said "It's not your fault." I didn't tell her that I felt to a degree it was *her* and *my father's* fault because the reason I joined the military, the reason I experienced those horrible things, the reason I had changed, was because *they* didn't make enough money to pay for my college. I knew this was irrational but I couldn't help feeling that way. But I didn't say anything.

Since I returned home, I had treated my sister poorly—I was bitter and my resentment ran amok where my sister was concerned. I had become the bully I hated. I was so horrible to her that she moved out. But after the session with Dr. Sword, she moved back in. She said she understood better why I was acting irrationally. I told her I was working on myself and she said she could see the results. We came to an understanding.

And my dad—my dad loves me so much and I know that! I know it! He wants the best for me in life and I was screwing up. After his meeting with Dr. Sword, he walked up to me and gave me the biggest bear hug. He said we were going to get through this together—as a family. My tired, closed down heart opened up—wide.

step 5: planning for the future

Once all of the skeletons (the past negatives) are out of the closet and their manifestations (present fatalistic and certain present hedonistic behaviors) have been examined, it's time to lay them to rest. We begin by making first short- and then long-range plans for a positive, brighter future.

In each succeeding session, we focus first on handling any recent past problems, with emphasis on learning from past negatives and focusing on past positives. We discuss how the problems were handled or, if things didn't turn out so well, how they could have been handled better.

Next, we discuss immediate day-to-day problems and formulate plans to tackle them. We give our clients homework, stuff they must do outside the therapeutic session to try out new patterns of behavior—under the safety of "I have to do it, they made me do it, it is my assignment."

Then plans are made for the next day, and then the next week, and then the next month . . . until we have sketched out plans for a far future positive. These future positive plans must include some selected present hedonism to offset the present fatalism in which most clients have been stuck. These "fun" things can take the form of anything from getting a facial, a pedicure, or a massage; to watching a funny movie; to taking a turn on the swings at the park with the kids.

Here's how Kara experienced the TPT process:

I went to my different therapy appointments—I had physical therapy as well as TPT!—and every day I felt like I was getting a little better. For the first time I felt understood.

In these early sessions, we focused on leaving the accident behind. In one session, Dr. Sword took me to Google Earth and showed me a bird's eye view of the accident site. Dr. Sword walked me through every stage of the accident until I ended up at the hospital. I was able to understand what had happened from a different perspective.

In another early session Dr. Sword said he wanted to shift focus from what was wrong with me to what I needed to do to get my life back in order. I had let all sorts of things go since the accident because of my injuries—like paying bills, shopping for groceries, things like that. Plus I was depressed and didn't feel like doing anything because I was stuck in present fatalism.

Dr. Sword taught me how to *not* get overwhelmed and to take things one at a time—to make a list of the things I wanted to accomplish and do one thing on that list each day. I started making lists right away, and when I crossed out something I felt good. Of course there's always more to add to the list, but I learned to keep on top of stuff so it didn't snowball and bowl me over.

We worked on me trying to accept myself for the way I am now and not compare myself to the way I used to be. This was really hard. I hated the way the accident left me. I used to be so active—I could do anything—go anywhere. Now I was all banged up and in horrible pain. Dr. Sword helped me see that even though I might never be the way I used to be, I'd be a whole lot better in time. He told me my future could be better than my past negatives, and not to base my future expectations on my pain. He taught me how to make plans to improve me physically and mentally—first by exercising, then by communicating better with Bud, and then by setting up appointments with specialists to help me with my chronic pain.

We talked about defensive driving and how to avoid being rear ended in the future. Since the accident, I had a fear of being hit from behind again. Instead of focusing on that fear, Dr. Sword taught me to have a plan so I could avoid being hit. I learned when I was driving I had to expect the unexpected and keep one eye on the rear view mirror whenever I had a foot on the brake or was stopped in a lane of moving traffic. He said I should always have a contingency plan in case someone failed to stop behind me. If I was going to be rear ended, I was to take my foot off the brake, put my head back on the headrest, and point my front wheels in the direction I wanted to be pushed.

We cleared my emotional freakouts so the medical doctors could figure out the many different physical things wrong with me. My negative memories were fading into my rear view mirror.

It's a given that clients will take a wrong turn or veer off course at least once in a while. Often they may revert to spending too much time looking into that rear view mirror instead of focusing on what is ahead of them. When this happens, we press PAUSE and review clients' patterning—that is, why and how they got off course. Then we press RESET by going over how they might have handled the situation differently and garnered more positive results. When we get back on the right road, we resume our voyage toward a brighter future with the PLAY button fully engaged.

step 6: living in the expanded present

Follow-up psychological test results tell us that our job is done when the PTSD client consistently has more past positive thoughts than past negative, is following through with future positive plans while taking care of present business, and is enjoying himself or herself with selected present hedonism.

The cycle of well-being (see Figure 3.3) starts in the present, with awareness and decision making. When a positive thought or attitude in the form of hopes and dreams is projected into the future, this maximizes the chance of a future positive time perspective. Once the person acts on the idea and it proves to be positive, it returns to the present, where it is automatically transformed into good memories and a past positive time perspective. This energy creates the expanded or holistic present.

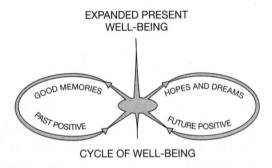

Figure 3.3   **Cycle of Well-Being**

⊙ getting to a balanced time perspective

TPT's goal is to help the client establish a balanced time perspective. For PTSD sufferers, the negative past far outweighs the present or future, overbalancing the system like an elephant on a seesaw.

The optimal temporal mix includes all time zones:

- The past grounds us. It gives us roots, connecting us to our identity and family.
- The future gives us wings to soar to new destinations and accept new challenges.
- The present gives us the ongoing energy we need to explore our world, inside and outside of ourselves.

Remember Figure 1.2 from Chapter One, the one that starts with all of that past baggage overbalancing the seesaw? Let's look at it again in the context of what you now understand about TPT.

the present is the balance point between past and future

As the figure shows, the *present* is the fulcrum — the balance point — between the past and the future.

The present is the point on which both the past and future can achieve balance. The present is the only place from which we can take action, but it's not the only place that action is felt. From the present, we can make plans for the future and make peace with the past. When one's present time perspective becomes more positive, the past doesn't seem quite so negative and the future looks more promising.

mental distress tips the balance toward the negative past

The *mental distress* portion of the illustration demonstrates what happens when the negatives of the past outweigh hope for a better future (see Figure 3.4). Here the past negatives have been stuffed into a junk box, overflowing and chaotic. The solid bar of the timeline runs out just past the balance point of the present — the past is so heavy that the future can't even find a place to sit, let alone balance the negative past. The future, in fact, is only a cloud of question marks.

Figure 3.4   **Mental Distress**

time perspective therapy extends future hopes

As *time perspective therapy* progresses, several things change: the negative junk from the past is packed up into a much more manageable suitcase — we've all got baggage, but we don't need to carry our entire basement with us! (See Figure 3.5.) The timeline extends much further into the future — so far, in fact, that we can see a positive, hopeful goal beginning to balance out the negative past. We are well on our way to achieving a balanced time perspective.

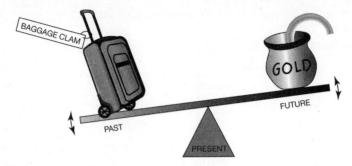

Figure 3.5   **Time Perspective Therapy in Progress**

*a balanced time perspective includes past, present, and future
working together in harmony*

In a *balanced time perspective,* a more positive past and a positive future
rest on the fulcrum of the present (see Figure 3.6). As future goals
become present realities, mental health improves. The positive things
that happened in the past once again become more readily accessible,
vivid memories, helping the past negatives shrink in importance. In this
highly desirable state (the *expanded or holistic present*), we see positive
relationships and experiences in our past and look forward to the yet
undisclosed gifts the future has in store for each of us. We understand
that this balance grows from planning our life ahead, while living out
our plans now, in the expanded present.

rick's perspective: the sailboat analogy

Rick writes,

> I sometimes explain the logic of balancing your past negatives
> with future goals by giving this example: when our sailboat tips
> too far and starts taking on water, we rightly fear our little boat
> will sink. The natural instinct is to run over to where the water is
> deepest and start bailing. *But this is absolutely the wrong thing
> to do!* Most likely, the extra weight will just cause the boat to tip
> further, take on more water, and capsize.
>
> As sailors know, there's a more effective strategy: when you start
> to take on water on one side of the boat, move to the opposite

side to reestablish the balance. Once the boat is stabilized the water will redistribute, becoming much more manageable to deal with. You can safely start bailing it out, and it may even flush out the stern with the momentum of the boat's forward motion.

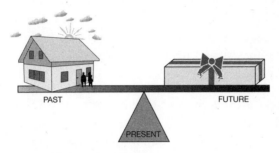

Figure 3.6   **Balanced Time Perspective**

o pro-social behavior: family and friends

PTSD sufferers feel miserable, angry, and hopeless. They can see that their behavior is alienating them from their social circle, which makes them feel worse. So it's not surprising that they tend to isolate themselves. For this reason, encouraging pro-social behavior is a vital part of their recovery, and helps contribute to their realization that the present has something good to offer. In time perspective therapy, we encourage maintaining healthy friendships and family relationships, and other pro-social behaviors.

Groups of peers are especially helpful. In our original work with veterans, we discovered that veterans' bonding with buddies, as they did while in the military, is an important part of their therapy, and that scheduled social meetings reinforce their sense of a brighter future. (Chapter Four discusses how this came about.) We thought that our Iraq War vet, Everest, might benefit from socializing with the World War II vets, even though they were much older. He recalls,

Dr. Sword had scheduled our fourth session on a holiday. When I got to his office, he told me he was taking me to a fast food restaurant for breakfast to meet some special people. I was hungry, so this was fine with me—especially since he was buying. When we got to the restaurant, there were ten of the original WWII 442nd Regimental Combat Veterans sitting around a table. Dr. Sword announced to these guys, who must have been near ninety years old, "Gentlemen, this is Everest, he's the new generation of 442!" These old guys cheered. They jumped up and they all reached out to shake my hand. They were grinning from ear to ear and so was I. One of them told me I was their first new member in sixty-five years. After knowing my family still loved me and were trying hard to understand me, I think this was the best I had felt since I returned from Iraq.

We've also introduced a small group of widows who have undergone TPT to each other and have found they are the best sounding boards for their own future planning. But group members do not have to be perfectly matched, nor do they have to think of themselves as being in "group therapy." Psychologically speaking, groups meet for pro-social experiences. In the case of the group of veterans, for example, they were simply talking, laughing, and enjoying food together. Even Kara—about as far away from their experience as possible—benefited from a dip into this social pool:

About a month into my stay, the Swords asked me if I wanted to come to a Wednesday afternoon veteran's group—made up of Vietnam vets, Gulf War vets, and Iraq vets—they had at their place. They were concerned that I wasn't doing anything other than going to physical therapy and coming to their office for TPT. Since Bud was gone, if I wasn't going to therapy, I was pretty much staying in the condo watching television. They knew that I worked mostly with men and thought maybe being around a bunch of guys would perk me up.

Well, that first Wednesday, I tell you, I never felt so accepted! Those veterans hugged me and made me feel like I was one of them. And ladies—they can cook! I went to a few of the Wednesday groups and before I left, I wanted to do something for these great guys so I made them all Native American dream catchers—a woven net, or web, on a hoop that is intended to catch the bad dreams and only let the good dreams through. When I handed one of the dream catchers to a

Vietnam vet, he said, "Now maybe I won't have so many nightmares!" That made me laugh and cry at the same time!

o planning a brighter future

For PTSD sufferers, who have for so long lived only in the past and immediate present, planning a brighter future means making plans for the long term, for themselves and their loved ones. In the beginning, they naturally allow their past negatives to overwhelm their outlook for the future. We ask them instead to focus on *the successes of their past* as paving stones they can use to establish their own path toward a more balanced time perspective, as they design and define it. We want them to realize they can help themselves, their families, and future generations by planning for a brighter future.

Now back in Alaska, Kara says,

> Although I've gotten much better and I'm stronger, I'm still injured so I can't go back to work at my old job. I'm thinking about taking another job with the state that won't be as stressful and won't remind me of the accident. I either watch *The River of Time* or listen to the relaxation CD every day. I still feel down sometimes—but it's not an all day, every day thing. I have to have more operations and this is scary to me. But it'll be worth it if they help me get closer to being my old self.
>
> Bud and I are getting along really good. He says he sees the positive changes in me. We're making long-range retirement plans—we want to spend winters in Maui and summers at our fishing lodge.

Kara's plans for the future are realistic, positive, and hopeful—and they are a huge part of her continuing recovery from PTSD. Planning for a brighter future is key to the success of TPT, because PTSD sufferers have a difficult time conceiving of a version of their future that does not contain more of the same pain. Many find it hard to believe such a future can even exist.

Everest, too, has a brighter future: "I am enrolled at the university...with the goal of becoming a psychiatrist," he says. "My intention is to work with veterans." Everest's symptoms have improved significantly, and he now has a focus. He was able to replace past negatives—the real-life war movies repeatedly playing in his head—with a vision of a positive future involving a pro-social career and long-term relationships.

The pro-social momentum of TPT is a potent agent for change that encourages other PTSD sufferers to work for a positive future for themselves and their families. The positive social momentum of seeing other PTSD sufferers who have actually achieved the desired goal of a future positive time perspective amid a fully balanced time perspective is a very powerful motivator.

o the z team backs up anecdotal evidence with hard data

Anecdotal evidence that time perspective therapy works is one thing, but we needed to gather hard data. To this end, the Z Team came together in 2009 and carried out the first longitudinal pilot study.[1]

encouraging results

In June 2009 San Francisco–based Z Team members Sarah Brunskill and Anthony Ferreras came to Maui for two weeks to conduct research on time perspective therapy. The team gathered data from thirty-two of the Swords' veteran clients. We had established their baseline data at the beginning of therapy by administering a battery of psychological tests: the Burns Depression Checklist, the Burns Anxiety Inventory, the Post-trauma Checklist for military, and later the ZTPI.

In psychological research a proven 30 percent improvement is typically considered significant. Generally, there is about a 20 percent improvement due to the halo effect[2] or the placebo effect[3]—that is, 20 percent of the people will get better, regardless of whether or not they got the "real" treatment or merely believed that they did. In our study, we were able to document—to a very high level of scientific confidence—that our veterans found improvements far greater than the placebo or halo effects could account for. The results were very encouraging. (The pilot study is detailed in Appendix B.)

hard data

The line graph in Figure 3.7 summarizes the ongoing longitudinal research project by the Z Team investigating TPT. Clients were given psychological tests for the three components of PTSD: trauma, depression and anxiety

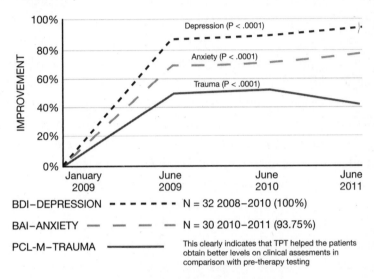

BDI–DEPRESSION – – – – – –   N = 32 2008–2010 (100%)

BAI–ANXIETY — — — — —   N = 30 2010–2011 (93.75%)

PCL-M–TRAUMA —————   This clearly indicates that TPT helped the patients obtain better levels on clinical assesments in comparison with pre-therapy testing

26 are 100% S/C PTSD disabled by VA
All have S/C PTSD rating with VA
ZERO SUICIDES

Figure 3.7   **TPT Pilot Study Results (2008–2011)**

Within the six-month time period from January 2009 to June 2009, levels of depression improved 89 percent, levels of anxiety improved 70 percent, and levels of trauma improved 52 percent. This shift occurred at very high levels of statistical confidence. The changes in depression and anxiety could only be accounted for by chance in fewer than one out of one thousand times. The changes in the levels of trauma could only be accounted for by chance in fewer than one out of one hundred times. This clearly indicated that TPT helped these veterans attain better levels on clinical assessments in comparison to their pre-therapy testing levels. Furthermore, it proved consistent with Sarah and Anthony's direct clinical observations of these vet clients' behavior, as well as the qualitative assessment of them by the Swords and also the clients' self-reports.

All thirty-two veterans were retested in June 2010. The improvements endured, with slight improvements over the one-year period from June 2009 to June 2010. This is an important finding: *the significant improvement in symptoms demonstrated in the first phase of the study was maintained, and nearly two-thirds of the cases improved over a one-year period.*

In our June 2011 retest, two veterans were removed from the study because we lost contact with them. *We noted that for the remaining thirty vets, their significant improvement in symptoms endured over a two-year period.* We discovered in follow-up interviews that the dip in trauma improvement from June 2010 to June 2011 was due to situational events that affect us all at some point in our lives, such as health issues and deaths in the family. Despite these normal life problems, the veterans continued to experience relief from trauma symptoms.

This indicates that TPT is not a temporary fix; with continued individual treatment, group treatment, or a combination of both, the gains made can be retained and even improved on. The positive changes noted are enduring, at least over the eighteen-month period we have studied. We assume now that such enhancements will continue and even get stronger.

TPT's post-therapy outcomes are proven in our pilot study results as well as in client follow-up, indicating that it can indeed be a long-lasting solution. TPT pilot study results indicate improvements between pre- and post-treatment over the three-and-a-half-year pilot study. Overall, 87 percent of clients reported decreased trauma and PTSD symptoms; astonishingly, 100 percent decreased their depression rating. These positive results indicate that TPT is proving to be an effective and enduring treatment for PTSD. (For a comparison of TPT effectiveness with that of CBT and prolonged exposure therapy, please see Appendix A.)

However, perhaps the most important thing is, during this time period these veterans have had *zero suicides, zero suicide attempts, zero divorces,* and *zero arrests.* They are enjoying socializing more with each other and assuming a new level of self-respect as honored and disabled American veterans rather than "crazy" war veterans. It's also gratifying to realize that we have had a 94 percent retention rate over the thirty months. This is unusually high, and a testimony to the acceptability and effectiveness of the program.[4]

the clinical trial

procedure
- All clients took an intake assessment comprising at least three of the following: the Burns Anxiety Inventory, the Burns Depression Checklist, the Post-trauma Diagnostic Scale (PDS), the Trauma Symptom Inventory, the Hamilton Anxiety Rating Scale, or the Beck Depression Inventory II.
- During this trial, researchers chose to administer a consistent set of tests to ensure that all clients from this point forward would have the same baseline clinical assessment tests.
- To establish if there had been a change in the levels of anxiety, depression, and PTSD, the same clinical assessments were given again six months after the start of TPT *with the addition of the ZTPI* to understand the client's perception of time.

participants
- n = 30 PTSD veterans (with pre- and post-data; see Appendix B for an explanation of the variables used)
- Mixed ethnicities, marital status, and combat history
- Age (m = 64.77, SD = 10.35)
- World War II, the Korean War, the Vietnam War, the Gulf War, and the Iraq War
- All living in Maui; clients of the Swords

main results
- There was a significant difference between pre- and post-data PTSD (t = 4.19, p = .001); depression (t = 7.08, p < .0001); and anxiety (t = 5.29, p < .0001) levels.

- This clearly indicates that something in TPT helped the clients obtain better levels on the clinical assessments in comparison to pre-therapy testing.
- Past negative thinking was found to be positively associated with post-data PTSD, depression, and anxiety levels ($r = .47$, $p = .006$). This indicates that the more past negative the client's current outlook, the higher his levels of PTSD, depression, and anxiety.

treatment impact — thirty vets with pre- and post-data
- Twenty-four clients (89 percent) with less depression
- Nineteen clients (70 percent) with less anxiety
- Fourteen clients (52 percent) with less PTSD

outcome
- Future orientation is negatively associated with post-data PTSD levels ($r = -.36$, $p = .04$). The greater the client's conception or grasp of his future, the lower the levels of PTSD the client had in the present.
- Present fatalism is positively associated with pre-data PTSD levels ($r = -.56$, $p = .013$). The more the client understands that his present is in his control and not part of uncontrollable fate, the less PTSD he had when he *entered* the program.
- Present fatalism is negatively associated with age ($r = -.45$, $p = .01$). The older the client, the more the client understands that his present is within his control.

As we have seen in this chapter, TPT has the power and simplicity to create a revolution in the treatment and prevention of trauma of all kinds. It can become a significant contribution to the future of psychology by teaching clients how to cope with their negative past in a more joy-filled present that creates new, optimistic future scenarios. In the next chapters we will take a deeper and more personal look at how TPT works with different populations.

○ to sum up

- The primary goal of TPT is the same regardless of what brought the client to therapy—achieving a balanced time perspective.
- The basics of TPT include the following: (1) understanding time perspectives, (2) respecting the trauma and understanding the concept of mental injury versus mental illness, (3) using breathing and visualization to self-soothe, (4) boosting past positives, (5) encouraging healthy present hedonism, (6) encouraging pro-social behavior, and (7) planning and acting on positive future goals.
- Initial psychological testing of clients includes a trauma severity indicator, a depression test (the Burns Depression Checklist), an anxiety test (the Burns Anxiety Inventory), and the ZTPI. These tests are scored by the therapist and discussed with the client during the next session. The ZTPI in particular provides the information needed for working in the context of TPT.
- Follow-up psychological test results tell us that our job is done when the PTSD client consistently has more past positive thoughts than past negative, is following through with future positive plans while taking care of present business, and is enjoying himself or herself with selected present hedonism.
- TPT's post-therapy outcomes are proven in our pilot study results as well as in client follow-up, indicating that it can indeed be a long-lasting solution. TPT pilot study results indicate improvements between pre- and post-treatment over the three-and-a-half-year pilot study. Overall, 87 percent of clients reported decreased trauma and PTSD symptoms; astonishingly, 100 percent decreased their depression rating. These positive results indicate that TPT is proving to be an effective and enduring treatment for PTSD.

now it's your turn: a brighter future

Allow yourself five uninterrupted minutes to relax in a safe place. Close your eyes. Breathe slowly, deeply, and rhythmically. Allow your body to relax deeper and deeper with each breath.

When you've completed four of these relaxing breaths, open your mind to the image of your brighter future. Try not to think too hard, just let it come. What does it look like? What are you doing? Who is with you? Where are you? What are you trying to achieve?

There are no "right" answers here! Perhaps your brighter future plan is social or financial, or has to do with your health. It could be as simple as planting a kitchen herb garden, starting an exercise program, or eating more healthfully, or as complicated as starting a business, learning a new skill, or instilling positive values in your child.

Now see yourself making a plan to actualize this brighter future. What will it take to achieve this goal? Take small steps that will be easy to achieve, and envision yourself making carefully planned, steady progress toward your brighter future.

part 2

the stories

4

war veterans, PTSD, and time perspective therapy

"At night, I wake up almost every hour," said Aki. "I only sleep about three hours a night. I wake up at about 3 a.m. and I cannot get back to sleep. So I just think about things . . . my mind goes back to Army times." The veteran who described this state of insomnia and nightmare to us was suffering from PTSD. But he was not a young Iraq War veteran who had lived with PTSD for a relatively short time. Nor was he a Gulf War vet, a Vietnam vet, or even a veteran of the Korean War. Aki is a veteran of World War II—a war that ended nearly seventy years ago. And for every night of every one of those seventy years, Aki lived alone with his dark thoughts, nightmares, and insomnia, unable to leave his negative past behind.

Thousands of American war veterans—from surviving World War II and Korean War vets in their seventies, eighties, and nineties; to Vietnam vets in their sixties; to today's young soldiers returning home from the Middle East—struggle with PTSD.[1] In the context of time perspective therapy (TPT), it is predictable and reliable that these war veterans are stuck in the past negative and present fatalistic time perspectives at the expense of both present and future.

○ why soldiers live in the present fatalistic time perspective

Fighting forces must, by definition, live in the present fatalistic time perspective: willing to die *on the spot*. They have no future time perspective—nor should they, if they are to be effective. But these present fatalistic fighting machines start life just like the rest of us. This attitude is instilled during basic training.

The military specifically trains troops to react properly *in the present*. In the process of being transformed from citizens into soldiers during basic training, young men and women learn to live in the present fatalistic time perspective, willing to forfeit their future to protect their country. It doesn't serve the military to have soldiers who are engaging the enemy while thinking about their future and the family they might raise, or about their past and their family waiting for them back home. This time perspective is drilled into our troops in basic training and becomes their mind-set throughout their military service. At a certain point, enlisted personnel accept their fate and stop thinking about the future.

This mind-set is a necessity on the battlefield; but when veterans return home, it no longer serves them. A fortunate number manage to get through wars unscathed and can return to normal life. But for those who face the horrors of battle, this mind-set easily transforms into the sense of a shortened or lost future, which is a major PTSD symptom. In the context of TPT, this loss of a much needed future time perspective may be a primary cause of the current epidemic of suicides after Middle East deployment among American soldiers.[2]

We have found TPT to be very effective in helping veterans escape the horrors of PTSD and return to the balanced time perspective they deserve: one encompassing past positive, selected present hedonistic, and future orientations. Helping them redefine and reset their time perspective (TP) from military metrics to the civilian metrics needed to cope in civilian life is a priceless gift we can offer our honored and valuable war veterans.

o why social networks are especially vital for vets

After leaving the military, veterans often feel out of place. They miss the social intensity of being part of a group of other young men and women with similar military backgrounds; they like being immersed in a group of like-minded people who understand them, and often seek out the company of other veterans. They tend to see civilians without military experience as somewhat inferior and not especially desirable as friends. Ironically, many veterans with PTSD avoid social contact altogether. This social avoidance is a symptom, not a solution. The solution is social acceptance, and encouragement from peers whom they respect and with whom they identify.

In many other nonmilitary settings, group therapy has been shown to be helpful in reducing isolation and social stigma.[3] Previous studies concur with our clinical experiences: clients who have shown signs of withdrawal, traumatic stress symptoms, or both have demonstrated improvements (such as enhanced relationships with family and medical personnel, improved symptom control, fewer mood disturbances, and an increase in social support) when placed in our group therapy program.

As the literature suggests, increasing a sense of belonging and community is an important part of reducing negative, violent, and self-destructive coping responses to adversity and also increasing pro-social civic engagement. Identifying, making sense out of, and responding to injustice are also important. Work by DuRant and colleagues and by Glover[4] suggests that a sense of purpose and an avenue of action in response to injustice are important factors in both promoting social resilience and reducing psychological symptoms and also engagement in violent behaviors among youth.

A social network for referral is invaluable for a sustainable TPT program for veterans, in particular a network of veterans who have successfully been through the TPT process and who will bring in new, qualified veterans in need of therapy. After PTSD vets have been referred to us, our individual work with them begins, including client education in regard to time perspectives and important counterbalancing skills of deep breathing and relaxation. We then explain the value of pro-social activity, and introduce them to other PTSD vets who also understand the value of a future positive time perspective. The outcome is building momentum toward a more positively reinforced and energized future time perspective, which in turn produces a balanced time perspective and subsequent symptom abatement.

"follow me!"

In the military, the older, more experienced troops have always been there for the younger, less experienced ones to "show them the ropes" and warn them of hidden dangers. This holds true for veterans as well.[5] Due to the intensity of their social network, it is much easier for PTSD vets to trust other PTSD vets who have achieved success with TPT than it is to trust and believe that a mental health professional can even understand them, much less help them. Those who are viewed as high-status individuals in their group, such as decorated members with a Silver Star, a Purple Heart, a Combat Infantry Badge, or the Congressional Medal of Honor, are seen as especially trustworthy in this regard.

According to DaSilva, Sanson, Smart, and Toumbourou,[6] pro-social attitudes and behaviors evolve from actual pro-social involvement, perceived rewards from involvement, attachment to others, and a firm belief in pro-social values. When this positive reinforcement cycle is activated and operational for PTSD vets, it becomes self-reinforcing. The PTSD vets who have indeed found a brighter future naturally become promoters of this approach for other PTSD vets. We have seen that PTSD vets appear to be happiest when they are establishing a brighter future for themselves *and also* assisting their fellow vets to follow them to that brighter future. As the Marines say, "Follow me!" In this way we work closely with the veterans' social and cultural values and means.

The social influence of peers on the PTSD vet's behavior is extremely powerful.[7] The involvement of peers and positive social modeling are essential components of TPT with veterans, as they easily recall times when their very lives depended on trusting more experienced troops who knew how to stay alive in battle. This intense and powerful social alliance has proven to be one of the most useful tools in the implementation of a successful TPT program. As the individuals start to move toward temporal balance and can share positive images and strategies in a supportive group structure, individual therapy and group therapy enhance and complement one another.[8]

rick's perspective: the importance of buddies

Richard Sword writes,

About seven years ago, a handful of veterans started showing up on the back *lanai* (porch) at our office on a weekday afternoon for what we call a *pau hana* (after work) social gathering. We didn't plan this; it just happened. One veteran started coming, and then he brought a friend. When other veterans would drive by and see their buddies' vehicles parked out front, they came inside too.

We wanted to leave our office available to them for this casual drop-in type of meeting because we knew that culturally, these Japanese Hawaiian vets needed more informality. They did not like a specific start time as we would on the mainland, so *pau hana* Maui time made perfect sense to all of them. We did this without charge to honor and respect them, and because we wanted to be there for them in their hour of need and provide a safe place for them to gather. We also wanted to demonstrate the sincerity of our commitment and love, our Aloha Spirit.

Philip Zimbardo, like a true Italian American, always says that you cannot have a family culture if you don't have family meals together. These men love to sit around to talk while cooking on the grill. For our veterans, having "family meals" together with their veteran brothers helped them create a family culture of nurturing.

In the process, they discovered that they shared similar types of problems. This gave them a greater sense of self-esteem and common bonding. It helped them to realize that they were not mentally ill, rather they were having the same types of reactions that the other GIs have. They were having a normal reaction to a normal military experience—in an understandably extreme form. They began to realize that PTSD is more of a mental injury than a mental illness. They naturally began to help each other focus on achieving a brighter future.

Then they asked if they could bring other veteran buddies who needed help to the meetings. As of this writing, the group ranges from fifteen to twenty-five veterans, and they accept nonvets—and women!—like Kara as part of the group.

Significantly, the more experienced veterans serve as role models and guides for the new-to-TPT vets. Good food and positive social interactions with their fellow veterans have made the therapeutic process a positive social and learning event instead of a visit to the "mental doctor." Many veterans say this is the most important time and highlight of their week.

peer power

In June 2009 San Francisco Z Team members Anthony Ferreras and Sarah Brunskill came to Maui to study our veterans' group interactions as they gathered data for the TPT pilot study. They both later confided that they were a little bit frightened and intimidated about coming out to Maui to study a group of combat veterans, most of whom were 100 percent service-connected PTSD disabled. They had no idea what they would find, but thought it would be something like *One Flew Over the Cuckoo's Nest*.

However, to their surprise and delight, they found veterans in Rick's war trauma group to be very social and funny individuals who greatly enjoyed their group gatherings and whose clinical symptoms from PTSD, anxiety, and depression were under good management, especially with the aid of a cohesive group that had a well-formed focus of achieving a brighter future for its veteran members. In this case, the whole has become greater than the sum of the parts.

The social component of TPT is one of its most important and criti-cal parts. The old saying, "He who suffers alone, suffers more intensely," is certainly true. The symptoms of avoidance that arise from PTSD and make veterans want to disassociate from other veterans or any reminders of the war can be mitigated when the social interactions are modeled and reprogrammed to remind them of the positive social bonding and goals that were forged in times of war and military service instead of the chaos and losses. These social interactions can become much more enjoyable and even pleasurable for the veterans. They look forward to just being able to be with each other and feel like they can understand and be understood by a group with whom they identify and feel com-fortable. We later applied this social component with our civilian clients and found it to be equally important in establishing a balanced time perspective.

For the most part, our TPT group of PTSD veterans is essen-tially leaderless. However, extremely important conversations go on; for example, they discuss their stress and how they cope with it, and they try to overcome their overreaction, anger, and social issues; or they talk about how to get along better with their significant others and families. It is not unusual for smaller groups to form in the yard or around the *lanai,* and little focus groups emerge around certain topics.

These group meetings offer veterans an opportunity to share notes about the VA benefits process as well as their progress in overcoming their PTSD, anxiety, and depression. This sharing of knowledge and experiences gives the vets a sense of camaraderie and identification with their group culture — with a future positive focus.

Many of these vets have lived in social isolation for forty or fifty years without even discussing with other veterans what their issues are. They harbored tremendous repressed anger and shame. It is interesting how some of them come in and see guys they've known since their school days without even realizing they were fellow veterans. They may have worked alongside each other for decades in their trade but never once discussed their veteran status. Now when they see each other, they openly discuss their veteran status, they feel pride, and their self-esteem returns.

This is part of a process that we find to be extremely important in terms of veterans' relationships. When they first start therapy, the norm is for them to have terrible relationships with family, friends, and themselves, and—often even worse—with the government for which they risked their lives. When the TP therapist assigns value and worth to the veterans and pays attention to them, treating them with dignity and respect, their self-esteem starts to come back. When they begin to meet with a group of veterans and form friendships with people they like, admire, trust, and respect—and realize the feelings are returned—their self-esteem receives another big boost.

○ encouraging pride

Veterans suffering from the nightmares and debilities of PTSD also experience a near-fatal blow to their pride in themselves and their accomplishments. So along with helping them gain a balanced time perspective, we also want to restore that sense of pride in themselves and their valuable service to their country as soldiers.

An important step in this process is to encourage a positive relationship with the VA and the government that they served while in the military. This is done by assisting them with the paperwork necessary to support their claims applications for a service-connected PTSD disability rating with the VA. When veterans realize that we are willing to help, and they have success with the VA because they have proper documentation, their self-esteem grows and shifts from negative to positive.

We tell them that they are not worn-out veterans, and that when they receive their disability rating with the Veterans Administration they will become living national treasures because our national treasury will write their checks. We explain to them that it is not the money, it is what the money means; that their government is trying to do the best it can to let them know that the service they paid to their country is not forgotten and is still appreciated. This means everything to their self-esteem and their sense of worth. It also reminds many of them of the reason they went to war in the first place.

sarah's perspective: the war trauma group

Sarah writes,

From my previous experiences of working with the veteran community, particularly those who are diagnosed with PTSD, I expected a very somber and withdrawn crowd. However, at the first Wednesday war trauma group meeting I found happiness, socialization, and laughter. After I became acquainted with the group, I began to ask them questions about their experiences and how working with their therapist had changed them.

One man in particular stood out from the group as a true example of this program. This veteran and his wife told me that prior to the program he had all of the classic signs of PTSD: night terrors, irritability, mood swings, social withdrawal, avoidance of certain stimuli, and so on. He was extremely resistant to seeking help, and actually had to be physically escorted to his therapist's office by eight fellow veterans he had known and trusted for many years. He was infuriated. He said, "I didn't want help. I did not want to think about those things again, I did not want to relive them..."

Finally, it was his wife who convinced him to see this new therapist. I asked her how he has changed since entering the program, and she described it as "life changing...He is so much happier now that he has his 'group,' his buddies, and sees what life can be...a much better future." They instinctively know what the others have been through and the struggles they face each day.

o military sexual trauma

In the past three years we have worked with four veteran clients, two female, two male, suffering from military sexual trauma (MST)/PTSD. In each case the individual was abused by a higher-up. All four veterans considered suicide; two of them made plans to carry out the act. Fortunately, to date they have not acted on their suicidal ideations. They continue to struggle with overwhelming feelings of shame and powerlessness. For various reasons, each chose not to report the incidences while in the armed services. Their traumas and symptoms were so severe that we referred them to Veterans Administration MST specialists.

Being sexually abused by a fellow GI, especially one in a position of power and trust, is devastating. Add to this the inability to communicate about the situation without severe personal and professional repercussions and we have a recipe for extreme depression and a potential for suicide.

Not long ago, NPR journalist Alix Spiegel reported on the suicide rate in young women who serve or have served in the military.[9] Jan Kemp, director of the U.S. Department of Veterans Affairs' National Suicide Prevention Hotline, said that one of her counselors received a call from a young woman who had recently returned from overseas. She had been in an argument with her husband, who then decided that he and their two young children would be better off without her. She suffered from PTSD and had a history of MST. She was tired of trying and had called the hotline to relay a message to her husband: it wasn't his fault; she was doing it for him. She had gathered a number of pills and said that she was going to take them after she had walked into the woods. The hotline attendant located the young woman's local VA office before the line went dead. He called them, and they contacted the young woman's husband, who gave the local authorities a description of her car. She was found in the woods, nearly unconscious; was carried to the hospital; and was saved. This story has a happy ending, but others do not.

Spiegel also reported that because there are fewer women than men in the military, women's issues receive less attention. Researchers McFarland, Kaplan, and Huguet conducted a study comparing the suicide rate between civilian and armed services women ages eighteen to thirty-four.[10] Using statistics culled from sixteen states, researchers found that armed services and veteran women were three times more likely to suffer death by suicide than civilian women. They noted that although anxiety disorders and PTSD are similar in men and women in the military, more women struggle with military rape and are concerned about their children. In an interview on this subject, Jan Kemp agreed that the increase in women's mental health issues is concerning. According to both Kaplan and Kemp, as more women serve in war, an increase in women's suicides is likely to follow.[11]

Although the veterans' stories in this chapter are all about men emotionally scarred on the field of battle, we must not ignore the women who also serve. The four MST/PTSD veteran clients responded to treatment and were helped to deal with their extreme traumas through a combination of time perspective therapy and the assistance of the VA MST professionals. (You will read one of their stories in Chapter Six.)

These men and women did not attend our PTSD group meetings, instead receiving individual and telephone counseling because of the sensitive nature of their trauma. They are working on forgiving their perpetrators while overcoming their anxiety, depression, and other symptoms. They each plotted a course to a viable and brighter future, which includes higher education. They have regained focus on the reason why they joined the armed services and have a heartfelt desire eventually to serve the country they dearly love, but now in the private sector.

"i can still feel the shock wave of the incoming artillery hitting us"
Aki, World War II Veteran

Aki is an eighty-eight-year-old Japanese American who joined the Army's all-Japanese American 442nd Regimental Combat Team (RCT) during World War II to prove his loyalty to the United States. Shortly after being deployed to Europe, he was sent as a rifleman replacement. In spring 1945, just two weeks before the end of World War II in Europe, he arrived at the front alone. He found himself on the Gothic Line—the Nazi line of defense in the mountains bordering Southern Germany and Northern Italy. He checked into the Command Post, which was also an aid station and was thought to be a safe haven, located in a large cave on the southern face of the mountains. But at 2:00 a.m. the Command Post took direct hits from a "short round" of American artillery friendly fire. All officers, medics, and wounded were killed instantly, leaving Aki, a private, in charge of his rifle company.

Psychological Diagnosis: Combat-related PTSD

When Japan attacked Pearl Harbor on December 7, 1941, we Japanese Americans had a hard time. On the mainland, Japanese were treated like prisoners of war and put in concentration camps;

the government called them "internment" camps. In Hawaii it was different—too many Japanese to put away. [Over 35 percent of Hawaii's population at the time comprised Japanese citizens.] Hawaii wasn't a state yet, it was a U.S. Territory; but we still had internment camps. They locked away the people that had strong ties with Japan. Many of us were ashamed; we thought of ourselves as true-blue Americans. Shame is very bad in Japanese culture. Some people committed *Seppuku,* Japanese ritual suicide; there were men in the internment camps on the mainland and in Hawaii who did this. They could not live with the shame.

The war had been going on for three years before the government trusted Japanese Americans enough to let us join the U.S. Army. Many of us joined right away. We became the 442nd [Regimental Combat Team]. We wanted to show American people that we were Americans too. We come from a Samurai warrior culture and wanted to prove ourselves. We were sent to Europe and fought in France, Italy, and Germany. We really took a beating—many of us were killed or wounded. I lost many friends. It was very sad and I will never forget how brave my buddies were.

The conditions were horrible—freezing! You are not used to snow or the cold when you are from Hawaii. We were very near the front where most of the fighting is going on—very close to the Nazis—at the Gothic Line. We were camped at the base of the mountain. The Command Post was high up the mountain in a big cave. One night my commander said they needed a rifleman at the Command Post. No one wanted to go so I volunteered. I made my way up the mountain in the dark to the Command Post. The cave was very big. The main Field Aid Station was in there because it was a safe place. There were many medics and many more wounded.

I had been sent as rifleman so I was on guard duty outside the Command Post when the sky lit up and there were explosions everywhere. We took direct hits into the cave...all the officers, all the medics, all the wounded were killed. There were only privates left...mostly we had been on guard duty. We were all in shock but we knew we had to make it back down to our base camp. When we got there, we found out we had been bombarded by friendly fire. Our own Army had killed our guys. They had tried to aim their big guns over the Command Post to kill the Germans, but the artillery shells fell short and destroyed everything... I can still feel the shock wave of the incoming artillery hitting us.

I have thought about this every day of my life...and I have thought about the way we [Japanese American soldiers] were treated while we were fighting in Europe. We helped liberate Rome [but] had to walk around the city so no one would see us... We were sent on suicide missions to fight brutal, bloody battles; we were expendable. In one battle, we went to save two hundred Texans who had gotten lost and were surrounded by Germans [the Battle of the Lost Texas Battalion]. We had almost 1,000 casualties—dead or wounded—but we saved those two hundred. The [members of the] 442 who survived were pushed aside and the Texans were made to be heroes... I do not begrudge the Texas Battalion, they could have been us. But I wonder if General Dahlquist would have risked any other battalion to save us... All these things have been in my mind for many, many years.

I never did get married, I was afraid to...too much responsibility. I lived with my parents until they passed away. Then I lived with my brothers, but I cannot stand them, so I moved out on my own. It is good to live alone... At night, I wake up almost every hour. I only sleep about three hours a night. I wake up at about 3 a.m. and I cannot get back to sleep. So I just think about things...my mind goes back to Army times.

I have seen Dr. Sword for some years for my PTSD. If not for him, I would not have my PTSD disability rating from the Veterans Administration. I could not understand the paperwork. He helped me fill all these forms out; they are very confusing. He wrote a report for me. When I got my disability rating, I thought maybe the government had not forgotten me. Maybe things had changed and they cared about the many Japanese who fought for them in WWII.

One day Dr. Sword asked if I would be part of the study for his new time perspective therapy. He said it was partly based on what he had learned from the 442nd. I said sure I would. He has done so much for me. He gave me psychological tests...I had taken some like this before when he wrote my report. I already knew I had bad PTSD. He told me about Dr. Zimbardo's theory and all about time perspective therapy. I liked the simple therapy. He knows I think about the war every day and every night so he told me to think of the good times. Even though we were in a bad situation [past negative], we laughed a lot [past positive]. And now if I start to think about all my friends that died and how they died [past negative], I think about the jokes we told and the songs we sung and the meals we tried to make with whatever we could find. One time we were camped near a field of onions and we made terrible onion soup with water from a close by stream—but we ate it and we laughed [past positive].

The next time I came for therapy Dr. Sword showed me a chart with my ZTPI [Zimbardo Time Perspective Inventory] scores—it didn't look too good. He showed me how the past negative and present fatalistic dots were too high... I didn't think too much about the good things that happened in the past (past positive) and I didn't do anything with anybody or have any fun (present hedonistic). I just liked to stay at home and work in my garden. I didn't think too much about the future—I didn't like to because I don't know how much time I have left.

Dr. Sword said I had to start doing things with other people. I had to work on my present hedonism. He told me that there was a group of 442nd [veterans] who met for coffee every morning and that I should go. He said it would help me get away from my present fatalism. Then he told me there was a 442nd Veterans Club that has socials every couple of months and I should go. I started going to the morning coffee meeting the next day and I really enjoyed seeing my old buddies...I hadn't seen them in decades. Dr. Sword told me when the next social was and I went. They had good Japanese food and sung karaoke and played bingo. I had a good time. It reminded me of the way I was brought up. In Japanese culture, we work together for the better of the whole.

When I saw Dr. Sword again he told me we should make some plans for the future. I had been having a hard time with how I feel about the Veterans Administration—the benefits I got weren't as much as I thought I deserved. Dr. Sword helped me with more paperwork. He told me we were working on my brighter future together. He said that I had something to look forward to—getting more benefits—and that I had to live a long life so I could enjoy them.

I see Dr. Sword every month and we go over how I am doing...I am doing good. I remember the past positives and practice being present hedonistic—I see my buddies every day. I got more benefits. I don't know how long my future will be, but at this point, it doesn't matter; it will be good. I am still part of the TPT study, and every year Dr. Sword shows me how I am doing and also how all the veterans in the study are doing—the dots are in the right place.

aki's cognitive behavioral therapy

Aki had received treatment for several years using cognitive behavioral therapy (CBT), positive psychology, and relaxation training. The therapists helped him obtain a 100 percent service-connected PTSD disability rating with the VA by writing and submitting a detailed psychological report on his behalf. This restored his sense of honor and his respect for the government for which he had fought so hard.

Like many Asian and Pacific Islander veterans, Aki was a symptom minimizer, an attitude that has been instilled and reinforced from childhood. Symptom minimizers can be severely depressed or anxious, yet "put on a happy face" in public. In psychological terms, Aki suffered from repression and denial. He suffered from frequent intrusive, distressing recollections and flashbacks even after more than sixty years. In combat, soldiers never get a good night's sleep. It's common for combat vets to suffer from sleep deprivation for the rest of their lives, and Aki continued to suffer from combat-related sleep disturbance, sleeping only about three hours every night.

aki's time perspective therapy

Aki's time perspective therapy began sixty-four years after World War II. Although rapport had already been established during their CBT sessions, in the beginning the therapists were concerned that at Aki's advanced age TPT would not be effective. He had received CBT for three years prior to the advent of TPT. There was no need to review his past or his past negatives, as they had been covered in previous CBT sessions, so the therapists moved right into introducing TPT.

The therapists were very surprised when, in that first TPT session, Aki quickly grasped the concept of Temporal Theory (TT) and TPT, which the therapists explained and reviewed in a cross-culturally sensitive manner. He liked TPT's simplicity and positive focus. Whenever he had past negative thoughts — of the scores of his buddies who had died in the war, for example — he was asked to remember the past positives: the heroic deeds they performed, the funny experiences, and their close camaraderie. This was surprisingly easy for him to do.

In the second TPT session, the therapists suggested pro-social behavior and selected present hedonism in the form of meeting with surviving 442nd buddies, who were already convening at a local fast-food restaurant. This would help replace Aki's present fatalism, and the isolation and avoidance he had imposed on himself for decades. The therapists sought to further extend selected present hedonism by encouraging him to participate in World War II 442nd Veterans Club social activities. Aki himself pointed out that the pro-social group focus portion of TPT was in keeping with the social nature of the Japanese 442nd culture, which emphasizes the goals of the group above the agenda of the individual. He was eager to reestablish the close ties he had known with his buddies. This bonding elevated his mood and his sense of future hope and social belonging.

In the third TPT session the therapists focused on a future positive TP, and encouraged Aki to work toward a positive relationship with the VA. His service-connected PTSD disability rating had been established prior to his receiving TPT; having the social status of a disabled veteran has been very positive for his self-esteem and gives him more reason to go on with his life at his advanced age. TPT concepts worked well for him culturally, and reminded him of the way he had been brought up — working together and focusing on past positives rather than past negatives, and planning for a future positive beyond one's lifetime.

In the fourth TPT session, Aki was asked to expand on his future positive time perspective. His future positive plans include (1) living until he is 100; (2) maintaining his excellent health by walking three miles each day, a habit he developed while in TPT; and (3) attending the annual 442nd RCT conventions in Las Vegas.

aki's brighter future

TPT proved highly effective for Aki. He says that he feels this therapy has been very important for him. His social bonding with his World War II unit was so intense that in the nearly seventy years since the war ended, he has never made close friends outside his elite fighting unit. However, since his experience with TPT and his success with selected present hedonism, his social interactions with his old military buddies are more frequent and positive. In fact, he meets with his buddies for coffee every morning. These relationships, along with past positive memories, propel him toward a brighter future. He recently attended the World War II 442nd RCT's Congressional Gold Medal Ceremony (CGMC), in which he was awarded his medal by speaker of the house John Boehner in Washington, DC, as well as the State CGMC in Honolulu, in which he was honored by both Secretary of Veterans Affairs General Erik Shinseki (retired) and U.S. Army General Joseph Peterson.

aki's pre-TPT and post-TPT psychological test results

Interpreting the Graphs: In the clinical graph on the left in Figure 4.1, Aki's psychological test scores show an excellent profile of improvement over the course of treatment. With TPT, this veteran's depression and anxiety scores fell significantly, from severe to extreme and severe, respectively, to within the normal range. His trauma went from high severe into the mild to moderate range, taking him from the severe stage of PTSD to a fairly normal level of functioning and lifestyle.

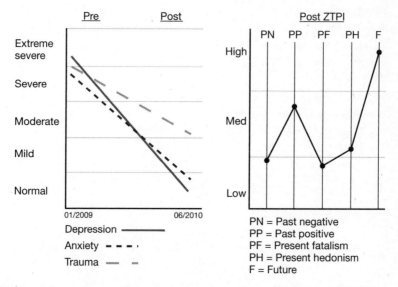

Figure 4.1   Aki—World War II Veteran—Psychological Test Graphs

His post ZTPI scores ("post" means after TPT treatment) also reflect improvement. It is interesting to note that he maintained his low past negative and high-medium past positive outlook, even with the horrors he endured at the end of World War II. He now lives with low present fatalism, low-medium present hedonism, and high future orientations. When he looks back on his life, the good overwhelms the bad. Aki feels that his life is within his control, and that if he tries, he can make it even better. This gives him a wonderfully positive outlook for the future, even at the age of eighty-eight.

Viewed together, these graphs indicate significant improvement and normalization of his PTSD with a brighter outlook for the future and significant drops in depression, anxiety, and trauma.

"i didn't want to shoot villagers"

mike, korean war veteran

Mike is an eighty-year-old Korean War veteran of American Japanese ancestry. He participated in the bloody Battle of T-Bone Hill (also called Pork-Chop Hill), in which human waves of villagers were used by the North Korean Communist forces as shields against U.S. forces. "We took between 2,000 and 2,500 incoming artillery rounds right on top of our position in less than 20 minutes," Mike recalls. "I never thought I would survive that battle."

psychological diagnosis: combat-related PTSD

I was too young to be in the military during World War II. But five years later, when war broke out in Korea, I enlisted. We were all gung ho! We would be heroes—remembered like the guys who fought in WWII. But some WWII veterans I fought alongside of in Korea told me that Korea was much worse than WWII. There was very poor leadership—it was every man for himself. The unity and quality of command had broken down. Our purpose for being there was in question.

In December 1952 I was part of the Battle of T-Bone Hill... It was horrible. The Communist Chinese who were trying to take over

Korea used Korean villagers as human shields. We took between 2,000 and 2,500 incoming artillery rounds right on top of our position in less than 20 minutes. I never thought I would survive that battle ...

I didn't want to shoot villagers——old men, women, children...but the Communists would round up villagers and force them to march in front of their soldiers or they would execute all the rest of their relatives... The villagers sacrificed themselves to save their families. At first we didn't know what to do but...we just started shooting and killing everyone we could before the Communists got to our position. Villagers dropped, and there would be more behind them... We killed so many innocent people...but we defended our vital position.

Three days later, we came down the hill. I found out my best friend had been killed. I think I went crazy for a while. Before T-Bone Hill—before I found out my best buddy was dead—I would fight the enemy one-on-one and take them as prisoners. But after that...I killed the enemy. The Communists didn't give my friend a chance—they didn't take him prisoner. So I took no prisoners.

When I returned home, I got a job as a union carpenter and worked until I was sixty-two. I retired as soon as I could because I was burned out. I had gotten married late in life and had no children. I knew I had some problems. My temper got me into trouble at work...I had a hard time communicating with my wife.

I went to the VA for help but the process was all red tape. I felt like a forgotten soldier from a forgotten war. When I was at the VA, I saw a fellow GI who had been at the Battle of T-Bone Hill with me. He said he had PTSD and was getting help from the VA and Dr. Sword. He said Dr. Sword would help me. I went to see him and he helped me get my VA benefits. I saw him every month for four years.

One day when I was at his office for an appointment he asked me to be in a research study for his new therapy. I was honored. He gave me psychological tests and said we'd talk about them next time. He told me about Temporal Theory and time perspective therapy. It all made sense to me. My wife had made me promise to tell Dr. Sword about how I like to go out every night at 2:45 a.m. for walks. I think I liked to go because it made me feel like I was on patrol—guard duty. I told Dr. Sword that I was killing two birds with one stone: I was getting my exercise and

I was trying to find the punks that sprayed dirty words all over my fence. I wanted to find them and teach them a lesson. I had caught them one night and scared them off by waving my arms around and jumping up and down—acting crazy. They had come back a few nights later and sprayed my fence again.

Dr. Sword said I was acting present fatalistic. He said that instead of putting myself in danger like that I should do something called selected present hedonism. He asked me to consider going to the Korean War Veterans meetings and also the Veterans of Foreign Wars. Dr. Sword knew I liked to garden and raise flowers. Sometimes I brought them to his office. He said my flowers were nice and I should enter them in a flower show. This would do double duty; it would be present hedonistic because it's something I like to do and also it was future positive because the flower show was in the future.

In my next TPT appointment, Dr. Sword asked me to tell him about some of my past positive recollections about Korea and my life. Most of my past thoughts were about Korea. It was easy for me to remember how close we GIs felt to each other. I told Dr. Sword I had been going to the Veterans of Foreign Wars meeting hall almost every day and spending time with old buddies. We talked about past positives—the good things we remembered—not past negatives. Dr. Sword said as soon as I started thinking about the human shields and the killing—the past negatives—I should replace them and think of the good friendships, the good times, the good feelings, the past positives. I told Dr. Sword that since our last appointment I had been doing Selected Present Hedonism and expanded my green house and was growing orchids.

I guess I am a worrywart because at the third TPT appointment I told Dr. Sword I was being present fatalistic because I was very concerned about all the wars in the Middle East. He said it's good to "Think globally, act locally." I couldn't do much about the wars but I could do good things in my life and for the people in my life. I was going to enter some of my new orchids in the orchid show in a few months and I started thinking maybe I should ask my wife if she wanted to help me with the orchids. Dr. Sword said my future is more important than my past. He said that I had been past negative and present fatalistic but I was learning how to balance my time perspectives by being past positive, selected present hedonistic and planning for my future positive.

Every month when I go to see Dr. Sword, there are issues I have; but we talk them out and I leave his office in a better frame of mind. Sometimes my wife comes with me. Sometimes I bring Dr. Sword orchids. I go to either the Korean War Veterans meetings or the VFW meeting hall several times a week. I listen to other veterans when they have problems and try to help them. Dr. Sword told me this is pro-social behavior. Every day I take my wife to a local coffee house where other older veterans hang out. It's nice to see everybody.

Through TPT, I realized that focusing on the future is the best way to help the past. You cannot change the past but you can change the future. I am really glad I came to get this therapy. If not for this I would be down in the dumps. When I went to the VA for therapy, they did not help; but this process definitely helped me. I thank my Korean vet buddy who sent me...I will never forget this to my dying day.

mike's cognitive behavioral therapy

Like Aki, Mike is a symptom minimizer. Mike had been brought in for therapy by a fellow veteran who recognized his chronic and severe PTSD symptoms. He had been in therapy for four years before TPT was developed and had received his 100 percent service-connected PTSD disability rating from the Veterans Administration. Mike had been treated with seventy-six individual therapy sessions of CBT, positive psychology, and media-based relaxation training before he started TPT.

mike's time perspective therapy

In Mike's first TPT session, he agreed to participate in the TPT pilot study and was given a battery of psychological tests. TT and TPT were explained, and he easily grasped these concepts.

The therapist's immediate concern was his present fatalistic practice of taking very early morning walks (2:45 a.m.), partially as a form of exercise and partially in the hope of a physical confrontation with youth gangs. Engaging in dangerous activities that involve high personal risk is common with many PTSD vets. The major concern was that at his age, he was no match for a gang. These gangs had taken to spray painting graffiti on his fence, and he was intent on "teach[ing] them a lesson." (It should be pointed out that Mike had *not* seen the movie *Gran Torino*.) He had already had one physical confrontation in which he scared the gang away by "acting crazy."

The therapist suggested that Mike spend pro-social selected present hedonistic time with his fellow Korean War veterans (KWVs) at their meeting place during the day. Because Mike enjoyed gardening, the therapist suggested he focus on his exotic plants and enter them in flower shows (a present hedonistic and future positive activity).

In the second TPT session, the therapist explained that when past negative flashbacks and thoughts about the Korean War entered his mind, Mike was to replace them with past positive memories. When asked what these memories might be, he recalled the camaraderie he had shared with his fellow GIs. He said that since he had begun going to the KWV meeting hall almost every day, he was remembering more past positives. He greatly enjoyed the company of people with whom he shared experiences. He said, "We don't talk too much about the bad times—we talk about the good times and what we are up to." Mike was progressing rapidly in TPT. In this same session, he stated that he was practicing selected present hedonism by expanding his greenhouse and growing orchids.

In the third TPT session, Mike was greatly concerned about world events and the wars in the Middle East (present fatalistic). He was reminded to focus instead on what he could do to make a difference in his life and the lives of those around him. He addressed his future positive in this session when he stated he was entering his first orchid show in the coming months. In his personal relationship with his wife he was very private, but he did mention he would ask his wife to help him with his orchids. When introduced to the idea that his future is much more important than his past, he realized and understood how biased his time perspective was toward past negative and present fatalistic orientations. He began the work of making the time he has left as productive and enjoyable as possible.

The fourth TPT session focused on a brighter future. Mike's future plans were simple: to win a ribbon in the county orchid show and to continue to help fellow veterans. To this end, he has married his selected present hedonism of caring for his flowers and his buddies with his future positive goals.

mike's brighter future

Mike continues his TPT sessions on a monthly basis. He has taken to assisting other Korean War veterans suffering from PTSD, acting as a counselor of sorts. Fortunately, he has curtailed his dangerous, present fatalistic midnight patrol walks. His selected present hedonistic bonding with fellow Korean War veterans elevated his mood, sense of future hope, and sense of social belonging to an important group he identifies with.

Having the social status of a disabled veteran has been very positive for his self-esteem and gives him more reason to go on with his life at his advanced age. "It is not the money; it is what the money means." This has not cured his PTSD, but certainly has palliated the symptoms of chronic and severe PTSD and assisted him in finding meaning and renewed enjoyment in life and a brighter future. Since he learned to check and balance his time perspective, his mood has substantially improved, as evidenced in his psychological test results.

Mike felt like "a forgotten soldier from a forgotten war" when therapy began. Once he understood the positive message of working toward a balanced time perspective his symptoms abated dramatically. Now he feels like an honored Disabled American Veteran who has turned his present fatalistic, antisocial withdrawal symptoms into pro-social, selected present hedonistic coping behaviors by attempting to help other veterans through the Korean War Veterans Association. His love of orchids and his desire to win a ribbon in upcoming flower shows adds an artistic dimension to his brighter future.

mike's pre-TPT and post-TPT test results

Interpreting the Graphs: This is an excellent case, showing dramatic improvements in anxiety, depression, and trauma. In the clinical graph on the left in Figure 4.2, Mike's depression, anxiety, and trauma scores have all sharply declined from the severe (depression) and severe to extreme (anxiety and trauma) levels to within the normal range.

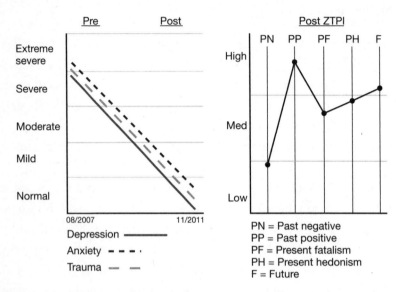

Figure 4.2   Mike—Korean War Veteran—Psychological Test Graphs

Mike's post ZTPI scores are consistent with his significant increase in mental health in regard to his time perspective ratings, even though his war trauma was extreme. He is able to maintain a low to medium past negative and very high past positive time perspective. He has a high-medium degree of present fatalism and a healthy (high-medium) degree of present hedonism. His high future score suggests that his future looks bright, as does his prolonged recovery from his PTSD.

Although Mike's PTSD maintained a severe level for over fifty years prior to treatment, it is clear from the psychological testing and consistency between tests that this veteran has made significant strides to overcome and normalize his chronic and severe PTSD.

"the rush of taking a human life was my addiction"

ed, vietnam war veteran

Ed is a sixty-year-old Vietnam War veteran. His Hawaiian father and grandfather taught excellent traditional hunting and water skills, which the military felt placed him in a special category: he was selected to be part of a Brown Water (River Patrol) Navy Special Forces unit known as the Black Berets. He underwent intense physical and mental training prior to deployment in Vietnam. Part of his training was to learn the Vietnamese language.

While in Vietnam, he worked alongside Navy Seals, Mobile Riverines, and Sea Wolves on covert missions. They would frequently "grease" villages or the countryside—killing every living thing in sight: man, woman, and child, as well as the farm animals. Ed grew to enjoy killing humans. (It is one of the darker sides of military missions, a real form of systemic evil in action.)

He participated in covert missions during the renowned 1968 Tet Offensive and was "ready to die." While on one of these missions, Ed's home base was destroyed and many buddies were killed in action (KIA) or wounded in action (WIA). On one mission they fired on and killed an old woman with a baby; this incident continues to disturb him greatly. During his tour in Vietnam, many of his buddies, including his best friend, were KIA; many others were WIA, leaving him with intense rage and survivor's guilt.

psychological diagnosis: combat-related PTSD

I am pure Hawaiian and grew up steeped in Hawaiian culture. I attended Kamehameha School, which is college prep. My education was not only academic but also rich in the knowledge of how to be self-sufficient. My father and grandfather taught me everything they knew to live and survive. I was very comfortable in the water; I could dive, spear fish, throw net. I knew how to gather seaweeds and all the edible shellfish. I was trained to hunt with guns, knives, and crossbow. I knew how to build things and grow food. It was a very good way to be raised.

I was drafted to go to Vietnam and decided to enlist in the US Navy. When they found out about my survival skills, I was tapped to be in the Navy Special Forces Unit as a Black Beret. Our training was physically, psychologically, and mentally intense. We had to be proficient in the Vietnamese language. We were trained to dehumanize "the enemy." They prepared us for a variety of tortures—we were prepared to die. Once we were in-country [Vietnam], I found it hard at first to kill the Vietnamese...they looked like Hawaiians. But that changed. I was constantly on covert missions, living on the river, living in the jungle.

It was routine to "grease" villages—to kill every man, woman, child, and all the livestock. In time, all of them were the enemy—animals in my eyes. I lost more buddies than I can count, including my best friend. I have flashbacks to him all shot up and bloody, dying in my arms. I also have flashbacks to an old woman in a *sampan* [a flat-bottom skiff with two oars]...she had a little baby she was holding. It was crying. She begged me not to shoot her but I had my orders. I killed her and the baby... The adrenaline rush of being covert, of taking a human life, of living in the jungle and on the river, was my addiction.

When I got back home, I became a fireman. I lived for the adrenaline rush. I was a good leader, good at my job, and became fire chief. I married and had children. The whole time I was living in denial. I repressed my true feelings about the war and myself. This rage grew inside me and became increasingly difficult for me to control. My survivor's guilt made me physically ill sometimes. Every day I questioned God. Why did he take my buddies, my best friend, and not me? Why didn't He kill me? I had killed so many.

A couple of my firemen had been to Dr. Sword, and they introduced me to Vietnam veterans who Dr. Sword had helped. All of them knew the symptoms of PTSD and they told me I had it very bad. I didn't want to hear it. My wife had been telling me this for years. Outwardly, I refused to believe I had PTSD. And yet I had taken early retirement because I couldn't handle the stress of the job anymore. I felt like Peter in the Bible, denying he knew Jesus...I denied to everyone that I had it. But deep inside, I kept my PTSD close to me. The flashbacks and nightmares were my punishment.

Five Vietnam veterans bullied me into having an appointment with Dr. Sword. I did not trust this [Caucasian-looking man]. In my mind, I had an invisible M-16 and I was prepared to blow him away. All the vets were in the meeting with me—they knew I'd run out the back door if I had a chance. Dr. Sword named off PTSD symptoms. The veterans were all nodding their heads, especially about rage, isolation, and avoidance. They didn't know about the nightmares I had every night, the yelling in my sleep, the soaked sheets, my wife huddled in a corner because she was afraid I was going to kill her. I didn't nod my head. I stared at Dr. Sword and tried to scare him. He gave me a questionnaire to fill out and told me that when I was ready, his wife, Rose, would interview me for a report for the Veterans Administration so I could apply for VA benefits and try to get a PTSD disability rating. On my way out, Dr. Sword introduced me to Rose. He explained she is part Hawaiian and that her father was a lifer Marine and had served two tours in Vietnam.

It took a few weeks of convincing from my new vet buddies, but I finally filled out the questionnaire; it was very hard for me to complete. I didn't want to see how my PTSD affected my loved ones. I had five very intense appointments with Rose. It took time but all of the poison was drawn out of me. I told her things I had not told anyone. She wrote everything down for my VA report. She did not judge me. In those appointments I realized that I had become an adrenaline junkie in Vietnam and by working for the fire department I had my constant fix. We took out the skeletons in my closet and laid them to rest. I started to feel a little better about myself.

I had met with Doc a few times before he and Rose developed TPT. In my first TPT session, Doc explained Dr. Zimbardo's Temporal Theory. I remembered Dr. Zimbardo from his Stanford Prison Experiment and how good people could do bad things. Doc went over TPT and how it works. I understood the concept—seeking balance by replacing positive for negative and making plans for the future, but it seemed too easy to me, like a magic wand. But I was willing to give it a try. I agreed to be part of his TPT pilot study and took some psychological tests. Doc showed me his website and we watched *The River of Time*. I was supposed to watch it every day; I'm not proficient at the computer—but I didn't tell him that.

My next appointment, we went over my test scores. We already knew about my trauma, depression, and anxiety. The new information came from Dr. Zimbardo's ZTPI. It validated my other scores—I had a very high past negative and high present fatalism. Past positive, present hedonism and future—forget about it. Doc wanted to work on my past negatives and said as soon as I start to have a flashback or negative thought about Vietnam, I should think about something positive instead. Every day I had Past Negative flashbacks, especially to my buddy dying in my arms and the old woman and the baby I killed ...

Doc asked me about some past positives, some good things I remembered about my best buddy. There were plenty. Even though we were scared shitless most of the time, we joked around and laughed a lot. Doc told me to replace my buddy's death scene with memories of the jokes and laughter and the smiles. Doc also explained how I lived a real-life Stanford Prison Experiment when I was in Vietnam. I was young and following orders. I understood this but it still didn't take the pain away.

I told him about how I beat myself up in my job—thinking about all the lives lost because I wasn't fast enough. He said I was a hero and saved far more lives than were lost on the job and that I should replace those past negative thoughts with the past positives. I told him some of the past positives like carrying people out of burning buildings, helping a lady give birth, and pulling people out of vehicles with the Jaws of Life—and climbing down a mountainside to extract a woman from her car, which had gone over the cliff. These were the past positives I should recall whenever I started to think about past negatives.

In the third TPT appointment we discussed my propensity toward present fatalism. I told him it was all I knew; isolating myself because I couldn't deal with people anymore, staying home and working around the house on projects I kept coming up with to keep busy. Doc said being pro-social would help me with my depression and get me out of the house. For my first pro-social selected present hedonistic project, I took Doc up on his offer and went to my first war trauma meeting. It opened up a whole new world to me. I met other veterans who understood me. I joined the Disabled American Veterans and got to know vets who needed help around the house. For my selected present hedonism I repaired fences, built rock walls and resurfaced drive ways. I felt appreciated and really good about helping out my buddies.

Doc helped me plan for a brighter future in my fourth TPT appointment. I didn't think about the future—it seemed so hopeless. But Doc pointed out to me that I had already started making short-range future positive plans by having a list of projects to do for fellow vets. I realized he was right. Doc wanted me to work on my relationship with my wife, which seemed okay to me until he asked me when was the last time I took a trip or spent any extended length of time with her. I was ashamed to tell him not since our honeymoon in the seventies. He suggested I consider making future positive plans to take her somewhere on a second honeymoon. I thought this was a good idea. My poor wife had put up with so much from me over the years. She has loved me through the worst of my life and now I was feeling more like young Ed. I called my wife during the appointment and asked her if she wanted to go away with me and she jumped at the chance—got on the phone and thanked Doc. Doc got on the computer and we made travel arrangements for a couple of months later for me and my wife to go to Las Vegas. That's where our honeymoon was.

I see Doc when I feel I need to for TPT, and I go to the war trauma meetings about every two months. I'm very busy with all the projects I have helping other vets. They exhaust me and help me sleep at night. I still have trouble with all my past negatives—they creep in more often than I'd like to admit. But I'm working on remembering the past positives. I admitted to Doc that I don't really use computers so he gave me *The River of Time* DVD so I can watch it once in a while. I think my wife watches it more than I do. My wife and I have been to Las Vegas and now, in our Brighter Future, we plan on an extended vacation—renting an RV and visiting National Parks.

ed's cognitive behavioral therapy

After Ed got out of the military, he wandered aimlessly for a couple of years before joining the fire department. The thrill in this new career was saving lives (pro-social) instead of taking them (anti-social). Due to his intelligence and heroic feats of courage, he was promoted to a high-ranking position in the fire department. In therapy, he realized he had found a way to make up for the killing in Vietnam by doing the opposite; he also realized he was able to continue the adrenaline rush in a way acceptable to society.

When the therapists commenced therapy, Ed's service-connected PTSD had forced him into early retirement. He approached therapy with great distrust and reservation. He did not understand why he was so wound up and angry all the time. His repression and denial would not allow him to admit he suffered from PTSD. His veteran friends insisted on his coming in for therapy because they recognized his extreme anger and overreaction as clear indicators of the severity of his PTSD from Vietnam. It took a "squad" of five veterans to physically bring him to the office; he appeared to be carrying an invisible M-16 and assumed a full combat posture and look while in the waiting room.

Ed commenced therapy prior to the advent of TPT. In these early sessions he was skeptical about therapy and distrustful of the therapist. He was assisted in filing for a service-connected PTSD claim with the Veterans Administration. CBT was employed.

ed's time perspective therapy

The first TPT session was devoted to TT and TPT education. Ed agreed to participate in the TPT pilot study. He was quick to grasp TT concepts and had many questions concerning TPT. He appeared to understand the goal: a balanced time perspective would ameliorate his chronic and severe PTSD symptoms. Ed took psychological tests, the results of which would be discussed in the next TPT session. Ed's past negative traumatic wartime experiences had been covered in previous sessions and were not discussed. The therapist showed him *The River of Time* relaxation video, and asked Ed to watch it on a daily basis.

In the second TPT session, Ed's psychological test results were reviewed. Test scores revealed that Ed suffered from borderline severe to extreme trauma, severe depression, extreme anxiety, and panic attacks. His initial ZTPI results indicated extremely high past negative and present fatalism scores, and extremely low past positive and present hedonism scores.

Ed was asked to replace his past negative Vietnam War flashbacks and intrusive thoughts with past positive memories from his war and postwar experiences. When he found himself having thoughts about his best buddy being killed, he was asked to recall good feelings and good times — past positives he had with his buddy. He shared that they had used humor to help them cope with terrifying and horrendous conditions, so the therapist asked him to immediately overlay his sad memories of loss with past positive recollections. If he started to spiral into dark past negative thoughts about the love of killing he developed while in Vietnam that caused him to feel self-hatred, he was to replace them with past positive memories of his heroic actions and the many people he had saved while in the fire department. He recounted numerous past positive incidents, such as saving people's lives by pulling them from burning wreckage and crushed vehicles. Because Ed had said he was aware of Zimbardo's Stanford Prison Experiment,[12] a correlation was drawn between the traumatic experience for Zimbardo's prisoners and Ed's traumatic experiences and his behavior in Vietnam.

Unfortunately, this led Ed to recollections of past negative experiences in the fire department — the occasions his efforts "failed." The therapist stopped him before he could get too far into more recent past negatives and brought him back to past positives. Ed would prove to be a difficult case because, in his mind, his extreme past negatives far surpassed his past positives. However, he was asked to work diligently toward replacing his daily past negative flashbacks with past positives.

In the third TPT session, the therapist noted that Ed lived a life of present fatalism and did nothing for enjoyment: present hedonism was not on his radar. To address this behavior, the therapist asked Ed, who had been self-isolating since retirement from the fire department, to participate in pro-social selected present hedonism by attending war trauma group meetings. He found the understanding and camaraderie he had missed since Vietnam in this group of compassionate veterans. Through the simple act of being with others of like mind at these meetings, his expanded selected present hedonistic and pro-social behavior bloomed. He met members of the Disabled

American Veterans and started participating in fundraisers. He also helped fellow veterans in need of assistance around the home in undertaking small construction projects, building rock walls, and resurfacing driveways.

Having set the groundwork for creating a future positive, the fourth TPT session was dedicated to empowering Ed to plan and work toward a brighter future. He found that he enjoyed the selected present hedonism of helping fellow veterans. His many skills were greatly appreciated, and he quickly developed a long list of projects that would take months to complete. He looked forward to spending time with these veterans in his future. On the home front, Ed and his wife had not been on a vacation since their honeymoon. During this session, Ed made plans for him and his wife to return to Las Vegas, where they had taken their honeymoon.

In follow-up TPT sessions, Ed's frequent backslides into past negatives were addressed by repeatedly refocusing on past positives. Because he was not especially computer savvy, he was given a DVD of *The River of Time* so he could practice the calming breathing technique and reinforce what he had learned in TPT.

ed's brighter future

Ed never put together how, throughout his decades in the fire department, he had planned for everyone else's future but lived a life of present fatalism. He could see no future for himself or direction for his life. His present fatalism caused him to self-isolate at home, working on projects to keep his mind off Vietnam. When he realized how he had trapped himself in present fatalism at the expense of his future, he began to purposefully change.

Once he realized that his TP therapist sincerely wanted to help him achieve a brighter future, he opened up. He still struggles with his extreme past negatives but continues to work on replacing them with past positives. The selected present hedonism of the weekly trauma group meetings allowed him to connect, relax, and enjoy his fellow veterans and actualize a more positive and brighter future. He notes that the sense of accomplishment and joy he feels by helping his buddies repair and build things are an important part of his brighter future. And, perhaps most important, the second honeymoon he took with his wife was so successful they are now planning another trip. With additional TPT, Ed can continue to achieve a balanced time perspective.

ed's pre-TPT and post-TPT test results

Interpreting the Graphs: In the clinical graph on the left in Figure 4.3, Ed's scores improved in all three categories; greatest progress was made in depression, in which he went from a high-severe score to within the low-normal range. His trauma scores indicate that he went from high severe to the borderline between mild and normal. Although his initial extreme anxiety score has improved and is now in the borderline mild to moderate range, it is an aspect his therapists continue to monitor.

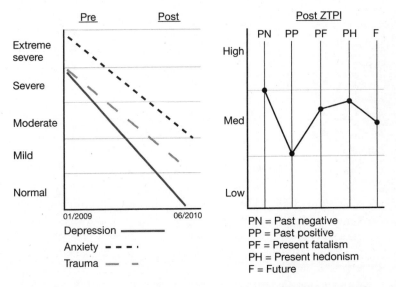

Figure 4.3   Ed—Vietnam War Veteran—Psychological Test Graphs

His post ZTPI results reflect some of his continued difficulties, especially with anxiety and trauma. He continues to hold on to his past negative trauma from Vietnam, and he has trouble recalling past positives. His present fatalism, present hedonism, and future scores are all in the medium range.

He continues to hold on to anxiety about his future, which is a diagnostic criterion for PTSD. His past negative score is medium to high, whereas his past positive score is medium to low. He believes this is due to his inability to save as many lives as he took in Vietnam.

"it's etched forever in my memory"
sean, gulf war veteran

Sean was deployed to Saudi Arabia shortly before the start of Operation Desert Storm, the Gulf War. He was a driver and helicopter mechanic. He was devastated when a female major he had been assigned to as a driver was killed in a helicopter crash along with four of his friends. He participated in recovering the bodies and transporting them from the scene. He also participated in body recovery along the heavily bombed "Highway of Death" in Kuwait. The sight and smell of the severely charred dead bodies and body parts haunt him to this day in nightmares; flashbacks; and recurrent, intrusive, distressing recollections of these horrible events.

At age thirty-nine, Sean is highly intelligent and very thoughtful. He did not want to go into detail in regard to his service-connected PTSD stressors, or triggers—the reasons he initially sought therapy; but he touched on his most severe stressor in his description of the TPT process.

psychological diagnosis: combat-related PTSD

That first TPT session was exciting. Doc explained Dr. Zimbardo's Temporal Theory, which I found fascinating. Doc went on to explain time perspective therapy. I was familiar with CBT and positive psychology and had gone through some Prolonged Exposure therapy—which only made me worse. This new therapy was intriguing. It was so simple. I asked Doc why somebody hadn't thought of this before. Doc said sometimes things are hiding in plain sight.

Doc asked me to take some tests: trauma, depression, anxiety, and Dr. Zimbardo's ZTPI. I scored the tests and, in the case of the ZTPI, plotted the graph. Doc reviewed the results with me. It was interesting that the ZTPI reinforced my other test results; my past negative was greatest followed by a high present fatalism score, high present hedonism score, very low past positive score, and practically nonexistent future time perspective. Doc mentioned we'd be working on balancing my time perspectives in future appointments. He went online and we watched *The River of Time* video. It was very relaxing and I knew I'd have no problem watching it every day, as Doc requested.

We focused on replacing my past negative flashbacks with past positive memories in the second TPT session. I have several recurring flashbacks, but there's one that is particularly upsetting to me; it has to do with the death of a major I was close to. I was her driver in the Middle East. She was a very intelligent person and could discuss any topic, from quantum physics to politics. She opened my mind to things I hadn't considered. I think, to her, I was like a smart little brother. I loved our conversations. When her helicopter was shot down and all my buddies aboard were killed . . . well, there is no word I can think of to express the way I felt.

I was sent to retrieve their bodies. Seeing her in that condition—it's etched forever in my memory. Doc asked me to replace this extreme past negative with the past positive recollections of our conversations; to focus on the way she expanded my awareness; that I honored her when I remembered the knowledge she had passed on to me. We discussed the importance of displacing past negatives with past positives.

We worked on my predisposition toward present fatalism in our third TPT session. For years, my attitude was affected by my past negatives which made me think present fatalistically—I was trapped in a deep hole. The only time I felt alive was when I pushed the envelope and did something extremely present hedonistic—and dangerous. At night, I drove my car or motorcycle twice and sometimes three times over the speed limit. Nothing made me feel more alive than being on that line between life and death. Doc said that if I died during one of my stunts, I'd never have children and the world would be a poorer place. Who knew what great things my progeny might accomplish?

I do have an ego, and this appealed to my sense of self-worth. He suggested the easiest way for me to overcome my present fatalism was to change my focus to the most positive thing in my life, my girlfriend. My girlfriend was the best—smart, beautiful, loving, affectionate—perfect for me. We lived together, but I had increasingly been ignoring her. I'd tinker on my electronics projects at home all day and into the night, then I'd take off for a ride. Doc suggested I include her in my plans for healthy selected present hedonism.

My girlfriend loved anything to do with nature; it was one of the things about her that attracted me. We did things together early in our relationship; but as my PTSD symptoms increased, my present fatalism caused me to isolate at home. Doc suggested I practice selected present hedonism by taking my girlfriend out in nature, to the beach and hiking. That weekend we went on the first of our many adventures. We were re-bonding.

I love anything to do with aerodynamics; my home projects included building remote control helicopters and airplanes. I started taking my girlfriend with me to try them out, which is something I hadn't considered prior to selected present hedonism. I wanted to do these things by myself, but my girlfriend liked that I was including her and I found I enjoyed her company.

In the session we also talked about my being more pro-social instead of anti-social as a way for me to deal with my present fatalistic depression. Pro-social behavior was another form of selected present hedonism. Doc asked me to come to war trauma meetings. I have a difficult time expressing the transformation that happened inside me at that first meeting...I was in the presence of brothers who had been in the shadows like I was, but they had come out to stand in the light. I wanted that. It was extraordinary.

In the fourth session, we discussed how I have trouble handling normal, daily activities. My present fatalism would get a grip on me and not let go. I had things I wanted to accomplish, but I was easily sidetracked. At the end of the day, I had completed nothing. It was incredibly frustrating and I'd go into a rage. Doc suggested a simple thing: make a list and stick to it. If I got sidetracked, come back to the list. At the end of the day, I would feel positive about what I had accomplished instead of feeling frustrated...if I hadn't completed what I wanted that day, I could finish it the next day. Why hadn't I thought of that?

We moved on, and made plans for my Future Positive. In high school I developed a love of antique vehicles. When I mentioned this to Doc, he went online to different websites and I saw a couple of antiques that looked good. I made a plan to save up and buy a car and motorcycle in my Brighter Future. Of course, the most important part of my brighter future was my girlfriend. We had been together for a couple of years but because of my PTSD, we hadn't been anywhere together so I made future positive plans for a vacation.

I continue to see Doc for TPT, especially when my present fatalism rears its head, but I'm done with the risky extreme present hedonism. I learned to make short- and long-range plans for a brighter future. My girlfriend and I became engaged and got married—we had a large wedding that took future positive planning. We had a wonderful honeymoon, we traveled all over the Pacific Northwest. That took some future positive planning. We got pregnant and have a beautiful baby girl—that took some future positive planning!

Doc and TPT have given me hope for a future positive. I've learned how to balance my Time Perspectives. I understand I'll probably always suffer from PTSD, but TPT really helps.

sean's cognitive behavioral therapy

After serving in the military, Sean returned to Maui and took a job working at the observatory on Maui's ten-thousand-foot mountain, Haleakala. He deliberately isolated himself, choosing a job that demanded he sleep during the day and work in isolation at night. He shared in an early (pre-TPT) therapy session that the only place he felt safe was locked inside the observatory—with no windows, no doors, and an excellent surveillance system.

After ten years of isolation, Sean felt it was time to come down off the mountain; he secured a position in the aviation industry as an airline mechanic at the local airport. Unfortunately, he was soon overwhelmed by being around people and the stress of his job. All the reminders on the flight line that triggered his PTSD symptoms surfaced. He had lost his concentration and ability to follow through in purposeful serial acts that are standard routine. Because Sean was an airline mechanic, this was not acceptable; it posed a significant danger to others. He was ordered to stop that work. Fortunately, he was able to obtain a 100 percent service-connected PTSD disability rating from the Veterans Administration.

sean's time perspective therapy

Sean had been to over forty therapy sessions and already received his 100 percent service-connected PTSD disability rating from the Veterans Administration with assistance from the therapists' office prior to the establishment of TPT. He agreed to participate in the TPT pilot study and commenced TPT.

Sean is extremely bright. In the first TPT session, he eagerly absorbed Zimbardo's Temporal Theory as well as TPT concepts. He took the psychological tests, scored them himself, and reviewed his test results with the therapist to ensure he interpreted the results correctly. His ZTPI results indicated high past negative, high present fatalism, high present hedonism, low past positive, and low future scores. Sean was asked to watch the video *The River of Time* on a daily basis.

Because both Sean and the therapist knew about Sean's past negatives from previous therapy sessions, the therapist asked Sean to begin replacing past negative flashbacks and thoughts with past positive memories, especially positive memories of his friends who had died. His most recurrent past negative flashback was to retrieving the mangled body of the major from the helicopter crash. He recalled specific intellectual conversations they had had, and the good feelings he had knowing there was another person with whom he could communicate. The therapist asked him to replace his past negative flashbacks with these past positives, and remember that the knowledge gained from her would live within him. Sean was given relaxation CDs to assist him in reducing his stress level.

The third session addressed Sean's high present fatalism. The therapist suggested he focus on the positive things in his present, especially his relationship with his compassionate and loving girlfriend, rather than his propensity to act recklessly and present hedonistically. His extreme present fatalistic suicidal ideations were discussed in detail; Sean wrestled with a desire to die in a car accident. When the therapist suggested that the world would experience a loss without the benefit of Sean's contribution to the continuing gene pool, this was an "Ah ha!" moment for Sean.

The therapist suggested that instead of being present fatalistic and self-isolating at home, Sean should practice selected present hedonism by taking his girlfriend, who loved nature, to the beach and hiking. Sean was a very quick study, and turned these selected present hedonistic outings into adventures and educational experiences for him and his girlfriend. He also had a love of aerodynamics and was encouraged in his selected present hedonism to enjoy remote control planes and helicopters, which he assembled himself. He was asked to attend war trauma group meetings to expand pro-social selected present hedonism. He valued the bonds he made with fellow veterans, and especially benefited from their discussions about personal relationships.

Sean's future positive was the main focus of the fourth TPT session. However, his coping skills were addressed first; he had trouble dealing with day-to-day problems and would become present fatalistic — overwhelmed to the point of losing his temper. The therapist suggested he become a list-maker and focus on completing a few items on the list each day. He was asked to focus on feeling positive about what he had accomplished rather than negative about what he didn't, and to understand that tomorrow he could complete more tasks.

In regard to his future positive, Sean revived a high school interest in antique automobiles and motorcycles, and made plans to purchase one of each after going online with the therapist to discuss makes and models. His relationship with his girlfriend was progressing, and they made future positive plans for their first vacation together.

sean's brighter future

In subsequent sessions, Sean's day-to-day problems were sorted out, and many were adequately resolved. His brighter future included detailed marriage plans, which were executed flawlessly, followed by plans to be an exceptional prenatal parent and then an excellent parent to the baby born to him and his new wife. He now understands the importance of a future positive time perspective and how this balances the negative experience of his military past. He has been able to find happiness and is no longer a danger to himself or others. Sean continues to battle with the serious effects of combat-related PTSD, but is learning to cope with the help of time perspective therapy.

sean's pre-TPT and post-TPT test results

Interpreting the Graphs: The clinical graph on the left in Figure 4.4 exhibits typical improvements from TPT. Clinical scores of depression, anxiety, and trauma have all significantly dropped. Sean's depression score went from severe to borderline normal. His anxiety score lowered from severe to the borderline between moderate and mild. His trauma score went from the borderline between severe and extremely severe to moderate.

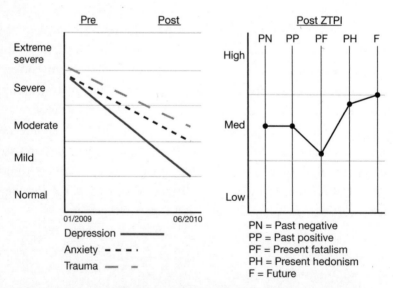

Figure 4.4   Sean—Gulf War Veteran—Psychological Test Graphs

In regard to his post ZTPI scores, his past negative and past positive scores are both in the medium range. His present fatalism score in the low-medium range coincides with his elevated (high-medium) sense of selected present hedonism. His future score is on the borderline between medium and high, and it indicates hope for a brighter future.

"something snapped inside me"
everest, iraq war veteran

Everest is a twenty-six-year-old Iraq War veteran. He was a smart, fun-loving boy when he was deployed to Iraq at the age of nineteen. There he headed up a team of four older men. At first he had a difficult time leading due to his age, but he proved himself by saving them with his instincts and quick action during a mission in which two insurgents were killed and a heavy weapons cache was confiscated. This combat was tough, but things took a turn for the worse when Everest was assigned to serve as an escort for detainees at Abu Ghraib prison outside Baghdad.

psychological diagnosis: combat-related PTSD

I've always been interested in psychology; figuring out why people do what they do is fascinating to me. I had a lot of great friends growing up. We had a good time—joking, laughing; lots of fun. I took AP psychology when I was a senior in high school, with the intention of becoming a psychologist one day. But my parents couldn't afford to put me through college so I joined the US Army 442nd Regimental Combat Team as soon as I graduated, knowing that I'd be able to receive assistance when I was discharged.[13] One of my uncles and a close cousin were in the National Guard and had been deployed, so I thought there might be a chance I'd see them in-country...I didn't realize how mentally damaged I'd be when I came home.

When I was nineteen, I was deployed to Balad, Iraq, stationed out of Anaconda LSA [Logistics Supply Area]. I had a few jobs. Since I was qualified in all weapons I was weapons NCO [Non-Commissioned Officer], I was part of the QRF [Quick Reaction Force], I was an assistant medic for troops and villagers and went on humanitarian missions; I was part of MIT [Mobile Intelligence Team] and detainee escort at Abu Ghraib.

I guess I scored high on military testing because I was placed in a team leader position—which was hard because the guys I was in charge of were all older than me. There was a lot of posturing going on. For a while I put up with insults and put downs 24/7. I knew that age doesn't necessarily beget intelligence, knowledge, or wisdom. I knew I had to prove myself to my team in order to gain their respect, so that's what I did. I have this thought that in Vietnam, the officers and soldiers were trained—they were hardened... In Iraq, the troops were Nintendo-playing couch potatoes. I toughened up and became a smart, hard leader.

When I track back to the start of my PTSD, I'm led to an incident at Abu Ghraib. I was escorting two detainees to a helicopter for deportation when one, an older guy, started running. I didn't want to shoot, so once I caught up I stopped him with a head butt. I was wearing my night optics helmet—it acted like a weapon. He went down and I ran back to get the other detainee in the helicopter. Then I ran back to get the guy who tried to run. He was dead. It's hard to describe how I felt other than to say I was in shock. The doctor who performed the autopsy knew I felt bad. She told me the guy had been suffering from terminal cancer and when she opened him up, he was full of tumors—close to dying. I know she was trying to make me feel better, but I didn't.

I can't stand bullying or physical abuse; especially when I see a male taking advantage of a female—it does something to me... I was on patrol and had just rounded the corner of an alley when I saw a civilian Iraqi man hitting and kicking a woman; two young children were there crying. Something snapped inside me. I ran up, yelling at him in Arabic to stop. He wouldn't. I swung my M-4 rifle at the man [and] cracked his head wide open. I didn't mean to hit him that hard... I just wanted him to stop.

It was strange—I didn't feel remorse. I dragged him behind a dumpster. The little children were clinging to the woman's skirts. She came up to me, crying, "Thank you, bless you" in Arabic. She grabbed my hand and started kissing it. I kept shaking my head—I needed to get out of there... I cleaned my weapon as I walked back to the street and continued patrol... I knew something inside me wasn't right ...

The nail in the coffin for me was when I was responding to our company's convoy being hit. We were informed that four of our

GIs were KIA, killed in action. I was acting as medic. When the situation was secure, I ran up to the scene to see what needed to be done—who I could help. Some of our responders were assisting the wounded. Others were gently handling the bodies of the four dead GIs. I went up to see who they were. I knew two of them...my uncle and my cousin. Break down? Yeah. The happy go lucky Everest died that day. I cried until I felt numb. I didn't and couldn't cry again for years. Love, sorrow, grief—I couldn't feel them. I could only feel hatred and uncontrollable rage.

I was twenty-two when I got home. I knew I needed help so I went to a State Veterans Service officer and asked for benefits. I wanted psychological treatment and maybe funding for school. He turned me down without even looking at the merits of my case. This sent me into deeper depression. I lived at home with my parents. I was able to hold it together enough to get a job as a pharmacy technician and tried to keep busy, to keep my mind off of Iraq. When I wasn't working, I holed up in my room, plotting and planning ways to off people. Old friends and family members found out I was back and called the house but I didn't want to talk to or see anybody.

My PTSD symptoms were like a monster inside me, waiting to be provoked. I was so ready to overreact and act out. Anything could set me off. I had these horrific, violent thoughts; thoughts of homicide and suicide. Thoughts I don't want to share because they're too horrible. I finally got in to see the VA psychiatrist and he prescribed medications. While the meds helped during the day, at night, they distorted my dreams and nightmares. The recent past would mix with my time in Iraq and I didn't know who was who or what was real. At times I thought I was back in Iraq and I mistook family members for Iraqis. It was terrifying. I'd wake up feeling like I was having a heart attack—heart palpitating, gasping for breath; I'd be drenched in sweat. I was sleep deprived and on edge...I would constantly pick fights with my younger sister and get in arguments with my parents. I was so miserable. I didn't want to live anymore. I overmedicated myself and hoped I would never wake up. My mom saved me.

The only person I felt even remotely close to is an uncle who is a police officer. He's a really good man. He's also a member of the federal disaster response team. I knew my parents were talking to him about me and that kind of pissed me off. But sometimes I'd talk to him too. He's a good listener; he didn't judge me. I didn't tell him everything, but I told him I was angry about being turned down for veteran's services and benefits. I guess I told him enough for him to suggest I see this doctor who specializes in trauma and PTSD he had met on the federal disaster response team.

My uncle called to make the appointment with Dr. Sword, which I didn't show up for. I wasn't ready. I had studied psychology—it was about the past; I didn't want to go there consciously. I knew I needed help but I just couldn't do it. Then my mother called to make me an appointment. I was at home at the time and my mom told me the person on the other end wanted to talk to me. This lady said her name was Rose and she asked me if I was ready. I thought, "Who is this, questioning me?" I was kind of belligerent. She told me that any help they had to offer wouldn't work unless I was ready to deal. She said that generally when people make appointments for someone else, there's a good chance that someone else doesn't want therapy—the person making the call wants them to come in and it's a waste of everyone's time. I thought "Damn—she talks straight!" I told her that she was talking to me now and that I *would* come in. I was scared. Nobody knew my inner thoughts, my demons. I didn't want to be judged and found incompetent.

I was late for my appointment with Dr. Sword. Rose was waiting for me at the door. She didn't say anything about me being late—just smiled, introduced herself, and said we'd be working together once in a while. She introduced me to Dr. Sword. He knew my uncle pretty well and I admire how he broke the ice—talking about family, acknowledging I was with the 442nd and how he worked with the old WWII 442 veterans.

That first session is a blur. I know I hinted at some of my stressors and some of the things that trigger my flashbacks. But I wasn't comfortable talking about my "crazy" thoughts—about thinking of ways to take out people that pissed me off or ways to commit suicide...those things came out later. We set up weekly appointments with Dr. Sword for therapy as well as a series of two appointments with Rose. She would interview me, document my traumatic experiences in Iraq, and start on a report Dr. Sword was going to submit to the Veterans Administration. I left there with the feeling these people wanted to help me.

My first interview session with Rose was a three-hour emotional marathon. I thought counselors were supposed to be made of stone but when I started talking about how I used to be growing up and how I was "now," Rose's eyes teared up. I thought—why is it she can feel and I can't? Then I told her about what happened in Iraq. While she was typing what I said, these tears were streaming down her face. I felt something wet on my cheek—I was crying. It was such a relief to cry, to know I could cry, to know I could feel...

In my next session with Dr. Sword, he explained about PTSD being a mental wound, not a mental illness or disease. This made me feel better somehow. Apparently, I'd already taken the first steps towards healing by talking about my traumatic Iraq experiences. We talked about goals and I told him one of my major objectives was to get off medications. He suggested another goal should be to have some hope for the future. I thought that was a nice idea but the future looked pretty bleak to me.

I had a second marathon session with Rose but it wasn't as emotional as the first. Since my previous session, I had looked up PTSD symptoms on the Internet. It didn't surprise me when she asked questions about my sleep patterns, did I avoid people and certain situations or places, what made me angry, how I was doing at work, how I related to family members. Then she asked if I minded my parents meeting with her or Dr. Sword so they could be informed about PTSD. She said although I was her and Dr. Sword's focus, they were also concerned about how my family was handling things. I told her it was okay with me so she set it up for the next week.

In my third session with Dr. Sword, he gave me psych tests and explained how I suffered from severe to extreme trauma, depression, and anxiety. This was no surprise. He brought up Type A behavior because of my anger issues. I was familiar with it through my studies and I knew exactly what he was talking about. We immediately went to work modifying my behavior starting with slowing down my breathing; I would do this whenever I started to feel angry or frustrated. I would slow down my movements, relax my muscles, lower the tone, timber and volume of my voice and think things through instead of reacting or overreacting in a military style the way I did in Iraq. These are simple things that are hard to do when you're starting to spin out of control. But that day I made a vow to myself to be more conscious of my behavior. I wasn't in the military anymore.

My mom met with Rose while my father and sister met with Dr. Sword. After their meeting, my mom told me she learned a lot about PTSD and how it affects everyone in the family. This made me feel guilty. I guess it showed because my mom hugged me and said, "It's not your fault." I didn't tell her that I felt to a degree it was *her* and *my father's* fault because the reason I joined the military, the reason I experienced those horrible things, the reason I had changed, was because *they* didn't make enough money to pay for my college. I knew this was irrational but I couldn't help feeling that way. But I didn't say anything.

Since I returned home, I had treated my sister poorly—I was bitter and my resentment ran amok where my sister was concerned. I had become the bully I hated. I was so horrible to her, she moved out. But after the session with Dr. Sword, she moved back in. She said she understood better why I was acting irrationally. I told her I was working on myself and she said she could see the results. We came to an understanding. And my dad—my dad loves me so much and I know that! I know it! He wants the best for me in life and I was screwing up. After his meeting with Dr. Sword, he walked up to me and gave me the biggest bear hug. He said we were going to get through this together—as a family. My tired, closed down heart opened up—wide.

Dr. Sword had scheduled our fourth session on a holiday. When I got to his office, he told me he was taking me to a fast food restaurant for breakfast to meet some special people. I was hungry so this was fine with me—especially since he was buying. When we got to the restaurant, there were ten of the original WWII 442nd Regimental Combat Veterans sitting around a table. Dr. Sword announced to these guys who must have been near ninety years old, "Gentlemen, this is Everest, he's the new generation of 442!" These old guys cheered, jumped up and they all reached out to shake my hand. They were grinning from ear to ear and so was I. One of them told me I was their first new member in sixty-five years. After knowing my family still loved me and were trying hard to understand me, I think this was the best I had felt since I returned from Iraq.

Dr. Sword and Rose helped me open a PTSD disability claim with the Veterans Administration with the psych report they wrote.

They encouraged me to keep seeing my VA doctors. They knew I wasn't socializing so they invited me to attend the Wednesday veterans' group meetings. I went to a few and actually enjoyed being around fellow veterans. I saw the VA psychiatrist about every three months—he'd check on my medications. During one of my meetings with the psychiatrist, he suggested I be placed on an emergency 100 percent PTSD disabled basis but I turned him down because I wanted to go to school. I told this to Dr. Sword and he told me to listen to the VA psychiatrist because I wasn't yet in the right frame of mind to go to school. I couldn't concentrate and my short term memory was shot—it was very difficult to remember things I had read. I went back to the psychiatrist and he suggested I attend an eight week veteran PTSD rehab program at a large veterans' facility. Since I was in process with the VA for a PTSD disability rating, I thought I might as well try it. I told Dr. Sword I was leaving the following week.

I called Dr. Sword every week I was at PRRP [Post-Traumatic Stress Residential Rehabilitation Program]. I was doing fine. I can't really talk about what we did other than to say it was extremely difficult and at times I wanted to escape—but I think every one of us felt that way at one time or another.

When I returned from rehab, my disability rating had come through. I was now able to collect my benefits and go to school… The Swords asked if I wanted to be a member of the Z Team. This was a chance in a lifetime for me. I helped the researchers Dr. Zimbardo sent from the Bay Area with the initial pilot study they conducted on veterans.

My brighter future? I am enrolled at the university and am working towards my degree in medicine with the goal of becoming a psychiatrist. I know firsthand the effects of war. My intention is to work with veterans, especially those returning from the Middle East.

everest's time perspective therapy

Everest returned from Iraq and took a job in pharmaceuticals. This young veteran had studied advanced placement psychology as a senior in high school and was very interested in dissecting the cause of his personality change. He suffered from severe to extreme PTSD symptoms, including frequent suicidal and homicidal ideations.

The severity of Everest's combat-related PTSD necessitated concurrent individual therapy with both Swords. Everest's first session with Rick focused on establishing rapport through conversation and discussion. It was apparent that the normal TPT protocol of past, present, and future would need to be modified. Instead of following TPT's logical progression from past to present to future, it was necessary to boost not only past positives but also future positive goals to offset his extreme past negatives. His first individual session with Rosemary Sword was a three-hour intensive in which Everest shared his military-related past negative experiences. His suicidal ideations with plan (firearm) as well as his homicidal ideations without plan were of paramount concern. He agreed not to act on these ideations and to call the Swords when he felt overwhelmed by these thoughts. Everest's second session with Rick focused on PTSD and its symptoms. Rick explained Temporal Theory and time perspective therapy. Everest's background in psychology allowed him to grasp these concepts quickly and recognize the importance of letting go of his past trauma to move forward with his life.

Before his second three-hour intensive TPT session with Rose, Everest had educated himself concerning PTSD and was prepared to discuss his severe and often extreme symptoms, which had caused him to be present fatalistic. To assist in his recovery, his family members were asked to attend sessions without Everest.

In the third session with Rick, psychological tests were administered and explained that confirmed severe to extreme trauma, depression, and anxiety. Also, as Everest was dealing with anger issues through negative present hedonism, Type A behavior was discussed. Rick immediately encouraged Everest to employ behavior modification, whereby Everest was to practice breathing and deep muscle relaxation techniques, as well as slowing down movements and lowering his voice tone, timber, and volume.

In separate sessions, Rose met with Everest's mother while Rick met with his father and sister, explaining PTSD and its symptoms, Temporal

Theory, and time perspective therapy. All family members were asked to use compassion and understanding with Everest.

In the interest of reestablishing Everest's self-esteem and helping him cope with his present fatalism by experiencing a taste of present hedonism, the fourth session was held at a fast food restaurant where Everest met a group of original WWII 442nd RTC veterans. He was greeted warmly. The spontaneity of this encounter, coupled with the realization of the unconditional love of his family, were the major turning points in Everest's TPT. Shortly after this meeting he expanded his selected present hedonism by sporadically attending the war trauma group meetings. He was encouraged to continue seeing a VA psychiatrist every few months to monitor his prescription medications.

In subsequent sessions, Rick and Everest discussed Everest's plans for his future positive. Although he wanted to attend a university and get his degree right away, he was asked to continue working on his coping skills; his PTSD symptoms, especially his inability to concentrate, were still severe. Everest's VA psychiatrist enrolled him in an eight-week intensive Post-Traumatic Stress Residential Rehabilitation Program at Tripler Army Hospital, which commenced the following week. Everest checked in with the doctor once a week during the PRRP process.

Upon his PRRP course completion, Everest received his PTSD disability rating. He was asked to join the Z Team and assisted in research and the TPT pilot study.

everest's brighter future

Over the course of therapy and through intermittent attendance at the weekly war trauma group sessions, Everest decided to attend a university with the academic goal of completing medical school and becoming a psychiatrist. Although he will always suffer from PTSD, his symptoms have improved significantly, and he now has a focus: it is his greatest desire to help fellow veterans suffering from similar disabilities. Through time perspective therapy, he was able to replace the real-life war movies that repeatedly played in his head with the hopeful vision of a positive future that includes a pro-social career and long-term relationships.

everest's pre-TPT and post-TPT test results

Everest was an original member of the Z Team in early 2009 and did not participate in the TPT pilot study. He graciously agreed to share his story for the purpose of this book. Respecting his wishes, there are no graphs to present. However, he has given permission to share his psychological test scores (see Appendix C).

o to sum up

- Thousands of American war veterans from all wars struggle with PTSD.[14] It is predictable that these war veterans are stuck in the past negative and present fatalistic time perspectives, at the expense of both present and future.
- TPT has been found to be very effective in helping veterans return to the balanced time perspective they deserve: a positive past, selected present hedonism, and a positive future.
- Increasing a sense of belonging and community is an important part of reducing negative, violent, and self-destructive coping responses to adversity and also of increasing pro-social civic engagement. Pro-social war trauma groups are especially beneficial for PTSD vets who miss the camaraderie of military life and the guidance of more experienced peers.
- Restoring veterans' pride in themselves and their service is encouraged by helping them foster a positive relationship with the Veterans Administration and the government that they served while in the military. This is done by assisting them with the paperwork necessary to support their claims applications for a service-connected PTSD disability rating.
- Women war veterans also suffer from PTSD, particularly as a result of rape and sexual harassment classified as military sexual trauma.

5

everyday trauma, PTSD, and time perspective therapy

"I heard all sorts of car horns going off," remembers Sherman, twenty-four.

> Then I heard tires squealing and metal hitting metal. I looked into my rear view mirror right when I felt this huge impact and heard a really loud crunching sound. There were giant tires on the back of my car and I was being pushed forward. I looked in front of me and I was being pushed right toward a big propane tank on the side of the highway. All the cars in front of me were scrambling to get away as fast as they could. I thought I was dead for sure. I prayed to Great Spirit to take care of my family. I thought of Grandpa and Grandma and all my ancestors and how I would see them very soon. The propane tank came towards me so fast! I closed my eyes as my car slammed into it...

Trauma followed by PTSD can be caused by natural disasters, such as hurricanes, floods, and earthquakes, and by large-scale tragedies, such as 9/11, as the following box makes clear. It can also be a result of physical assault, prolonged abuse, plane crashes, and a myriad of other causes. But—as it was for Sherman—the leading cause of PTSD in the general population is motor vehicle accidents. Car accidents are the number one trauma for men and the second most frequent trauma for women.[1] (The number one trauma for women is sexual assault,[2] which is addressed in the following chapter.)

It's likely that you know someone who has been in a car accident, or that you have been in one yourself. Many people who have been in accidents are likely to have suffered from PTSD to some degree, and have been able to work through it on their own. Others, like the people in this chapter, need some assistance. One of the wonders of being human is our incredible diversity. Each of us handles situations in our own unique way—for better, but sometimes for worse.

In our clinical practice about half our nonmilitary clients suffering from PTSD were in motor vehicle accidents (MVAs), most of them serious enough to cause personal injury.[3] The people you will read about in the following case studies are fine people who found themselves in extraordinary and horrifying circumstances. Three of the four case studies relate to MVAs, and demonstrate how these people's lives were changed forever by something that happens in the blink of an eye. The first case study is about a phone call that pushed a 9-1-1 operator over the edge and into the deep, dark chasm of severe PTSD. The fourth case study concerns a good cop forced into a bad situation, with a deadly outcome. Their extreme traumas negatively affected every aspect of their lives, and the lives of their family members; yet they were able to get their lives back, balance their time perspective, and live their brighter future through the systematic application of time perspective therapy (TPT).

how TPT can help treat disaster-related PTSD

In 2005 Hurricane Katrina made landfall in southern Louisiana, ultimately causing more 1,800 deaths and an estimated $81 billion in property damage. Ordinary people lost their lives, their families, their friends, their pets, their homes, their jobs, and even their city. And their stress didn't end as the storm subsided. According to the National Institute of Mental Health,

A study of Hurricane Katrina survivors found that, over time, more people were having problems with PTSD, depression, and related mental disorders... As communities try to rebuild after a mass trauma, people may experience ongoing stress from loss of jobs and schools, and trouble paying bills, finding housing, and getting health care. This delay in community recovery may in turn delay recovery from PTSD.[4]

Following the aftermath of a recent earthquake, Richard Sword was dispatched by the federal government to assist with disaster-related stress control; to assess and provide treatment for stress reactions of federal disaster response team members; and, when necessary, to provide support for local families of the deceased.[5] But it quickly became apparent that his primary mission was to bolster the morale of the disaster workers. The team was diverse—comprising not only medical professionals but also firefighters, homicide detectives, mortuary operations personnel, coroners, security, forensic odontolologists (specially trained dentists who help identify unknown remains), a physical anthropologist, and the incident command staff. Their deployment had come at great personal expense to each of its members: disaster team members take leave from their regular jobs and their families and travel great distances in difficult circumstances to rescue others and relieve suffering. The compensation provided is, in most cases, substantially less than they would normally receive. In addition, the devastation and destruction they were dealing with every moment of every day was taking an unexpected—to them—and ever-escalating emotional and psychological toll.

Depression and fatalism almost inevitably took hold of the team—it seemed impossible to give them the emergency and ongoing help they needed to survive and rebuild. Rick's goal was clear: to change their temporal outlook from negative to positive. They needed immediate help to avoid deteriorating from having a highly charged future positive time perspective—"We're going to give them the help they need!"—to having a past negative and present fatalistic time perspectives—"What can we do? This situation is hopeless."

Rick began by focusing on the team's mission, goals, and desired future outcomes rather than on the enormous challenges of the present situation. He emphasized the impact that the team's intervention was already making on the local people; he also spoke about how the team's social networking from diverse locations around the world after they left the scene would continue to create a better future for those affected by the earthquake.

Rick then invited the team members to talk to him to establish a practical therapeutic relationship. Some later commented that they found it refreshing not to hear "psychobabble," but rather a practical, common-sense approach that focused on their most valuable resource—time. All professional disaster workers are acutely aware of the importance of time. Often it simply runs out. But everyone has heard the stories about an individual's miraculous survival a week or ten days after it was presumed that everyone must be dead. This is the exception, not the rule, however; time is truly the greatest adversary of disaster teams. They cannot function adequately without a rapid and appropriate response.

During and after therapy sessions, team members quickly emerged from their depression and frustration about not being able to do more, moving toward being interested in networking and getting to know and appreciate their fellow team members. This paradigm shift was observed across the entire population of this socially intense group of dedicated professionals. They began to enjoy local culture and network with others. They were excited to be where they had chosen to go, rather than depressed to be stuck there.

After they had returned home, the team gathered for an after-action debriefing. A number of team members stated how positively this team operated in comparison to other teams in the same disaster field response scenario. "Other teams commented on the cohesive, friendly spirit of our team," said one, "and some individuals from these other teams caught on to the time perspective thing."

Rick told them that that they had been working with a new model for disaster workers called time perspective therapy. He explained Temporal Theory and TPT, and how he had employed this therapy after realizing

that things in the field were not working out as expected. Some team members expressed distrust and even disdain for previous mental health treatment they had received in disaster field response scenarios, seeing it as not particularly useful. The homicide detectives, veterans of the World Trade Center bombings on 9/11, commented that their TPT experience made this different from previous response episodes. They described TPT as a "breath of fresh air," and definitely more useful than prior approaches they had encountered in disaster field response scenarios.

Finally, the team's administrative officer reported,

This new approach is very user friendly. Our team listened with acceptance because it was not like the old psychology we were previously exposed to. [TPT] did not have the problems associated with the old way psychology has worked in the past. Dr. Sword put it in terms of Time, and that, we all understand ... time [perspective] therapy made a big impact on our mission.[6]

People suffering from PTSD often seem to have changed irrevocably from the people they were before the trauma, but each person still lives on, hidden deep inside the defenses and anxieties. We have found that understanding our clients' pre-situational personality is vitally important in helping them heal. Once we understand who they were—and help them hold on to that person—we can look at how the traumatic situation has changed their thoughts, feelings, and behavior and affected various aspects of their lives. Our goal is to find the healthy core of the inner person and to liberate her or him from the cloud of the terrible, traumatic experience that has impaired daily functioning. Gradually, that original person does emerge. And as that person develops a balanced time perspective, he or she begins to look toward a brighter future.

"the call that broke the camel's back"
mary

Mary comes from a long line of law enforcement professionals. But when Mary wanted to carry on the tradition, her father objected. So instead of becoming the first female cop in the county, Mary became the wife of a police officer, and soon after the mother of two children.

As the years progressed, Mary's desire to do something meaningful for her community became all consuming. When the county implemented a 9-1-1 emergency response system, she felt that being a dispatcher was something she could do to help people and not put her life in jeopardy.

For twenty-three years, Mary served as a 9-1-1 dispatcher. In the department, Mary was known for her warm, maternal voice. She had an incredible ability to calmly guide the caller while simultaneously directing the proper emergency service to the situation (for example, the fire department to fires, police and ambulances to traffic accidents). Mary loved her job, but being on the receiving end of life-or-death calls takes an incredible toll on the operator.

Then, at age fifty-eight, she received what she refers to as "the call that broke the camel's back. A little boy called and said his mother wasn't breathing ... " After this tragic incident, Mary started calling in sick, afraid to go to work, and when she did she cried on the job. Mary's commander recognized that she was overwhelmed by job stress. He placed her on temporary disability and referred her to the therapist, being familiar with the therapist's PTSD work with the police department and the local and national disaster teams.

Psychological Diagnosis: *PTSD due to chronic and severe on-the-job stress as a 9-1-1 emergency dispatcher for emergency medical response, police, and fire departments*

Law enforcement is very big in my family. My grandfather was chief of police. Dad followed in his footsteps and was chief of police. My uncles were police officers. I have three brothers, and they are police officers. I am the only girl. After I graduated from high school, women were allowed into the police force. I wanted to carry on the tradition too and prove myself to my father and my family, but I was voted down. Dad didn't want me to put my life on the line. Like most men of his generation, he didn't think a woman could handle the stress. In those days, being a female police officer was a battle fought on a very steep hill.

I lived at home, worked at a department store. Then I met my husband—he's a cop. We had two children. They were my life; I really enjoyed being a stay at home mom. But once they were in school, I wanted to better myself. I went to college part time and got my AA degree. I got a job as an office manager. I was very content. My husband was promoted, my kids were doing good. Then, in my mid-thirties, I heard the county was going to implement a new system called 9-1-1. I thought, *Here is something I can do and not put my life in jeopardy ... I can help people and work with the police department, the fire department, and emergency medical services.*

I have been working as a 9-1-1 dispatcher for nearly twenty-five years. My kids grew up and got their college degrees. Of course, one decided to become a police officer, but the other broke the mold—he's a prosecuting attorney. My husband is the captain of the SWAT team. I have learned so much about people by being a dispatcher ... people can be so resilient. I thought I was very good at removing myself from the situation and maintaining calm. My commander would compliment me on how composed I was under stress.

But I found out one thing that really bothered me, and that is all the children who are abused, who have zero parental guidance. Their parents are usually on drugs. I told my husband how I felt, and that I wanted to take some of these kids in. He's an honorable man. He agreed, and so we became foster parents in special emergency cases. Sometimes we would have kids for a few days. The longest we had a couple of children was for a few years.

I loved my job. Helping people in dire circumstances feels so good most of the time ... and at others, it's so sad... One night, I got the call that broke the camel's back.

A little boy called and said his mother wasn't breathing. I went through the protocol, calmed him down, found out where he lived ... the whole time he was crying. I told him to be brave and that his mother needed him to stay calm. I kept him on the line and heard the ambulance arrive ... but it was too late. I could hear the little boy screaming for his mother to wake up ... and something snapped inside me... It just destroyed me.

I was sick and afraid to go to work. I didn't want to get another call like that. I forced myself to go, but I cried all day. My husband's familiar with PTSD and he said that's probably what I had. My commander is such a good man. He saw that I was really stressed out and there was no way I could maintain calm under pressure. I went on TDI [temporary disability insurance]. He said I needed to get help and told me I should see this therapist who worked with the police department and was on the state and national disaster teams. He could help me.

I felt funny going to see a therapist. I thought counseling was only for veterans and couples with marriage problems. I was shy and didn't want to talk. But he was so nice—he made me feel relaxed. He asked about me and my family. I told him I love my husband and my kids and my family, I loved being a foster parent. I told him about growing up in a family of cops and how happy I was when I became a dispatcher.

Then he asked about the 9-1-1 call, the little boy crying for his mother. I told him that I thought about my own sons and what if this had happened to them ... I couldn't disassociate myself from the little boy or his mother ... I was so upset and cried so hard, I couldn't breathe. The therapist told me to focus only on my breathing. I closed my eyes and he talked and had me visualize walking on a path with beautiful flowers. I was able to catch my breath and felt really relaxed. He explained Temporal Theory and TPT to me and said we would be working intensely together so I could get back to work and feel confident again.

In our next meeting we talked about my past negative experiences. I realized during emergency calls that I had been doing the opposite of what I was supposed to do: I realized that part of me was imagining exactly what was happening on the scene when I should have been concentrating on staying at the dispatch office. He said that I had to stay grounded and let the emergency teams do their jobs in the field and not project myself to the scene. It was hard to admit, but I also realized that I liked the adrenaline rush and the excitement of what has happening.

I had taken psychological tests and the ZTPI [Zimbardo Time Perspective Inventory] at the end of my first TPT session. Three tests—the trauma, depression, and anxiety—were all severe. My therapist told me that they showed I had PTSD. My ZTPI scores showed that even though I knew I had a lot of past positives in my life, my past negative was higher and that I had become present fatalistic. My present hedonistic score was off the bottom of the chart. I didn't do anything fun, and I realized I hadn't basically since my kids had moved out of the house. I was afraid of my past and afraid of the future because I didn't want to get another call I couldn't handle. I realized that I liked being in control of the present. I liked being a dispatcher—I guided emergency responders and helped save lives—when everything worked right.

The TP [time perspective] therapist explained to me how your breath and your heart rate are connected, and that I could control my heart rate by taking control of my breathing. Then he proved it to me by showing me breathing exercises to help me slow down my heart rate when I get anxious. We watched a time perspective video together. It was very helpful for me and showed me how to balance my Time Perspectives. After that meeting, I watched the video every day and practiced the breathing.

In our next session we talked about how I could replace my past negatives with past positives. When I thought about the little boy, I would immediately think about how I helped guide people to deliver babies. I love babies and children, so another past positive for me is remembering the kids my husband and I fostered. These good thoughts are very meaningful and helpful for me. We went over my breathing and heart rate and I did the breathing exercises again. We talked about how I was handling things at home and I told him I was doing okay, the housework was getting done and I was cooking meals. I was going through closets and catching up on my reading. He said it was good for me to keep busy.

In my fourth session, the TP therapist said it was time to talk about selected present hedonism. I told him when I thought of "hedonism," it wasn't an especially good thing. He explained that the key word was *selected:* It probably wasn't good for people to do anything to excess, but that if you chose to enjoy yourself or reward yourself once in a while, it *was* a good thing. He asked me if I did anything fun with my husband or anything for myself. My husband and I were all about work, coming home, eating dinner, and watching reality television shows. He suggested we make "date nights" at least every two weeks so we could get out and enjoy each other's company outside the home. He also said that it would be healthy for me if I did something nice for myself once in a while. I told him I used to get pedicures but I had been too depressed to do anything like that. He said maybe it was time to treat myself again. I liked these ideas and discussed them with my husband. He took me out to dinner that night. After two weeks, I was doing well enough to return to work.

I still saw the TP therapist, but only twice a month. Whenever a 9-1-1 call came through that didn't work out, or whenever I went past negative by thinking about calls that didn't work out,

I learned to think about past positives—the good things I've done, the things that *did* work out. There were many more past positives than past negatives. My therapist made me feel better about myself. He helped me get my confidence and self-esteem back. He told me I provide a great service to my community and that I'd raised good kids. He told me I gave a stable environment and love to the foster children I cared for. I'm very grateful to my husband for his support, my commander for realizing I need help, and to my therapist—he showed me how to stay focused on the job and helps me see all the good things in my life.

Now I go to TP therapy once a month. I still get calls that cause me stress and it helps to know I will see my therapist and he'll help talk me through them. Lately we've been talking about my brighter future. I'll be retiring in a few years, and so will my husband. I never really thought about my future, what I'd do when I retire. When my therapist asked me what I'd like to do, I couldn't think of anything. Then he asked me what I liked to do in the past. When I think back in my life to what made me the happiest, my best past positive, it was being a mother and a foster parent. Being a foster parent was very rewarding. My husband and I were able to give these children something they had never experienced—three square meals and a safe and secure home. I talked to my husband and he's agreed with me. When we retire, we'll be foster parents again.

mary's time perspective therapy

Mary's narrow conception of therapy caused her to be apprehensive during her first TPT session. But within a few minutes she relaxed enough to review her background and then explained "the call that broke the camel's back." She sobbed uncontrollably, gasping for breath, while describing how the little boy cried for his mother. The therapist became concerned about Mary's inability to breathe properly, and led her through a soothing visualization, explaining to her that she could use this exercise during times of stress or anxiety. The therapist administered psychological tests, and then went on to explain Temporal Theory and TPT, noting that Mary would begin intensive therapy in the next session. It was determined that Mary would receive therapy twice a week for two weeks, with the intention of reestablishing Mary's confidence and self-esteem. At the end of two weeks they would decide whether or not she was ready to return to work.

In the following session, the therapist reviewed Mary's psychological test results with her. They indicated chronic and severe PTSD. Special emphasis was placed on her ZTPI scores, which indicated very high past negative and very high present fatalistic orientations. The therapist introduced Mary to the guided visualization video and administered a deep, rhythmic breathing technique to be used in conjunction with the video. Mary was asked to practice this breathing technique whenever she started to feel upset or anxious. The therapist explained the connection between breath and heart rate, and told Mary she could control her heart rate by taking control of her breath.

The third session dealt with replacing past negatives with past positives. Mary and the therapist tapped Mary's love of babies and children as an essential source of past positives with which to replace her past negatives. To monitor her progress and ensure that she was properly practicing anxiety and stress reduction through slow, rhythmic breathing, they reviewed the breathing exercise. The therapist surveyed Mary's day-to-day coping skills and was satisfied with her resolve to stay busy, thereby keeping her mind occupied.

The fourth session addressed Mary's lack of selected present hedonism. Her ZTPI indicated extremely low present hedonism. After speaking with Mary about this situation, it became apparent that both Mary and her husband did nothing outside the home together and that Mary had ceased doing anything for herself. It was suggested that she and her husband have date nights approximately twice a month, and that Mary do at least one nice thing for herself at minimum every few weeks. After this session, it was determined that Mary was equipped to return to work.

Mary was compliant. She watched the video, listened to stress-reduction CDs, and practiced her breathing. Her sessions were decreased to twice a month for a few months. In a subsequent session it came to light that Mary had been present fatalistically projecting herself *into* each emergency call and becoming overly involved in the imagined scene. The therapist suggested that Mary stay grounded in her body at her station and let the emergency medical teams, police officers, and fire department personnel to do their jobs in the field.

Mary had become addicted to the adrenaline and excitement of living in the present fatalistic moment. She feared the past, feared the future, and tried to control the present by being a 9-1-1 dispatcher—guiding these important different agencies—until it all caved in on her. Now, instead of focusing on past negatives, Mary learned to focus on the past positives she had accomplished: the babies she helped deliver, the lives she helped save, the great service she had provided for her community throughout her long career, and all the good things she had done for her family. After years of denying herself enjoyment, Mary embraced selected present hedonism with date nights with her husband and by indulging herself with pedicures.

mary's brighter future

Mary continues TPT on a monthly basis, and therapy recently helped her plan for a brighter future. Because Mary had never really thought about what she would do when she retired, the therapist asked her what she liked to do in the past. It didn't take long for Mary to relate that she loved being a mother, and that some of her fondest memories were of raising her children and being a foster parent.

Mary and her husband have an excellent relationship. They look forward to continuing their shared selected present hedonism and spending their golden years in a not-too-distant future positive. She has a sense of purpose for the future, having decided that when she retires she will once again be a foster parent and offer abused children the opportunity to know a mother's care and unconditional love. She has regained continuity as well as her motivation to continue serving her community until retirement. Mary now knows how to pace herself, remaining intact and effective in a most stressful job.

mary's pre-TPT and post-TPT test results

Interpreting the Graphs: The clinical graph on the left in Figure 5.1 indicates typical improvement following time perspective therapy. Mary's depression lowered from severe to the high-normal range. Her anxiety lowered from severe to mild; and her trauma dropped from severe to extreme to the borderline between mild and moderate.

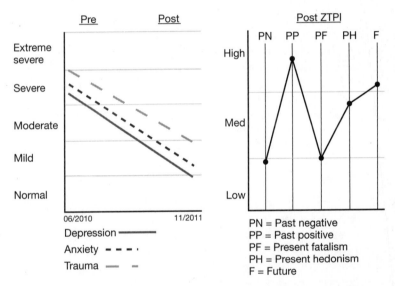

Figure 5.1   **Mary—Civilian with PTSD—Psychological Test Graphs**

Mary's post ZTPI scores on the right indicate that Mary is leaving her past negative traumas behind and looking forward to her future positive. Her past negative score has dropped to the low to medium range, whereas her past positive score is now very high. Her present fatalism score is on the borderline between low and medium, and she raised her present hedonism score to a healthy high medium while maintaining a high and brighter future outlook.

"i felt totally inadequate"

jenny

At age forty-six, Jenny has had more than her share of tragedy, and an indomitable sense of survival. She became a paraplegic after an accidental fall from a ladder, but with the help of her husband—her primary caregiver—she came back to have a full and productive life. Then tragedy struck again—and again.

Psychological Diagnosis: Exacerbated preexisting PTSD due to a motor vehicle accident

I married the love of my life and we were happy as could be. We had been married for fifteen years when I fell from a ladder and fractured my spine. My husband was incredible. After we realized I would never walk again, he suggested that we sell our house and move to Hawaii—it was always our dream. We bought land and designed a house for my special needs. We both adapted to my wheelchair and made the absolute best of our lives together. I learned to roll with the punches in childhood. My mother is naturally depressed all the time, and that made her a naturally negative person. I knew when I grew up I didn't want to be either of those things!

Then one day, five years later after my accident, my husband was riding his motorcycle and was hit by a truck and killed.

Before he died, I had never allowed myself to experience that depth of depression. I was so far down that my friends were concerned. One suggested I seek grief counseling. I guess I'm pretty strong, because after a few sessions, I was in the acceptance phase of grief and no longer needed counseling.

About a year ago, on Halloween night, I was in my car waiting at a stop sign. I was on my way home after partying at a restaurant with my friends when a huge lifted pickup truck—the kind with giant tires—came speeding around a corner and drove right over the hood of my car! I was rocked so violently that my car was halfway in the oncoming lane. My purse, with my cell phone in it, fell from the passenger seat to the floorboard as far away from me as it could be. Luckily my wheelchair wasn't damaged—it was folded up in the back seat. I was scared to death! *What* had just happened? I looked in my rear view mirror and saw that the truck had stopped a little way down the road, which had no street lights. So it was dark! These two guys jumped out of the giant truck and started running up to me. I was in shock ... my mind was racing ... I thought they were coming back to hurt me and steal my purse.

When they reached my car, one guy looked at me, looked down at my purse on the floorboard and then checked out the wheelchair in the backseat. The other guy was checking out the damage to my car. I was crying, telling them I had to use a wheelchair and could they please help me—call 9-1-1 and help me get out of the car ... I was afraid it might explode. They stood there talking to each other for a few seconds and then they ran back to their car and took off!

I tried to start my car but it wouldn't ... I was afraid another car would come around the corner and crash into me. I couldn't get out of my car ... all I could do was sit there and cry hysterically. In a little while, the police and an ambulance showed up—someone in a house nearby heard the accident and dialed 9-1-1. Truthfully, the paramedics couldn't tell if I was injured or not because I already had spinal injuries. I told them I was okay because I didn't want to go to the hospital. The cops—God bless them—took down all the information I could remember and one of them got my car started. They followed me home and helped me into the house.

I stayed home for a month, afraid to go out. I didn't feel like seeing or talking to anybody. When I realized I was severely depressed again and seemed to be getting worse, I called and booked a double appointment with my therapist. I wanted to get over this depression. I had in the past and I knew I could again. I wanted to get on with my life.

When I told her what happened, my therapist suspected I had PTSD. She told me about Temporal Theory and time perspective therapy, which had been developed since I'd last seen her. I took psychological tests and they indicated I suffered from severe PTSD. She also administered the ZTPI—my past negative/present fatalistic scores were really high and my past positive/present hedonistic/future scores were really low. I was so depressed; it felt like I was in a pit of depression.

I hadn't been the type of person to fear death—after my husband died, I thought I was at peace with it. But the accident had changed all that. Having stared possible death in the face, I was now very afraid of dying. The accident caused all of these abandonment issues I thought I had dealt with after my husband died to resurface. I felt so inadequate—again! I had been a hearty, physically fit person before my fall. When I was first wheelchair bound, my ego was crushed. It took my husband and me years to get me pumped back up to a healthy state of mind. After this accident, I felt totally inadequate. I was depending on a friend to run errands for me because I was a paraplegic—I needed help! That first TPT appointment was the first time I had left the house in a month!

I wanted to talk about the recurrent dreams and nightmares I was having since the accident. After I described each dream, we figured out that they had to do with my fears. All of the anxiety I experienced during the day was replaying at night. She said that sometimes our dreams help us prepare for circumstances that might take place in the waking (real) world and that we can work through a lot of issues in our dreams. Knowing there were simple explanations to my nightmares made me more confident that I wasn't crazy. Then we talked about my low self-esteem. The month I'd been home I didn't care about my appearance, but my therapist pointed out that I was wearing a pretty dress, my hair was done, and I had makeup on. She said that anybody looking at me wouldn't know I was suffering from severe PTSD; that made me feel good about myself. I told her "Fake it till you make it" is my motto.

It's pretty easy to understand the principles of TPT and how they applied to me. My past negative car accident caused me a mental health set back and also caused my present fatalism; and my obsession with present fatalism made it impossible for me to think about my future.

I guess the worst thing the accident did—present fatalistically speaking—was make me totally lose trust in people. What kind of people would do that to a disabled person like me? I had a really hard time not thinking about these two guys doing a hit and run on me. I was afraid they knew where I lived and were going to come and hurt me. I was thinking about selling my house and moving away because I wanted to get away. I started to get upset, and my therapist led me through a guided meditation, which calmed me down. Before I left she told me that in our next session we'd work on replacing my past negatives with past positives; she gave me a couple of relaxation CDs to listen to so I could get down the breathing technique.

Between my first and second TPT session, I was practicing my breathing. Since we were going to be talking about past positives, I brought two of my favorite photo albums with me to my TPT session. The therapist explained that whenever I started to have past negative flashbacks or thoughts to the accident or anything else negative, I should replace them with past positives. That's when I pulled out the albums. We looked through the first one, which was of my life before my husband died. Every picture had a story and I was happy to share each one. Then we moved on to the second album, life after my husband died. And every picture in it had a wonderful story. At the end of the session I knew for sure that for every past negative in my life, I had a hundred past positives to remember.

In my next TPT session, our focus was my extreme present fatalism. Up until that day I had not attended one of my support group meetings—and that was hard not only on me but on everybody in the group, because I was the leader. I kept getting calls from members asking when I was going to come back but I wasn't up to socializing. But my therapist asked me to go back to the meetings as soon as possible. She said that not only was this pro-social selected present hedonism—which I needed—but it was also a good way to deal with my depression. Helping other people and spending time with them in a positive way takes your mind off your own problems. She said that by being a trusted person in my group, maybe I'd gain back the feelings of trust I had lost in the accident. I told her I would do it.

We went over my improvement in the next session. I was thinking past positives and leaving my past negatives where they belonged—behind me. I was practicing selected present hedonism and had returned to my support group. I felt really good about helping others with their problems and *not* thinking about mine. And I had started going out a couple nights each week—meeting friends for dinner, going to movies, and going out dancing. Yes, people in wheelchairs dance! Now it was time to make plans for my future positive. My fear of the men who ran over my car had developed into a real desire to sell my house and move closer to my family and old friends. I kind of thought this was irrational, but the therapist was supportive. I told her I was ready to let go of the past ... the house that my husband had built for me had served its purpose. It was our dream. But we had lived our dream, and now it was time to move on. And anyway, why should I live in this big house by myself when there's a family out there just waiting to enjoy it? After we talked it over, my therapist agreed that I had thought things through. And since this was the direction I wanted my future positive to take, we went online and started looking at local house sales to see what my house might be worth!

I had TPT down pat, but I still went to see my therapist until I moved. It turned out to be a terrible time to sell my house because of the economy; but I owned it free and clear and sold it to a wonderful family with a special needs child. I live in Arizona now with my best friend. I'm closer to my family and back in touch with all my old friends. TPT is a part of my life; it's second nature to me now.

My brighter future positive plans are: to buy a house here in Arizona; to start up a support group (there aren't any in the town I live in, but I've talked to a few folks who want to participate); and to write a memoir. Maybe someone will find it inspirational.

jenny's time perspective therapy

Before her car accident, Jenny had been in therapy for grief counseling when her husband was killed. They had been married for more than twenty years, and her husband's death had an extra impact on her life because he was her major caregiver. Jenny is incredibly resilient and had a positive attitude about life. She required only five sessions of grief therapy.

When Jenny commenced TPT for her motor vehicle accident, she suffered from severe PTSD, including nightmares and flashbacks — concerning not only her accident but also her husband's unexpected death. Her severe PTSD symptoms were confirmed through psychological testing. She suffered from a fear of mortality, a flare in abandonment issues, feelings of inadequacy, and low self-esteem. The therapist had already established rapport with Jenny and knew her to be extremely bright, with a fierce desire to be well and move forward in her life.

In this initial TPT session, the therapist asked Jenny to start with her nightmares, which they discussed and analyzed. She was made aware of how the fears and anxiety she experienced during the day were played out in her dreams. The therapist bolstered her low self-esteem during this and subsequent sessions by sincere compliments on her appearance and compassionate ways, which assuaged her feelings of inadequacy.

Jenny grasped the Temporal Theory and time perspective therapy very fast. Her ZTPI scores indicated very high past negative and very high present hedonistic orientations. She understood her recent past negative car accident had caused her a massive setback — the progress she had made after the loss of her husband completely evaporated — and this was the root of her present fatalism; it allowed her no room for a future time perspective. Jenny described her present fatalism as a "pit of depression." This normally past positive, compassionate, gregarious, outgoing, fun-loving woman was now isolating herself, guardedly screening her calls, and leaving her home only to attend appointments.

Jenny, the leader of a support group, had always been the person others turned to for counseling and assistance. But now, for the first time since she had accepted her husband's death, she depended on others. Her extreme present fatalism had caused her to lose faith in human kindness, and she obsessed over this. The therapist led Jenny in a guided meditation to familiarize her with a calming breathing technique, and asked Jenny to watch a relaxing TPT video on a daily basis and to practice the breathing technique when she felt she was feeling stressed and overwhelmed. Knowing that Jenny was keen on self-help education and information, she also directed her to information about TPT and Zimbardo's Temporal Theory that she could quickly access on the Internet.

In Jenny's second TPT session she mentioned she had been compliant in watching the DVD, listening to the CDs, and perusing all of the things Philip Zimbardo had posted on the Internet. She knew ahead of time that she was going to be asked to replace both her recent past negative car accident trauma and the resurgence of grief she was experiencing over the death of her husband with past positive recollections, and came to the session prepared to share her past positives. She brought two photo albums: one of her life with her husband, which included pictures of her prior to and after the accident that caused her to be paraplegic, and the other of her life after the loss of her husband.

As Jenny reviewed the albums with her therapist, she lovingly shared memories of her life with her husband as well as happy moments she garnered from being the leader of a support group that met at least once a week. She recounted fun times at social gatherings, and spoke about how before her recent trauma she had regularly gone out with friends — at least three nights a week, she said. She promised that from this point forward, whenever she started to feel flashbacks or intrusive past negative thoughts enter her mind, she would replace them with snapshots from her albums of the many past positives that filled her life.

The third TPT session focused on Jenny's extreme present fatalism. Since the motor vehicle accident, Jenny had stopped attending her support group meetings and no longer socialized. She was asked to resume her former selected present hedonistic, pro-social behavior by returning to her support group and going out with friends at least once a week. The therapist discussed how focusing once again on helping others was a healthy, nonmedicinal way of coping with depression. Furthermore, by restoring faith in herself, she might restore faith in humanity; for if someone as decent and good as she exists on the planet, surely others do too.

The fourth TPT session began with a review of Jenny's TPT progress (replacing past negatives with past positives and resuming selected present hedonism), and then focused on making plans for Jenny's future positive. The severity of her PTSD symptoms, especially her hyper-vigilance — although she knew it was irrational, she couldn't shake the fear that the men who had hit her knew where she lived and would come to her house and cause her harm — had caused her to rethink living by herself. She discussed future plans to sell her house and move to another state, closer to her family and childhood friends. She wanted a fresh start in her future positive. She and the therapist went online immediately to test the reality of this future plan: they checked local house sales. Then they discussed at length the many things she would accomplish in the near future.

In subsequent TPT sessions, Jenny learned to balance her time perspective effortlessly. She mastered the ability to replace past negatives with past positives, and practiced selected present hedonism by returning as the leader of her support group. No longer present fatalistic, she once again took pride in her lovely appearance and resumed her pro-social nights out with her many friends and acquaintances. She reconnected with her strong spiritual belief and no longer had a fear of mortality. The housing market was at an all-time low, but she owned her house outright; she placed it on the market and sold it to a family with a child with special needs who would make good use of it. Although she had learned to implement TPT after only six sessions, she chose to continue TPT for moral support until her move.

jenny's brighter future

Jenny is well prepared for the next chapter in her life. She quickly grasped TPT and continues to apply it. She recently relocated to Arizona, where she is closer to family and friends and lives with a companion she has known since high school. Her future positive plans include purchasing a home in Arizona, starting up a support group, and writing an inspirational book about her life.

jenny's pre-TPT and post-TPT test results

Interpreting the Graphs: In the clinical graph on the left in Figure 5.2, Jenny's extreme anxiety lowered to the borderline between mild and normal. Both her severe depression and here trauma lowered to the normal range.

Jenny's ZTPI graph on the right is consistent with her clinical graph. Her very low past negative has been offset with a very high past positive. This is indicative of strong psychological resilience and a positive outlook on life. Her medium present fatalism score is offset by her high present hedonism and future scores. Her prognosis is as positive as her future time perspective.

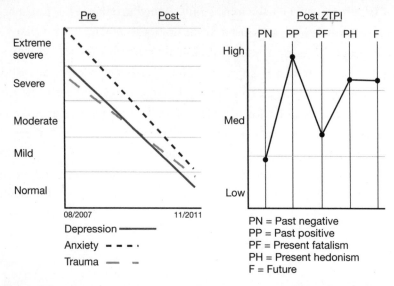

Figure 5.2   Jenny—Civilian with PTSD—Psychological Test Graphs

"i thought i was dead for sure"

sherman

Sherman was twenty-four, a young Native American man who had wisdom and maturity far beyond his years. He was married with two young children, was diligently working his way up the ladder in a construction firm, and was head of his extended family and chief of his tribe. He was co-foreman on the construction job site of a multimillion-dollar hotel complex when, driving home one night, he was caught in a horrendous multi-vehicle crash.

Psychological Diagnosis: PTSD due to a motor vehicle accident

I am twenty-four years old but I feel like I'm fifty. I was raised on a Native American reservation by my mother and my grandparents. I never knew my father. After my grandpa died, I became the chief of our tiny tribe. Grandma died a year after grandpa but our tribe grew when I got married young and had two little ones. Grandpa taught me how to build so that's how I provided for my family—through construction jobs. I moved our family off the reservation and to a place where construction jobs were plentiful.

I guess having a lot of responsibility at an early age showed because even though I was young, I was made co-foreman at the multi-million-dollar hotel job where I was working.

We started work at sunup and ended mid-afternoon. I was driving home after work and the traffic was backed up for miles. I called my wife to tell her I'd be late, when I heard all sorts of car horns going off. Then I heard tires squealing and metal hitting metal. I looked into my rear view mirror right when I felt this huge impact and heard a really loud crunching sound. There were giant tires on the back of my car and I was being pushed forward. I looked in front of me and I was being pushed right toward a big propane tank on the side of the highway. All the cars in front of me were scrambling to get away as fast as they could. I thought I was dead for sure. I prayed to Great Spirit to take care of my family. I thought of Grandpa and Grandma and all my ancestors and how I would see them very soon. The propane tank came towards me so fast! I closed my eyes as my car slammed into it. The noise was horrible.

Everything was real quiet for a while. I didn't feel any pain—I thought I had crossed over, but instead of light, there was darkness. When I opened my eyes, my ears opened too and I heard yelling and screaming. The airbag had deployed and I was coughing because of the powdery stuff inside the airbag. My car was accordioned between the truck behind me and the propane tank in front of me. I was covered in glass. I thanked Great Spirit and got the hell out my car—crawled through the driver's side window.

It looked like what you see in a disaster film—the air was full of smoke. Cars were parked in the middle of the highway at weird angles. People were getting out of their cars—they were hurt and bleeding ... walking around in shock ... a couple of people were laying in the highway. This semi-truck pulling two trailers full of cinders was on top of my car ... I remembered the propane tank and started jogging down the side of the highway further into the wreckage. I found myself saying the prayer my grandpa taught me: Oh, Great Spirit, whose voice I hear in the winds; whose breath gives life to the world, hear me. I come to you as one of your many children. I am small and weak. I need your strength and wisdom ...

As I was saying the prayer I saw that the truck hit at least six cars before it plowed into me. I started having a hard time seeing and thought I was sweating. When I wiped my forehead, my hand was covered in blood. I slowed to a walk and felt my head. There was a huge gaping gash—my scalp had been split open, but I didn't feel pain. That's when I saw my best buddy—he was heading home from work too. His car was all crunched up and he was unconscious.

I ran up to his car and tried to open the doors but they were all jammed shut. You know how they say an adrenaline rush can make you temporarily super strong? It's true. He was having a hard time breathing and the top of his scalp was split from ear to ear. I grabbed the door and practically pulled it off its hinges. I pulled him out of his car and laid him real gentle in the dirt. When I stood up for a second it felt like someone had turned a hose on my head and water was flowing down my back and I realized my head was bleeding a lot. I took off my t-shirt and ripped it in uneven halves. I wrapped my head first in the smaller half and then bandaged up my buddy's head as best I could. Then I sat in the dirt saying the Great Spirit prayer over and over, holding my buddy and rocking him … until the paramedics took us to the hospital.

I was pretty banged up. What with procedures and recuperating and physical therapy, it was three months until my doctor told me I had PTSD and should see a therapist. I was having bad flashbacks and nightmares. I was super aware of everything and anything that might be a threat to my family or me. My whole personality changed. I was constantly on edge. I'd pick fights with my wife and mother and yell at the little ones for just acting their ages.

I went to therapy as often as I could that first year. My doctors gave me pills for pain, pills for depression, pills for anxiety and pills to help me sleep, but I was raised not to take that stuff. My mom made me herbs and teas and tinctures instead. My therapist understood about native things, and explained the psychological language and what had happened to me in a way that made sense to me. My psych tests showed I had severe PTSD. We worked using CBT [cognitive behavioral therapy], and I listened to CDs, that helped me relax.

I got really depressed when I found out I was permanently injured and wouldn't be able to work in construction any more. My buddy with the split skull and I were in the same boat. He was hurt worse than me. Whenever I could, I hung out at his place—we played video games and told jokes. I tried to work as a dishwasher but my new temper got me fired. I was a skilled carpenter—a construction foreman—and here I was scraping food off plates! I got another job making pizzas. That didn't last a week; I got into an argument with a customer about cheese. So I stayed home and watched the little ones. My wife got a job and my mom had to work two jobs. I felt like such a failure. What kind of chief was I? I stopped going to my buddy's house because seeing him reminded me of the life I was supposed to have but never would.

I needed couples counseling and family counseling so my therapist met a few times with me and my wife and also with my mom. It helped that we were all able to talk about my PTSD and how I was different now. I had to leave the room when my wife and mom started getting into how mean I was... I never used to be mean. I was the calm one—the peacemaker. As a family we worked through my worst PTSD symptoms, like not having any sympathy for anybody else and not wanting to be around anybody. We all learned how to communicate better.

My therapist told me she was starting a six-week meditation group that included a few of her clients and some friends, and some other doctors. They asked if I wanted to be part of it—they thought it might help me get back in touch with my native side, my beliefs and the wisdom, which had been shot to shit since the accident. I talked it over with my wife and mom and they wanted me to do it. They thought maybe it would help with my anger. In the meditation meetings I learned how to breathe and focus my mind so I could control myself. It really helped me to learn how to calm down and focus on what I had to do and what's important.

I came in one day for therapy, and my therapist told me about this new therapy, TPT. She explained Temporal Theory and TPT to me and I took the ZTPI and the psych tests I'd taken before. The scores were pretty much the same as the year before: severe trauma, high depression, and extreme anxiety. My ZTPI scores were what I thought they'd be, given what she'd told me—my past negative was pretty high and so was my present fatalism—but I think they would have been a lot worse if I hadn't already had a year's worth of therapy. She said our goal was to up my past positive, present hedonistic and future scores, which were all pretty low, and lower my past negative and present fatalistic scores.

It all made sense to me. I was set to dump d-bag Sherman once and for all and get back to being a good chief. The therapist gave me a TPT DVD for relaxation, and said I should watch it every day, and that maybe my wife and mom would like it. I took the DVD home and made my wife and mom and kids sit with me—we watched it as a family. The little ones fell asleep, which was cool. Mom cried, and my wife held my hand; it's like we had this heart-opening experience together.

I really looked forward to the next TPT session. We worked a lot on past positives—I have a lot of past positives. Thinking of the good times was easy. When I started to think past negative—have flashbacks or just think negatively—I started to vision a happy time with my family or friends, or how good I did when I worked construction; and it changed the way I felt from not good to good.

Then we talked about pro-social selected present hedonism. My therapist said that I should get back to spending time with my buddies—invite them over for a barbecue. This way, I'd spend time with them and my family. My wife had been bugging me about how I'd ditched my friends after the accident, so I knew she'd be cool with it. We talked about me spending quality selected present hedonistic time with my family too—getting back in touch with nature and teaching my kids the things my grandpa taught me.

Before my next TPT session I had gotten together two or three times with my buddies to play pool, and for barbecues, and had taken my family out for short hikes. I had also been thinking a lot about my future, especially since I knew that's what we were going to talk about. When the therapist said we were going to plan my future positive, I told her I was already planning on going back to college because I wanted to get into green construction. Eco-friendly construction seemed to me to be the way of the future and I wanted in.

We talked about how my case was getting closer to closing, and she wanted to know what I was going to do once I got my settlement. After the accident I had to move my family into a tiny one bedroom condo. Mom slept on the couch and me, my wife, and kids were all in the same bed. I wanted to buy a small piece of property and build an eco-friendly house. Knowing that I'd have some financial relief coming really helped me see that my future positive could be a reality for me and my family. My wife and I started designing the house.

I went to TPT sessions until my case closed. Every session, we'd go over how I was doing. I had learned how to balance my time perspectives pretty fast but we still needed to make sure I was coping okay. Toward the end of my TPT, I enrolled in college and started taking courses in green construction. I liked being around people who all had the same goal. I also became my son's soccer coach. I had forgotten how much fun being around little ones can be.

My mom got married and moved out. I miss her but I'm happy for her. My wife and I get along good. We're looking at lots to buy in a neighborhood where we want to raise our little ones. I'm grateful to the Swords for helping me and my family—for showing me the way to a brighter future. Every day I thank Great Spirit for this opportunity to live, to be with my family and to act with the intention of helping others.

sherman's cognitive behavioral therapy

Sherman started therapy three months after the accident (before the advent of TPT) at the suggestion of his primary care physician, as he was experiencing major PTSD symptoms—flashbacks, nightmares, avoidance, isolation, panic attacks, irritability, distressing and intrusive recollections, and outbursts of anger and hyper-vigilance. For the first year, he received cross-cultural therapy, CBT, and relaxation media therapy. During that year Sherman discovered his physical injuries were permanent, and that he would never be able to return to heavy construction work. The company he worked for did not offer light-duty work, nor did any other construction companies.

For the first time in his young life, Sherman was unemployed and unemployable in his field of expertise. His wife, who had enjoyed being a stay-at-home mom for their two young children, now had to work. His mother, who was already working full-time, also took on a part-time job. Sherman, formerly the breadwinner and head of the family, was relegated to staying home with the children and looking after their needs until his wife or mother relieved him.

His PTSD symptoms caused problems in his family. Although he rarely lost his temper with his children, as soon as his wife or mother arrived home he would express his anger and frustrations through overreaction at the slightest perceived provocation. His low level of stress tolerance, coupled with sleep deprivation due to nightmares and physical pain, caused him to spend the vast majority of his time lost in negative thoughts and emotions. His Native American beliefs caused him to distrust Western medications; hence he did not take the prescribed pain, antidepressant, and anti-anxiety medications, relying instead on herbal remedies made by his mother. He progressively isolated himself at home, socializing only with the buddy whom he had pulled from the wrecked vehicle — but in time, not even with him.

Sherman brought his wife in for couples therapy and his mother in for family counseling. During these sessions, pre-accident Sherman was revealed as a wonderfully well-rounded worker, friend, and family man: intelligent, compassionate, caring, affectionate, fun-loving, generous, even-tempered, emotionally balanced, focused, gregarious, clean living, athletic, ethical, moral, and steeped in the Native American spiritual belief that we are all connected. He was an attentive husband and son, a deeply connected father, and a loyal friend. The severity of his personality change after the accident caused his therapist to consider accident-related brain damage, but that was ruled out by his physicians as well as by his general level of functioning.

Cross-cultural therapy helped Sherman reconnect with his Native American spirituality; he regained the ability to be empathetic with others. He joined a weekly relaxation meditation group hosted by the therapists, focusing on visualization and deep rhythmic breathing. After six weeks of meditation therapy he noted improvement in his coping skills and more easily gained control of his PTSD symptoms. By the time TPT was developed, Sherman was already well on the road to recovery.

sherman's time perspective therapy

At Sherman's first TPT session he was prepared to move forward in his life as quickly as possible. The therapist explained Temporal Theory and time perspective therapy, and his cultural background allowed him to easily grasp the concepts.

Sherman's psychological test scores indicated severe trauma, borderline severe depression, and extreme anxiety and panic. After taking the ZTPI, which indicated his orientations were still primarily past negative and present fatalistic, he decided to turn his life around. He was familiar with the relaxation breathing technique because of the meditation class, and he was also given a TPT relaxation DVD and asked to watch it daily.

In the second TPT session, Sherman was asked to replace his past negatives with past positives. Physical pain caused by the trauma is often a key flashback trigger for many people suffering from PTSD, and this was the case for Sherman. Whenever he started to have a past negative flashback to the accident or was reminded of it due to his chronic pain, he would think instead of a past positive memory. Sherman was normally a positive-thinking person and found it easy to recall happy, satisfying times in his personal life as well as his work life. He accepted the fact that although he could never go back in time to change what had happened, his perception of the incident and how it changed the course of his life were in his control. He felt he would have no problem overlaying past negatives with past positives.

In this session the therapist also suggested that Sherman expand his pro-social selected present hedonism to include not only his friends (he was getting together with them at least once a week) but also his family. Sherman absolved himself of the guilt he felt over his behavior toward those closest to him as he realized that the severity of his PTSD symptoms were the major cause. He was encouraged to include his wife and children in selected present hedonistic time, such as taking walks in nature; and he was also encouraged to get together with old friends and have them over for barbeques.

In the third TPT session, Sherman eagerly planned and plotted his future positive. He had decided to explore a career in green construction. He was due a legal monetary settlement for the accident, which greatly reduced his anxiety about immediately providing for his family. He shared his future positive plans of moving out of the cramped rental in which he and his family had been living after the accident. His future positive included purchasing a modest plot of land in a kid-friendly neighborhood. He also wanted to design a simple house and oversee its construction.

Sherman learned how to balance his time perspective quickly. In follow-up TPT sessions, the therapist reviewed Sherman's day-to-day coping skills and monitored his levels of anxiety and depression. He was doing very well, and discussions about a future positive career in green construction led him to enroll at the local college. He continued TPT until his case closed.

sherman's brighter future

Sherman's mother recently remarried and moved out, causing Sherman, at the age of twenty-four, to feel the bittersweet emotions of a father of the bride. His wife is now teaching full-time in their younger child's preschool, and makes nearly as much as she did at her two jobs. Sherman's older child is adjusting well to kindergarten, learning social skills, and participating in sports. Sherman is coaching his son's soccer and T-ball teams and is progressing toward his brighter future plan of a career in green construction.

Sherman's rapid comprehension of Temporal Theory and time perspective therapy allowed him to progress quickly. He is at ease relying on his own inner guidance to check and balance his time perspective and has completed TPT.

sherman's pre-TPT and post-TPT test results

Interpreting the Graphs: Sherman's clinical graph on the left in Figure 5.3 shows that his extreme anxiety level dropped to the borderline between severe and moderate. His trauma score went from the high end of severe to the low end of moderate, and his depression score lowered from the borderline between moderate and severe to the borderline between mild and moderate. This is indicative of good improvement via the therapeutic process over the period of his time perspective therapy. However, there is still room for him to continue decreasing his PTSD symptoms to more mild and normal levels.

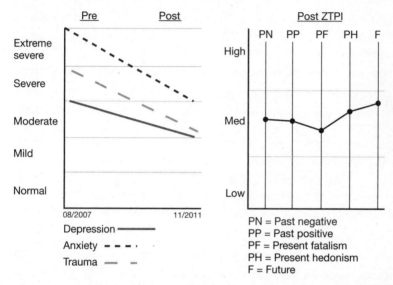

Figure 5.3   **Sherman—Civilian with PTSD—Psychological Test Graphs**

In his post ZTPI graph on the right, Sherman's scores are all in the medium range. His past negative memories are checked and balanced by his past positive recollections, providing him with an even keel. His lower-medium sense of present fatalism is balanced by his higher-medium sense of present hedonism. His high-medium future score suggests a positive prognosis and future outcome.

"i don't know if i killed her—it's worse if you don't know"

randall

Randall was thirty-five. He had been on the police force for ten years, enjoyed his job, and was well known and liked by both fellow officers and the citizens he served and protected. His beat was a small town and its surrounding neighborhoods—the same town in which he lived with his wife and children.

As head of the Neighborhood Watch Program, Randall spent most of his time educating people about the program. But one day he found himself joining three other police officers in hot pursuit of a stolen vehicle being driven at high speeds through his town by a methamphetamine addict.

Psychological Diagnosis: PTSD due to extreme work-related trauma

I was studying to be a priest before I got a different calling: to be a police officer. I thought it would be an exciting way to uphold God's laws through the police force; educating people about right from wrong, fighting the devil disguised as crime, that sort of thing. And that's what I did to the best of my ability for ten years.

I was head of the Neighborhood Watch Program. We are not a perfect community—we have a lot of illegal drug trafficking and a number of sexual predators, just like most places. My favorite thing about being a cop was meeting with groups of concerned citizens and helping them set up their neighborhoods. I taught them how to be on the lookout for meth labs, drug houses, pedophiles, dog abuse—there's a lot of pit bull dog fights going on that most people aren't aware of. Teaching people to be self-aware, neighborhood-aware, taking care of each other—that's where it's at. Showing people that cops were on their side and did good things—that's what I loved to do.

I had patrol duty too. I was on patrol one afternoon when I got a call that a stolen vehicle was being driven at high speed into on-coming traffic on a highway. It didn't take long for three other squad cars to catch up to the suspect. I was coming in the opposite direction and was told to cut the suspect off by blocking the road. The suspect entered the small town where I live. School had just been let out and there was a lot of traffic—kids were on the street. My kids would be walking home. My sirens were blaring and pedestrians were running to get out of the way. The street was jammed with cars. The suspect drove her vehicle up onto the sidewalk and nearly hit a kid on a bicycle. People were screaming. It was total chaos. She smashed into a store full of people—crashed through the window—glass shattered everywhere. I angled my car behind hers, blocking her escape. The other three officers pulled up behind me and we all exited our vehicles. Then she slammed her car into reverse and tried to peel out. Me and the other officers pulled our weapons—she clipped me as she reversed her vehicle. We all fired our weapons. She was killed instantly by a bullet to the temple. It was found lodged in the store wall. The other three bullets were found in her vehicle. They were all deformed beyond identification—we never found out which gun the fatal bullet came from.

I don't know if I killed her—I think it's worse if you don't know. It weighs on your mind, you can't stop wondering ... I was the Neighborhood Watch Officer, not a killer. All the officers involved, including me, were placed on administrative leave—we had to wait for forensics results. I would have had to take time off anyway because I was badly bruised from being clipped by the suspect's vehicle. When forensics came back inconclusive and we were told we could return to work, I couldn't do it.

I found out that the suspect's family lived in my subdivision—just down the street. I was super paranoid. She had been a known meth dealer. I made my wife and kids move to my in-laws' place, but I would not leave my property. I never left the house. I kept the blinds closed and constantly checked to make sure the doors and windows were locked. I made the bed up to look like someone was sleeping in it in case someone broke in. I slept in the closet. The police chief stopped by to check up on me and saw what I was doing... He told me I should see this therapist that worked with the police.

I was on medical leave for four years. I saw my therapist every week during that time. This was before time perspective therapy—he used CBT. It was helpful, but I had trouble with flashbacks and constant memories. There was no way I wouldn't be reminded of the incident because I lived in the town where the incident occurred. I wanted to get back to work, but I couldn't see myself doing community outreach with the Neighborhood Watch anymore—I didn't want to come in contact with anybody. I was afraid I'd run into the suspect's family. My wife and kids came back home after a few months. The kids picked up that something was wrong with daddy. I didn't want to do anything with them anymore—no trips to the mall or the playground. I was distant with my wife. But after a while I guess they got used to it, because they stopped complaining.

In the police department you have to stop therapy in order to get your badge and gun back, which meant I had to stop seeing my therapist. I felt I was doing well, and returned to work as a patrol officer. But I couldn't handle it. Some things happened I don't want to talk about. But they made me think that I might be too fast at using my weapon and I couldn't live with the guilt if that happened. The job was too overwhelming. I got a desk job and did well for three years. Then they wanted me to return to patrol duty. I couldn't do it. The police department released me. I needed to see my therapist again and start a vocational rehabilitation program so I could get a different job. Giving up the police force—the job I loved and had been called to do—was upsetting, but at the same time it was a relief.

When I went back to therapy, TPT had been developed and he wanted me to start it right away. In my first session back, we spent time catching up on what had happened the past few years and then he explained Temporal Theory and TPT. I took some psychological tests, then we watched a TPT relaxation video and practiced the breathing technique. My homework was to watch the video every day until the next session.

The next week we went over my test results. I had gotten better than when I had seen him years before; but now I was back to having severe PTSD. My highest ZTPI scores were past negative and present fatalism. I wanted to start over—get on with my life. I knew I had to bring up my past positives and lower my past negatives.

I'd have flashbacks several times every day; every time I had to drive by the incident site, or whenever I'd see a kid on a bike, or when I'd drive into our neighborhood and pass the suspect's family's house. My therapist said that when I started to have a past negative flashback I should think of a past positive, like working with Neighborhood Watch and visiting the schools, talking to the kids. I also had a problem with past negative thoughts about how I'd been since the incident—super paranoid, distant from my wife and children. My isolating behavior pushed my family and friends away. He showed me it was pretty easy for me to think of happier times—like playing with my kids at the playground, and family get-togethers, and spending time with my wife. There were a lot of past positive memories for me to remember. I started to feel like I could get a grip on my flashbacks and negative thoughts.

In my next session we tried to replace my present fatalism with selected present hedonism. Since the shooting incident I had completely stopped exercising and stopped socializing. Church had been a big part of our family life—it still was for my wife and kids. It was our main social community. But I hadn't been since the incident. And my therapist had talked to me about how important exercise was when I was in therapy before; it helps lessen depression. But I was happy just staying home, playing video games (present hedonism). He brought up exercise again and said it was selected present hedonism. He suggested I ask my wife and kids to come along. Then he suggested I go back to church. I had a harder time with this because everybody at church knew me, and I thought they might think of me as a killer. But my therapist said that for me, going to church was selected present hedonism and it was something pro-social to do with my family.

Well, I went to church. And the best thing happened to me on that first time back. A twelve-year-old girl came up to me and said she knew I was the neighborhood cop who stopped the crazy lady in the car. We stood there for a while kind of awkward. I thought she was going to yell at me—but her parents were standing behind her, smiling. She hugged me and said she was in the store that day with her mother and she was so afraid when the lady crashed into it. She thought she was going to die and I had made her feel safe. I was really surprised and got choked up. Then her mother and father hugged me. It felt like I had been healed of the guilt... Catching up with fellow parishioners, talking to my priest, getting back into the social swing made me feel accepted and more like my old self.

When I told my therapist all of this at my next appointment, he said I was doing well and that we would work on my future positive. I was trying to figure out what to do for vocational rehabilitation. He asked me what I was interested in—he knew I liked video games, but there wasn't much chance of a vocation for me with them. I did like anything to do with computers. After talking it through I decided to get into IT [information technology]. Maybe in my future positive I could combine some of the other things that interested me with computers and IT.

In our other sessions, we focused on making sure I knew how to balance time perspectives. I wasn't having so many past negative flashbacks because I was getting better and better at replacing them with past positives. It was really helpful that the suspect's family moved out of our neighborhood. I felt like I could freely breathe again.

Me and my family were practicing selected present hedonism together—we were jogging and lifting weights and riding our mountain bikes. It took a little time, but I got my family back and I lost twenty-five pounds! I enrolled in and graduated from college with my computer/IT certification. And I got a job working for Catholic Charities. I plan on working my way up in Catholic Charities and I want to be a deacon at church. I learned how to balance my time perspectives and completed my TPT earlier this year.

randall's cognitive behavioral therapy

Randall received CBT for several years prior to the development of time perspective therapy. He lived with a constant fight-or-flight response. It was impossible for him to avoid reminders of the incident, as he lived in the small town where the incident occurred. Randall was determined to return to work as a beat officer, but he did not want to appear in public and continued isolating himself in his house. His wife and children eventually returned home from living with Randall's in-laws, and his family adjusted to his disability.

Randall finally returned to work after four years of medical leave. However, several incidents occurred that caused him to fear he would be too quick to use his weapon again. He asked to be placed behind the desk, where he worked for three years. When he finally realized that he could not return to patrol he was released from the police department for further treatment and a vocational rehabilitation program.

randall's time perspective therapy

It was at this point that time perspective therapy was developed and employed. In the first session the therapist followed TPT protocol by conducting client education in regard to Temporal Theory and time perspective therapy. The therapist administered psychological tests, including the ZTPI. Randall viewed and then was given the TPT relaxation video; he was asked to watch it daily as part of his therapy. The therapist also reminded him to listen to relaxation CDs he had been given previously.

In the second TPT session, the therapist reviewed Randall's psychological test results with him, placing special emphasis on ZTPI scores. Randall understood the importance of changing his negatives to positives; he wanted to improve his state of mind, and therefore his life.

The therapist asked Randall to recall past positive memories he could use to replace his past negatives, explaining that whenever Randall started to have a past negative flashback to the shooting incident he was to immediately overlay it with an upbeat memory of being on the police force. Because Randall had been on the force for ten years prior to the incident, he was able to recall numerous past positive occasions when he was helpful — for instance, establishing Neighborhood Watch Programs and being selected to talk about the police force at elementary schools.

Randall also needed some help replacing non – work-related past negative thoughts (about how his post-shooting PTSD symptoms of avoidance, isolation, and paranoia had adversely affected his family) with past positives. He found that this was actually easy for him to accomplish. Whenever he found himself having past negative thoughts about Randall-with-extreme-PTSD-symptoms, he replaced them with memories of playing with his children, relaxed family gatherings, and spending one-on-one time with his wife.

In the third TPT session, Randall and the therapist worked on replacing present fatalism with selected present hedonism, which proved to be a more difficult task for Randall. At this time Randall was all fatalism, no hedonism. The therapist reminded him that in prior sessions, before TPT, they had discussed the importance of an exercise regimen to combat depression. Randall had not followed through, choosing to stay home and play video games instead. When the therapist explained that exercise could be viewed as a form of selected present hedonism, Randall reconsidered.

Randall started jogging, riding his mountain bike, and lifting weights, and eventually he asked his wife and children to join him in his selected present hedonism. With this, the family began to re-bond. Randall lost twenty-five pounds once he decided to get up off the couch and out of the house.

After the incident, Randall—a devout Catholic who had spent a few years in a seminary—had stopped going to church on Sundays with his wife and children. The therapist suggested that he consider rejoining his wife and children for church services for pro-social selected present hedonism. This led to renewed friendships and social gatherings with other families.

In the fourth TPT session, the therapist led Randall through the process of working toward a brighter future. Focus for his future positive was placed on his aptitude for and interest in computers, as well as his background in law enforcement. Consequently, he enrolled in a college specializing in IT.

Follow-up TPT sessions focused on reinforcing Randall's ability to balance his time perspective. In each session the therapist first assisted Randall with coping strategies for addressing day-to-day issues, such as improving communication with his family. Then Randall reviewed how he was accomplishing his selected present hedonism personally as well as with his family, and finally how his future positive plans were developing.

randall's brighter future

Randall completed an intensive eighteen-month computer trade school program and accepted a position in IT at Catholic Charities. His relationships with his wife and children are now stable. In his brighter future, he plans to expand his position at his workplace and become a deacon at his church. He has successfully been able to move on with his life and leave the shooting incident behind.

Randall's extreme present fatalism had caused him to be unable to enjoy anything. The therapist encouraged him to stop and smell the roses by practicing selected present hedonism and enjoying his life and family more. Randall felt comfortable with TPT and became adept at balancing his time perspective. With a focus on past positives, selected present hedonism, and his future positive, he successfully completed TPT.

randall's pre- TPT and post-TPT test results

Interpreting the Graphs: In the clinical graph on the left in Figure 5.4, Randall's trauma score dropped from severe to extreme to the borderline between moderate and severe; and his borderline severe to extreme anxiety and depression dropped to borderline moderate to mild. His clinical presentation agreed with clinical test scores.

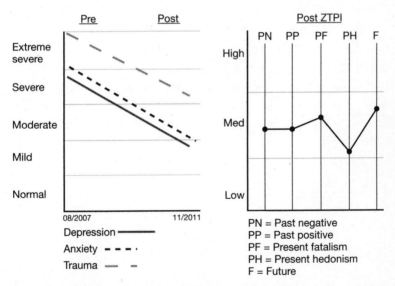

Figure 5.4   **Randall—Civilian with PTSD—Psychological Test Graphs**

His post ZTPI scores all fell within the medium range, with his past negative and past positive scores being nearly the same. In other words, he focuses on both past positive and past negative memories equally. He balances his past negative traumatic memories with past positive memories of his family and service to his community. However, his sense of present fatalism is higher than his present hedonism. His future time perspective outranks all others, indicating his brighter future is now his main focus.

o to sum up

- Trauma followed by PTSD can be caused by large-scale disasters, or can result from physical assault, prolonged abuse, plane crashes, and a myriad of other causes.
- The leading cause of PTSD in the general population is motor vehicle accidents.
- TPT has been used successfully with disaster workers to help them deal with stress-induced PTSD.
- TPT has been used effectively as the central component of family therapy in cases in which all family members have shared a common experience of disaster or loss.
- TPT is as relevant and appropriate for civilians with PTSD symptoms as it is for veterans suffering from war-based trauma.

6

women, PTSD, and time perspective therapy

"One night my father came into my bedroom and woke me up," said Iris.

> I knew what alcohol smelled like because my parents liked their cock-tails. That's how he smelled...When it was over, he told me that if I said anything to my mother, he'd break my mother's neck and beat me black and blue. He said, "And anyway, no one will believe you."

According to statistics from the National Center for PTSD, for every two women you pass on the street, see at the grocery store, or work with, one of them has suffered a traumatic event; and one out of every three women you know has suffered sexual assault. "Women are also more likely to be neglected or abused in childhood, to experience domestic violence, or to have a loved one suddenly die . . . and are more than twice as likely to develop PTSD as men after a trauma."[1]

Why twice as likely? The National Center for PTSD puts it in blunt terms:

- Women are more likely to experience sexual assault.

- Sexual assault is more likely than many other events to cause PTSD.
- *Women may be more likely to blame themselves for trauma experiences than men* [italics added].

According to the same source, women are more likely to develop PTSD if they

- Have a past mental health problem (e.g., depression or anxiety)
- Experienced a very severe or life-threatening trauma
- Were sexually assaulted
- Were injured during the event
- Had a severe reaction at the time of the event
- Experienced other stressful events afterwards
- Do not have good social support

In this chapter you'll read cases of sexual trauma from the victims' viewpoint, as well as a daughter's memory of hiding in a closet while her mother was being raped. You'll read about the tragedies of having loved ones die unexpectedly, of a competent woman being bullied by a coworker to the point of mental breakdown, and more. Although these stories are grim to read, containing such human suffering, the good news is that time perspective therapy (TPT) helped all of these women overcome their severe PTSD and find their footing on the road to a brighter future.

do hormones play a role in women's PTSD?

As scientific studies on women and PTSD emerge, we are finding an interesting correlation between women's physical makeup and PTSD.

Kerry Ressler of Emory University headed a team of scientists conducting a study on sixty-four traumatized clients (not combat veterans) at Grady Memorial Hospital in Atlanta, Georgia. Their findings: the hormone-like molecule PACAP (pituitary adenylate cyclase-activating polpypeptide), which regulates a person's stress response on a cellular level, was higher in clients with PTSD than in those who did not suffer from PTSD—and the association between PACAP and PTSD was significant *only in women*. A follow-up study including only traumatized women found that women with PTSD were also more likely to have a variation of a gene for PAC-1 (first procaspase-activating compound)—a synthesized chemical compound with anti-tumor potential that also responds to estrogen.[2]

This study provides a possible answer to the question of why some women respond differently than some men to traumatic situations and experiences.

> Ressler hypothesizes that estrogen, the primary female sex hormone, may amplify the effects of stress. The gene for the PACAP receptor can be turned on and off by estrogen. And the genetic variation his group identified lies within one of the sites in the PACAP receptor gene that is specifically sensitive to estrogen and may alter the way estrogen regulates the gene's activity.[3]

> According to Ressler and his colleagues, "These data may begin to explain sex-specific differences in PTSD diagnosis, symptoms and fear physiology."[4]

"and anyway, no one will believe you"

iris

Iris grew up in an affluent but highly dysfunctional household. Her father was a well-respected physician and a pillar of the community. Her parents "stayed married for appearances' sake . . ." At the age of twenty-five, Iris married a man she had known briefly. Two years later she had her only child, a daughter.

While she was pregnant, Iris discovered that her husband was having an affair, and she left her marriage. At twenty-eight, she was a single mother and assumed full custody of her infant daughter, Clarice. Iris had developed a pattern of having brief affairs, mostly with married men. "But I didn't bring them home or introduce them to Clarice."

At the age of forty-two, Iris had accomplished more than most people do in a lifetime: she had scaled mountains, dived out of airplanes, motorcycled across several states, run marathons, and made a comfortable living as a real estate executive. "I was originally looking for a therapist for my fifteen-year-old daughter," she explains.

Psychological Diagnosis: PTSD due to childhood sexual trauma and date rape

I had found a number of laxatives in Clarice's bedroom—I mean every type of laxative you could buy over the counter. I immediately thought she must have an eating disorder. This therapist had been recommended by a co-worker who had seen him. I ran an Internet search and spent some time on his website. I had taken a couple of psych courses in college and felt I knew a few things—I wanted a competent, well established professional, and he fit the bill. But in our get-acquainted session I realized it wasn't Clarice who needed therapy—it was me.

I went into the first session prepared, and told the therapist about the laxatives. I wanted to set Clarice up with an appointment as soon as possible. But he asked me to talk about myself—starting with my background. I thought he was wasting my time. I tried to brush it off. The past was done and I didn't see how going over my old stuff would help with Clarice's eating disorder. He was sort of insistent—in a nice way.

I hadn't thought about my past in a long time. I had buried it. I didn't want to talk about me. I was there for Clarice. I almost walked out. This wasn't going the way I wanted, and I told him. He said he understood if I wanted to leave, but that we might find clues to her behavior in my experiences. I thought about what he said and knew he was right. When I started talking, everything I had suppressed for years came out.

I was a child of privilege. My parents were pillars of the community. My father was a doctor and my mother was a homemaker. My father made a lot of money and my mother was intent on being the best mother around. She spent her time on nonprofit boards, attending meetings and fund raisers when she wasn't at the spa. When I was eight, my parents had an argument and my father started sleeping in the guest bedroom. Later I learned that my mother had found out my father was having an affair with one of his nurses. They stayed married for appearances' sake—and my mother didn't want to give up her lifestyle.

My parents argued a lot. I didn't see my father much. He'd come home late, after I was asleep. One night he came into my bedroom and woke me up. I knew what alcohol smelled like because my parents liked their cocktails. That's how he smelled. I don't want to go into details [of the abuse] because I get nauseous thinking about it...When it was over, he told me that if I said anything to my mother, he'd break my mother's neck and beat me black and blue. He said "And anyway, no one will believe you."

After that, I never knew when he'd come into my bedroom—sometimes weeks or months would go by. I locked my door one night but he had a way of unlocking it and told me that if I ever did that again he'd hurt my mother. I lived in absolute fear. I thought I was being punished, and I didn't know why. I'd pray to God and ask for forgiveness for whatever it was I had done to be punished. I promised God I'd be the best girl ever.

I thought that if I excelled in school and sports maybe my father would see that I didn't deserve to be punished. I didn't want to go home—I didn't feel safe. I was afraid every night. As time went by, I joined club after club to stay busy. I put on my happy face in public and became a good actress. I felt I had little control over my body; my father made sure of that. Then I realized the one thing I did have control of was what and how much I ate. I started throwing up after meals...Part of me didn't want to live because living meant being in constant fear of my father.

When I was sixteen, something happened. I can't explain it but I had had enough of being punished! I got up the courage to say something to my mother and asked her if I could see a therapist. She, in turn, accused my father, who, of course, denied his abuse. Since he's a doctor, he used medical terms and told my mother I was being hysterical and was probably mad at him for not buying me the car I wanted. My mother slapped me and called me a liar. But I saw fear in her eyes.

I realized right away that if my mother believed me, if she was truly a "good mother," she'd divorce my father and get me the hell out of there...but my mother was weak. She loved her lifestyle and chose her comfort over me. From that point forward, I knew my mother suspected my father, because at night she would open my bedroom door to see if he was with me. But he never came to my bedroom again. I started to feel a little safer at night. Gradually, I stopped throwing up.

I sent applications to Ivy League universities and was accepted by all of them. I chose the one farthest from home. Academically, I did very well. I studied psychology because I wanted to be a therapist to better understand myself and help others like me. I dove into the college scene...maybe I overindulged in drugs and alcohol...and I tried to find the love I missed from my father through sex with people I barely knew. But that's what you do in college, right?

One morning after partying with a group of kids I had just met, I woke up in a strange dorm room next to two guys—they were passed out. My crotch hurt and I was covered in sperm. All I could think about was taking a hot shower. I went back to my dorm and took a three-hour shower, but I just didn't feel clean. I thought about reporting the rape but I wasn't sure if it *was* rape. I remembered drinking everything I was given but I don't remember anything else. I had heard other girls talking and knew that sometimes if you said anything to authorities, the guys would get back at you. All the fear I felt growing up surged back...they could say it was my idea, call me a liar. I just wanted to get away and forget it.

I stopped drinking, drugging, and socializing. I focused on my studies. And I started vomiting again. I felt out of control and that old feeling of being in control through bulimia was strangely comforting. I finished out the year and then changed colleges. I told my parents I couldn't stand the cold weather. I switched majors because if I couldn't help myself, how could I possibly help others? I studied business. At this new university, I started over—reinvented myself. One way I did it was through extreme sports. Now I see that I had a death wish. At the time I thought I just wanted the adrenaline rush. Once I experienced the sport—bungee jumping, skydiving, cross-country motorcycle rides, running long distances—I moved on to the next.

I realized in this first session with Dr. Sword that I was running away. I've always run away!

I graduated at the top of my class and accepted a position at a large firm. I met a man—we had a whirlwind courtship; we married. I got pregnant and found out he was having an affair. We stayed together until I had Clarice. Then we divorced. I gave up the notion of ever being in a committed relationship. People weren't meant to be with just one person. I raised Clarice on my own. It wasn't easy and I was lucky to have good child care; having her didn't affect my ability to get promoted to a higher position. I started having affairs—mostly with married men—they were safe. But I didn't bring them home or introduce them to Clarice. I had very little contact with my parents. In fact I hadn't seen them in years. I didn't want to expose Clarice to my father...Clarice didn't ask about [her grandparents]; she didn't ask about her father either. It was just me and Clarice.

As she grew older Clarice gravitated to friends who had families—nice, wholesome people. She'd spend weekends at different friends' homes during the school year. If I wanted to take off somewhere for a week, her friends' mothers were very accommodating. I didn't understand until therapy that she was trying to find the family she didn't have...but this arrangement was great for me. I went rock and mountain climbing. I loved the feeling of running...I'd run marathons. I became bored being a business executive so I decided to switch careers and got into real estate, which was booming. I became a broker with a nationwide firm. I thought I was providing a good life for Clarice, and me. Then I found the laxatives in her bedroom.

Listening to myself talk in this session, I couldn't believe what was coming out of my mouth. I was really damaged goods. How could Clarice *not* have problems? The therapist thought I had PTSD from the sexual trauma I'd suffered as a child, which was made worse by my college experience. But he was optimistic. I was shaken and made another appointment for myself.

In our next session, I took a series of psychological tests, and they showed that I did have PTSD. They also showed that I suffered from severe trauma, severe depression, and severe anxiety! I thought I had dealt with my past traumas and put them behind me, but I hadn't. The therapist explained Temporal Theory and TPT, and then reviewed my ZTPI [Zimbardo Time Perspective Inventory] scores—which said it all: extreme past negative and extreme present hedonism. I had no past positive and no future perspective. It was clear I needed to work on healing myself before I could help my daughter. He wanted me to try to remember positive things from my past, but I told him my childhood was so lousy that I couldn't think of anything good. He kept pressing me for some good memories. It was a real struggle. I wracked my brain. Whenever I thought of growing up, I felt sick. He led me through a breathing technique that helped me focus.

Then I started remembering...I remembered lying on the grass in the backyard, looking up at the clouds and seeing animal shapes. I remembered riding my bicycle like a bat out of hell, feeling the wind in my hair and the wonder of my leg muscles pumping away. I remembered putting cookies and milk out for Santa on Christmas Eve, staring at the multicolored lights on our neighbors' houses, and the special smell of the Christmas tree. The therapist said that when I had negative thoughts about the past, I should replace them with these positive thoughts. I remember I told him, "I can do that." He gave me a DVD to watch and a CD to listen to to help me practice the breathing technique and help calm me.

In our next session we focused on the present... We worked out a way for me to talk to Clarice about the laxatives. I explained to Clarice how I suffered from bulimia. I wasn't comfortable telling her exactly what caused my bulimia, but I told her enough so she understood I'd been traumatized to the point I didn't think I had control of my life. For Clarice—she used laxatives because she didn't want to get fat. She told me she wanted to be trim like me. It was heartbreaking because she's perfect. We threw away the laxatives and made a deal to talk to each other whenever we felt the "urge to purge."

In the session, I realized that even though my professional life was together, I'd sort of turned into my mother! I didn't pay attention to Clarice. I was too busy thinking—thinking about how tired I was of uncommitted relationships with married men, how I wanted to be in a stable relationship, how I worried about my looks...and stand up paddle boarding—you stand on the surfboard and paddle with this long oar—my latest favorite thing to do. When the therapist asked what Clarice did because I was so busy, I told him the truth: I gave her some money and dropped her off at the mall or she'd spend the weekends at her friends' houses. The therapist suggested that I spend time getting to know Clarice and to start by asking her to go stand up paddle boarding with me (shared selected present hedonism). He also asked me to allow Clarice to have friends over and set aside date nights with her. I thought that after years of basically ignoring her, these things were the least I could do. I became Clarice's friends' new favorite mom.

Our next session was a few weeks later. I needed time to change my pattern. Clarice and her friends were a lot of fun, we all got along beautifully. The therapist said I was doing well and that he had a difficult task for me: to forgive my mother and father. He said I couldn't change what had happened and I couldn't change my parents, but I could change the way my past traumas affected me and how I carried them with me, either positively or negatively. He asked me to see my traumas in a different light—they made me a stronger person. I had created a rich, adventuresome past. He said that I wasn't alone, that a lot of people experience similar situations and I had the power to change how I passed on my experiences to Clarice.

He asked if I'd had a talk with Clarice about sex. She was fifteen. I knew she had sex education in school and thought that she'd already learned enough from her friends. He said that although she probably knew a lot, I shouldn't assume; he asked me to consider planning a time to talk to her about sex.

I was at a total loss and needed pointers. He suggested I tell her that sex could be an act of love or an act of aggression. Well, it had been more of a sport for me. He said it was my decision how much I wanted to share with Clarice. I had to think about it. I mentioned that Clarice had a hard time opening up to me when it was just the two of us, especially when she was having a problem. He suggested I practice listening to Clarice without judging her, and to "reflect back"—to restate what Clarice had said so we both knew I understood where she was coming from. He asked me to keep an open mind and to try to work things out with her together.

Our next session was all about the future. I have three years left with Clarice before she goes to college. We plan on taking road trips during the summer, visiting national parks, and maybe even bungee jumping. I want to make this time with Clarice special. In a way, I'm giving her the time I never had with my mother...the time I wish I had.

Taking Clarice and her friends paddle boarding was a blessing. Something totally unexpected happened—I met a man.

He's a professor at the university. He comes from a huge family and doesn't want to have children, thank God! He's smart, has a great sense of humor, knows how to express himself, and isn't demanding. He's the first truly mature man I've been with. Girls, don't give up hope. They ARE out there!

iris's time perspective therapy

Iris's first TPT session was devoted to covering her background. Iris didn't see the nutritional value in regurgitating "old stuff," but humored the therapist. Mining Iris's childhood yielded a wealth of surprising information, including her father's affair and her parent's marital separation inside their own house. Shortly after this conjugal separation, Iris's father started coming into her bedroom at night to sexually molest her, making threats about what he would do if she told anyone. Iris coped by keeping busy, being perfect, and staying out of the house. She earned straight A's in school, joined the soccer team, and ran track. She participated in numerous school clubs. She put on her "happy face" in public, seeming to be a well-adjusted, overachieving teenager. "I felt I had little control over my body; my father made sure of that." But the one thing she could control was what and how much she ate, and she started throwing up after meals. "Part of me didn't want to live because living meant being in constant fear of my father."

She was accepted into several outstanding universities and chose the one furthest from home. Like many college students, Iris overindulged in drugs and alcohol and "tried to find the love I missed from my father through sex with people I barely knew." After partying with a group of students she didn't know well, she woke to discover she'd been raped. She reacted by isolating herself, excelling in school, and throwing herself into extreme sports. "Now I see that I had a death wish," she reflects. "At the time I thought I just wanted the adrenaline rush." While recounting her many feats to the time perspective (TP) therapist, she realized, "I was running away. I've always run away!"

Iris raised her daughter, Clarice, as a single mother, neglecting her much as her own mother had done. But when Clarice was fifteen, Iris found numerous packages and bottles of laxatives in her daughter's bedroom and suspected that her daughter suffered from an eating disorder, just as she had as a teenager. "I don't want her to be like me. But I don't know what I'm doing wrong."

In subsequent sessions, the therapist educated Iris concerning Temporal Theory and TPT. Iris's ZTPI scores indicated very high past negative and present hedonistic orientations. The TP therapist explained that before Iris could help her daughter, she needed to work on healing herself by replacing her past negatives with past positives. They discussed how Iris had suffered from PTSD since she was eight years old. The therapist suggested that whenever Iris started thinking about her past negative, she should replace the thought as quickly as possible with a past positive thought. "I can do that," was her reply.

When discussing the present, Iris realized that although her professional life was "together," she'd "sort of turned into my mother! I don't pay attention to Clarice." The therapist suggested that to create a positive future for both her daughter and herself, Iris should work on improving her relationship with Clarice; thus Iris began to share her selected present hedonistic time with her daughter, enjoying stand up paddle boarding with her and having date nights on which the two of them would enjoy dinner and a movie together. Iris expanded her shared selected present hedonism further when the therapist suggested Iris open her home to her daughter's friends.

Then the TP therapist placed before Iris her most difficult task: to forgive her mother and father and thereby lay to rest her extremely traumatic past negative. The therapist explained that although Iris couldn't change what her parents did or didn't do, she could change the way her traumatic incidents affected her and how she carried her experiences forward: into a future positive or a future negative. Iris was asked to see the traumatic incidences in her life as factors contributing to making her a stronger person, a person with a rich history full of adventure.

The TP therapist made clear that Iris was not alone, that many women have had similar traumas, and that Iris had the power to change how she passed on her experiences to her daughter. One way Iris could accomplish this was by discussing with her daughter how sex could be not only an act of love but also an act of aggression. Another way was to widen the lines of communication with her daughter by active listening (the act of listening without judgment and reiterating back what one hears). Iris replied, "I'll work on it."

iris's brighter future

Iris gently confronted her daughter about her daughter's suspected eating disorder and explained how she had suffered from bulimia. Together they threw away the laxatives and have made a pact to talk to each other whenever either one feels the "urge to purge." By taking these difficult but important steps, Iris helped her daughter replace present fatalism with a shared future positive. Through selected present hedonism in the form of stand up paddle boarding, their bond strengthened, and Iris has become the new favorite mom of her daughter's friends. And — bonus! — Iris also connected with a physically fit university professor of literature with whom she has found a mature, stable relationship.

Iris's brighter future includes enjoying the remaining years she has with her daughter before her daughter goes off to college. They plan on taking road trips together during the summer, visiting national parks, and possibly bungee jumping. "I want to make this time with Clarice special. In a way, I'm giving her the time I never had with my mother . . . the time I wish I had."

iris's pre-TPT and post-TPT test results

Interpreting the Graphs: The clinical graph on the left in Figure 6.1 indicates typical improvements from time perspective therapy. Iris's clinical scores of depression, anxiety, and trauma have significantly dropped. Her depression score lowered from severe to mild; her anxiety score lowered from severe to the mild range; and her trauma score lowered from severe to extreme to mild.

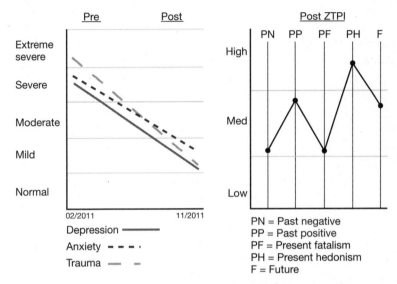

Figure 6.1   Iris—Woman with PTSD—Psychological Test Graphs

In Iris's post ZTPI scores on the right, her high present hedonism score correlates with her propensity to be a present hedonist. Both her past positive and future scores are in a healthy high-medium range. Her low-medium past negative and present fatalism scores indicate that Iris continues to occasionally struggle with her painful past traumas.

"i felt caught between a rock and a hard place"

eve

Eve, a highly intelligent young woman of thirty-three, was raised a "singular military brat." She traveled the world with her mother and father and loved learning about different cultures. While in college, she met a "solid young man from the Midwest." They married after graduation and settled into a comfortable routine. But when the economy took a downturn and Eve lost her job, she persuaded her husband of the benefits of her joining the military in an administrative role. After basic training, Eve and her husband moved to a military installation close enough to his workplace so he could commute.

Eve believed that establishing good working relationships with her coworkers involved occasionally going out for drinks after work. On one occasion, Eve's superior officer offered to buy Eve a drink. Eve had never heard of "date rape" drugs. But after accepting the drink from her supervisor, she was taken off the premises, raped, and driven back to her house.

Eve did not tell anybody about the rape for years, including and especially her husband. When her superior officer realized Eve wasn't interested in having an affair with him, he used his position to make her life miserable by mocking her work and telling her she would never advance. Eve's personality changed; this once secure, sociable young woman became paralyzed with fear. After years of struggling with PTSD symptoms, she sought therapy.

Psychological Diagnosis: PTSD due to military sexual trauma (MST)

I was a singular military brat... My father was career military and I have had the privilege of living all over the world. I developed a love of different cultures. I was an excellent student and did well in college. While there, I met a solid young man from the Midwest, and after graduation, we married. I had a management position at a factory and my husband worked at a nearby college. We were comfortable. When the economy started spiraling down and the factory downsized, they got rid of middle management and I lost my job. I spoke with my parents and my father suggested the military—the benefits were good. It's what I knew. It was secure; and if I was in administration, I wouldn't really be in harm's way. I convinced my husband it was a good idea. I completed basic training and we moved to a military installation close enough for him to commute to work.

I was assigned a position in administrative. I was very efficient and orderly. I had good relationships with both my co-workers and superiors. On occasion, I'd go to the enlisted personnel club with my co-workers after work. In the military there are clubs for enlisted personnel and other clubs for officers. Officers are restricted from going to enlisted service personnel clubs and enlisted personnel are restricted from going to officers' clubs. That's the way it's set up.

Then one evening, my superior officer was at the enlisted personnel club. He offered to buy me a drink. I didn't think much of it at the time, but he put something in it. I'm a slow drinker. About a third of the way through it, I became disoriented. He told my co-workers he was going to take me home. I couldn't speak coherently and I could barely walk. He took me to his car and drove somewhere—I don't know where, it was dark. He raped me and then he drove me home. I remember taking a shower and talking with my husband, who thought I was inebriated. He wasn't angry with me; he knew I was at the club with my co-workers. He told me to sleep it off.

I puzzled over what had happened. After researching on the Internet, I concluded that I had been given Flunitrazepam or a roofie, the date-rape drug. I didn't talk to anybody about the rape. I especially didn't want my husband to know.

The next day, my superior officer started coming on to me. I felt caught between a rock and a hard place. There was no way I was going to take up with him—I was incredibly angry! I didn't think there was anybody for me to complain to. It was my word against his. And anyway, I thought that if you report an MST, your career was over. I made sure I was with someone at all times. I never told my husband about what was happening on the job. I stopped going out with my co-workers. My superior officer finally realized I wasn't interested and he made my life miserable... He'd make demeaning remarks and criticize my work in front of my co-workers... he told everybody that I was doing such a bad job, I'd never get anywhere. I felt paralyzed with fear.

I was a mess... the stress was too great. I avoided my husband; I had no friends to talk to. I was afraid to leave the apartment and had to force myself each morning to get up and go to work. My job performance suffered greatly. I had no hope for promotion. I was afraid of men, especially those in roles of authority. I finally told my husband about being raped but it was too late; I was afraid to have sex with him... I couldn't get the rape out of my mind. We divorced.

After I completed my tour of duty I asked for and received a transfer. I relocated and made friends with my new co-workers and my new superior officers. I socialized with my co-workers and started to feel close to them. I know I was an excellent worker. Then my new supervisor asked me out. I diplomatically refused. But I started getting shaky again. And the cycle repeated. My supervisor started talking negatively about me behind my back. He would blame me for other people's mistakes and credited others for my work and accomplishments. My psychological symptoms flared: hyper-vigilance, fears, isolation and avoidance. I needed help.

Although I had made friends with my co-workers, I didn't feel I could talk to them about what was going on at work—even though they saw how I was being treated by my supervisor. Since I was new on the job, I was in a probationary period. I was back to isolating—staying in my apartment all the time. I watched self-help videos and practiced yoga. I read books.

I spent a lot of time on the Internet searching for articles about and by other women who had been raped or discriminated against. The only time I left my apartment was to go to the grocery store or to the bookstore. I had been calling in sick until I realized the military wasn't for me, so I requested early discharge.

I had heard about this therapist through veterans. In my first appointment, I reviewed my MST and explained why I didn't report it. I had been studying the personality traits of persons in positions of power and shared my findings with him. It seemed that this second go-around of MST was worse than the first, even though I hadn't been physically assaulted. There are paralyzing aspects of being in this position—under the thumb of a person drunk with power—and they are magnified by ten when you've been date-raped by your superior.

The therapist explained Temporal Theory and TPT, and I took four psychological tests: one for trauma, one for depression, another for anxiety and the ZTPI. He said that we'd go over the results in our next session and that we'd start TPT.

In the next session, he explained that I suffered from chronic and severe PTSD, and we discussed how MST is a type of PTSD. My test results indicated extreme trauma, severe depression, and extreme anxiety with panic attacks. He asked me to focus on past positive relationships and experiences instead of the past negatives that crowded my memories and thoughts. The past negatives had overshadowed any past positives for so long it took me some time to try to remember them. But eventually I did...I remembered how good I felt when I completed a project; I had a cat and I loved it like a child; my academic achievements; when people complimented me for anything—the way I looked or a job well done. It was a start. I used these past positives when a past negative started to creep into my consciousness. The therapist had given me a TPT relaxation video, and I watched it every day to help me cope. I practiced the breathing technique he showed me several times each day.

In the next session, we focused on my present fatalistic tendencies of avoidance and isolation and worked towards selected present hedonism. I used to have good social skills and the therapist wanted me to draw on these to make new friends. He invited me to the veterans' war trauma meetings at his office to help get my feet wet. This was a huge step for me to take—being around men—but it was a safe environment.

At my first meeting, I felt like a lamb going to slaughter. I was frightened and reminded of the bad things men had done to me in the military. But when the therapist introduced me as a fellow veteran, my fear evaporated. They were respectful; and although they didn't know what the cause of my PTSD was, they showed me a lot of compassion. I felt safe. I continue to attend these meetings once a month and I've made true friends, which speaks volumes. I felt better about myself—I *could* have friends that were men and not be terrified. It was quite a boost for my self-esteem.

In a subsequent TPT session, we continued our discussion about my present fatalistic inclinations and how since I'd been raped, I had difficulty making female friends... People, including women, don't understand what you go through emotionally, mentally, physically—unless it's happened to them. They think you in some way invited it, or that you're lying. They don't believe you can be naïve or trusting of others or innocent. They judge you. People's inability to be compassionate and understanding makes you not want to trust anybody. I realized this was present fatalistic thinking and that I somehow had to turn it around.

The therapist wanted me to further develop selected present hedonism, and he suggested I be on the lookout for opportunities to choose and make a female friend. Once I set my mind to it, it happened fairly fast. I was at a bookstore and struck up a conversation with another woman interested in the same book. We talked for a while and realized we had a lot in common so we went and had coffee... She invited me to a yoga class and I'm going!

In our more recent TPT sessions, he has been helping me make short- and long-range plans for the future, which I had given up on. I decided to get out of my condo and visit the bookstore weekly. I hadn't seen my parents for a couple of years and I made arrangements to go home for a visit. And through TPT, I've opened my mind to the possibility of being in a relationship. I'm not there yet, but I'm not opposed to the idea anymore. I've been planning my brighter future... I want to counsel people who have suffered trauma. Since I have a master's degree, I'm looking into getting my license in social work. I've learned important aspects of myself through TPT, one of them being that working with numerous personalities—especially power trippers—doesn't work for me. So my plan for the future includes opening my own office!

eve's time perspective therapy

Eve is a verbally expressive individual. She had researched the psychological effects of date rape as well as the personality traits of persons in positions of power, and shared her findings with the TP therapist. She reviewed the origin of her MST/PTSD and explained how at her new job, her symptoms had returned in even greater force. Eve had become alienated from her coworkers and did not feel she could talk to them about the sexual harassment she was experiencing. Unfortunately, she was a new hire and did not pass her probationary period.

The TP therapist listened attentively to Eve. Her past negative trauma developed into present fatalism in the form of a fear of men, as well as a fear or people she considered "inebriated with power." These feelings had so overtaken her life that she withdrew into herself. She had no social contacts and isolated herself in her apartment, only leaving to get groceries or books to read. She was obsessed with her past negative experiences, which fueled her present fatalism—she searched the Internet, seeking for articles about and by other women who had been raped or discriminated against.

The therapist took Eve's interest in educating herself to heart, and directed her to informational Web sites as well as Philip Zimbardo's book *The Time Paradox*. He also administered psychological tests, including the ZTPI.

In the next TPT session, the therapist and Eve reviewed her test results. She suffered from extreme trauma, severe depression, and severe to extreme anxiety including panic attacks—chronic and severe MST/PTSD. Her ZTPI results indicated high past negative, high present fatalism, low past positive, low present hedonism, and low future scores. The therapist suggested Eve replace her past negative flashbacks and thoughts with memories of past positive relationships and experiences. Eve did not think this was possible at first, but was eventually able to recall past positives she could draw on whenever her extreme past negatives surfaced.

The third session addressed Eve's present fatalistic propensity to avoid social contact and self-isolate. The therapist suggested she draw on her personal resources and social skills to develop new friendships and move forward into positive social circles (selected present hedonism). She was invited to join other veterans in the war trauma group. At first, Eve was hesitant. "I felt like a lamb going to slaughter," she said. But when Eve was shown respect and compassion by her fellow veterans, she relaxed and started to enjoy the safe haven presented to her in the group. She found she could relate to the veterans and began forming friendships with men, who thought of her as a family member rather than an object. As her fear receded, her self-esteem returned.

Eve's fourth TPT session was a continued exploration of past negative and present fatalistic orientations and how they affected Eve's ability to relate to women. She felt judged and misunderstood. To further enhance Eve's social life with selected present hedonism, the TP therapist suggested she scout for a female friend and explained that she had control over whom she chose to be friends with. The TP therapist was delighted when, in a recent TPT session, Eve told of how she had spontaneously formed a friendship with a woman, and how they had planned to attend a yoga class together.

eve's brighter future

The fifth TPT session focused on Eve's brighter future. Both short- and long-range plans were discussed—weekly bookstore visits instead of self-isolating in her condo, a trip back home to visit her parents, and research into an occupational field she was passionate about. She was compliant in that she diligently watched relaxation videos, was mindful of her actions (intent on being more pro-social), and was motivated to move on with her life in a positive, sustainable way.

Eve continues individual TPT and attends war trauma group meetings once a month. She proved to herself that she had the ability to embrace selected present hedonism by making a new woman friend, and by enjoying the camaraderie she felt with her veteran buddies. These important connections to others opened her eyes to the possibility of creating a larger social circle of friends and acquaintances. She has learned the art of discernment and once again trusts people. She is even open to the possibility of a future romantic relationship.

Careerwise, Eve wants to be a counselor and help others who have been traumatized. This is a healthy, pro-social means of dealing with her past negative trauma in a future positive way. By helping others, perhaps she will further overlay her past negative trauma with positive interaction and further improve her self-esteem. Because she does not feel she can work in a normal office setting "with numerous personalities — especially power trippers," her brighter future plans include being her own boss. She is working conscientiously toward her goals.

eve's pre-TPT and post-TPT test results

Interpreting the Graphs: The clinical graph on the left in Figure 6.2 indicates improvement from time perspective therapy. Eve's depression dropped from severe to the borderline between normal and mild; and her anxiety lowered from severe to extreme to moderate. Eve's most significant improvement can be seen in her trauma score, which dropped from severe to extreme to mild.

In her post ZTPI scores on the right, her present hedonism score elevated to the lower portion of the high range and is nearly as lofty as her highest score, past positive; her borderline-high future score is a close third. Eve's low present fatalism and low-medium past negative scores indicate that she has made good improvement in replacing the traumatic experiences of her past with positive memories and a future positive orientation.

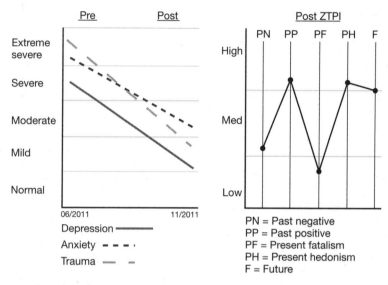

Figure 6.2   Eve — Woman with PTSD — Psychological Test Graphs

"i felt like i was half a person"

faith

Faith, age fifty, is a beautiful woman. Raised a "strict Roman Catholic," she attended parochial school and was known as "a good girl." In high school, she dated "a couple of guys...but I never even kissed them!" Secretly, she was attracted to a young man, Peter, a couple of years her senior. "But I never thought he'd be interested in me. He was so popular!" To her delight, in her senior year of high school, Peter asked her out. After a three-year courtship—which survived their two-year long-distance relationship while Faith attended business college out of town—they married. "I was so scared—I had only lived with my parents and then with a girlfriend on campus...I had never been with a man. But I was so in love with Peter."

Faith and Peter were opposites: where Faith was shy and withdrawn, Peter was outgoing and expressive. They enjoyed a good life and spent

quality time together, including weekly outings and social gatherings with Peter's numerous friends; "Peter's friends and their spouses became my close friends." Peter worked for the state and slowly climbed the administrative ladder while Faith worked as an accountant for a large corporation. They had two children and were active in both extracurricular school and sports activities. They continued their devotion to each other, family, and the church for nearly three decades. In time, Peter retired and established a family business along with their grown children.

Then, during the 2009–2010 winter holidays, Peter suddenly died. It was a shock. Faith's strong spiritual beliefs saw her through the first five months after Peter's passing; but her grief increased, and a friend became concerned that Faith might also be having possible symptoms of PTSD. She suggested that Faith seek therapy.

Psychological Diagnosis: *PTSD exacerbated by grief due to witnessing the unexpected death of her husband*

My husband, Peter, was very macho—he was a firefighter and he had a background in emergency medical care—he wouldn't go to the doctor when he was sick. If he needed stitches, he'd sew them himself! So I was surprised when he asked me to take him to the clinic the day after New Year, 2010. I knew he must really have had a bad flu. There was a skeleton crew at the clinic so we waited and waited. Peter grew weaker and weaker. After about five hours of waiting, we finally saw the doctor. He said Peter had the stomach flu so I took him home. But the whole drive home, the light was going out of Peter's eyes . . . it was four in the afternoon and he said it was dark.

When we got home, our children took over and helped Peter into our bedroom. I was confused and numb about what was happening. I kept thinking, *The doctor sent me home with a dying man.* My kids wanted me out of the bedroom because I guess I looked—well, I don't know how I looked, but they were afraid for me. When I was leaving the room I glanced at Peter. He was very weak but he motioned for me to come to him. By this time, he couldn't talk but he kept gesturing to me so I thought he wanted to tell me something. He looked deeply in my eyes—his eyes so full of love—and I put my ear near his mouth. He leaned in and kissed me on the cheek . . . I knew he was trying to convey something to me—I just didn't know it was good bye.

The ambulance came and Peter was taken to the hospital. He died a few hours later of a ruptured appendix.

You never think that the one and only man you've slept beside for twenty-eight years won't be there anymore...that he might be taken before his time...that he won't be there to kiss and touch and love. You never think that there will be no more family holidays together . . that the grandchildren yet to come will never know how wonderful their grandpa was...I was devastated. How could I handle everything Peter did? I couldn't think about it.

I returned to work a couple of weeks after Peter died—I don't think I was really ready, but I didn't want to lose my job. I thought I was handling everything okay but then I started having severe chest pains. I took a series of tests and the doctor said there was nothing wrong with my heart. He said I was having panic attacks. He sent me to see a psychiatrist who prescribed anti-anxiety and anti-depression medications. I took them but I didn't think they helped very much. You have to understand that it was so hard for me going to the clinic for these appointments...because it was the doctor at the clinic that sent me home with Peter. Every time I went to the clinic, I would have flashbacks to Peter's dying... How could they have sent me home with a dying man?

Four or five months after Peter died, I bumped into a friend and she told me that this therapist had helped her daughter who lost her young husband in a car accident. I had been going to the clinic for help but I thought it was a good idea to see someone outside.

The first time I saw the TP therapist I cried and cried. I told her what happened to Peter and how I wasn't myself anymore—I felt like I was half a person. She explained the stages of grief (denial, anger, bargaining, depression and acceptance), and that along with being in the denial stage of grief, I probably also had PTSD because I was there when my husband died. She told me about Temporal Theory and TPT and she gave me a TPT relaxation video to watch as often as I could—it had a breathing technique that would help calm me. I was supposed to watch it every day. I took some psychological tests, and we set up sessions once a week.

In the next session, I admitted I didn't watch the DVD. I wanted to talk about Peter and the clinic and what happened at the hospital. I wasn't ready to stop grieving.

In following sessions, I told the TP therapist that I wasn't doing a good job at work because I was having flashbacks and my mind would just race. She helped me understand that I was suffering from PTSD symptoms. I still hadn't watched the DVD. I couldn't sleep at night—I missed my husband so much! I slept with his shirts—they still smelled like him. I made my daughter, Belle, sleep with me. Sometimes I'd wake up in the night and she wouldn't be there. I'd find her in her own bed—she'd tell me that she couldn't handle all the crying and the praying. But every night, she'd stay with me until I fell asleep.

All of Peter's personal things were where he left them. His watch was on his nightstand, his toiletries were in the bathroom, the shoes he took off before he came into the house the last time were still near the doorway. Many months had gone by, but I hadn't moved or put away any of his things. Part of me was still waiting for him to come home from work.

I was still in denial—I wanted to think I was doing better than I really was, so I cut back my therapy sessions to twice a month. But I was becoming obsessed about finding answers to why Peter had been taken . . . I went to church services—not just of my faith, but every faith I could find. I was very, very angry—not at the doctor who misdiagnosed Peter; I knew he was just trying to finish up his day and get home to his family. I was rageful towards the clinic for being understaffed . . . and I realized I was mad at Peter for leaving me!

Throughout the sessions, the TP therapist listened. She tried to get me to focus on the positive things that had happened in my life before Peter's death but I couldn't really go there—it was too painful. Then she suggested I do simple, fun things with my daughter, Belle. I told her I didn't think I deserved to have fun—my husband was dead, my life was over, I was afraid. I couldn't even think about a future without Peter. But I would try—and those times I did go out with Belle, I forgot my sorrow for a while. But it always came back because I would think about Peter. I was having a good time without him.

The TP therapist was concerned about my kids, and in every session she would ask how they were doing. My son is a lot like Peter—men who think you should handle things on your own. But Belle had told me she wanted some help, so she started therapy.

She met with the TP therapist four times. I don't know what happened in those sessions but Belle seemed so much more confident and had a way of calming me. I found out later that Belle was learning ways to help me and the rest of the family.

I stopped eating—food didn't taste like anything. I would go to visit Peter's grave by myself, and in my mind I would see him down there. He would talk to me. I felt so sorrowful—it's like he was trying to pull me into the grave with him. It got so bad that one day I checked myself into the psych ward at the hospital. I stayed for four days.

You know, the people in the psych ward were just like you or me. They weren't crazy; they were just having a hard time with life. We met in a group every day and my psychiatrist visited me. He told me I had become "situationally psychotic"; that this wasn't normal for me. Because of Peter's death, I went overboard. He was a little miffed with me because I had cut back my therapy sessions. Then he increased my medications and told me I had to see my therapist every week. I hadn't even told her that I was in the hospital, but my psychiatrist called her and told her what had happened.

In my first session after the hospital, the TP therapist explained how we can have subconscious thoughts of suicide. My faith wouldn't allow me to kill myself—but by not eating, and thinking that Peter was trying to pull me into the grave with him, I showed that I didn't want to live. She explained that the trauma of Peter's death caused me to have not a mental illness but a mental injury. By going to the hospital, I proved to myself that I wanted to live.

She asked me to talk about all of the good things—the Past Positives—in my life before Peter died. She told me that all these good things were still inside me and that all the trauma and heartache I had experienced since Peter's death made me a stronger woman. She knew that I believe I'll see Peter again one day and that we could continue to have a different sort of relationship and that Peter wouldn't want me to be sad or give up on life. She also said at my age, I was very rich in experience. I listened and I believed.

Whenever I had flashbacks or started to have negative thoughts, I replaced them with one of the positive memories I had of life with Peter. I still felt like I didn't deserve to have fun, but each weekend Belle and I would go somewhere—the aquarium, a winery, or just for long scenic drives. It was good to get out among people and nature. Then I started noticing the paintings in the therapist's office—they had been there the whole time, but I had never been aware of them! I started seeing flowers and noticing how blue the sky was...it was like I had suddenly been reborn.

Lots of negative things happened in my life after this. The business Peter and our children owned was going bankrupt and the company where I had worked at for thirty years closed. But in our sessions, the TP therapist talked about not just turning lemons into lemonade, but something even better—maybe lemon meringue pie! She helped me plot and plan my future.

Things started to change, and I started to change things too. My kids and I saved the business and I got a job closer to home. I repainted the interior and exterior of the house and rearranged the master bedroom. I kept some of Peter's most cherished things but I gave away most of his clothes and tools to friends and family. I celebrated Peter's birthday with a cake and every holiday, I start off the meal by acknowledging him rather than ignoring him. After a while, my psychiatrist thought I was doing well so he decreased my prescription medication dosages. [Note: As of the writing of this book she is no longer taking them.]

One part of planning for my future positive that caused me a lot of problems was being a single lady. I had gone from my father's house to Peter's house. I had never really dated anybody and I didn't want to be thought of as a "floozy" or husband-stealer—that is so not me! But with this change in me, I wasn't so afraid anymore. So I asked a man out for coffee!

Both Peter and I have known him for thirty years. He's the only man outside of family members I feel comfortable with. He's very respectful and considerate. He never pressures me. He owns his own home and is retired. He doesn't need anything or want anything from me other than company. I've known him for more than half my life and he has always been a kind and good friend. We go to church together and Bible study, to the movies and out for meals, we drive around sightseeing. I'm having so much fun!

My future? It looks bright!

faith's time perspective therapy

Faith had been experiencing severe chest pains, which were explained to her by her cardiologist as panic attacks. Her primary care physician suggested she see a psychiatrist, who prescribed anti-anxiety and antidepressant medications, which she did not feel were helping her much. She explained how difficult it was for her to go to the clinic for assistance, as it was the doctor at the clinic who sent her home with a dying man. For this reason she embraced the idea of seeing a private therapist; she would rather pay out of pocket than have to go to the clinic every two weeks.

During the first session, the TP therapist explained the basics of grief, PTSD, and TPT, and asked Faith to watch a TPT relaxation video every day until the next session. Over the first two months of treatment, Faith rode the roller coaster of grief and PTSD symptoms. She was not compliant with either her psychiatrist's or her psychologist's suggestions. She admitted to not watching the video, and was becoming increasingly obsessive-compulsive, attending every religious service available to her and incessantly praying. Psychological tests were administered, with the following results: her trauma and depression were severe, and her anxiety was extreme. Her ZTPI revealed high past negative, low past positive, high present fatalism, extremely low present hedonism, and moderately low future scores.

She continued to work, but her performance suffered due to her lack of concentration. She was also extremely angry, not so much at the overworked doctor who misdiagnosed her husband but at the clinic itself—and at her husband for leaving her. Every time she had a doctor's appointment for a routine checkup, or went to see her psychiatrist, cardiologist, ob-gyn, or ophthalmologist, she had to go to the clinic. And every time she was at the clinic she suffered severe flashbacks to her husband's death. At the depth of her despair, she checked herself into the psychiatric ward at the hospital.

In the meantime, Faith's daughter, Belle, commenced TPT. Belle shared her insightful perspective of her mother's PTSD and grief as well as how the rest of the family was faring. Belle is very intelligent, with an excellent background in psychology. She explained that her brother was a lot like his father and did not see the value in therapy. However, she was excited to learn new ways to cope with the grief, stress, and anxiety that blanketed their family. Belle understood the importance of positivity rather than negativity. She quickly grasped Temporal Theory and TPT and immediately began implementing what she learned. After four TPT sessions in which she was given tools to help herself, her mother, and other family members, she felt equipped to handle future scenarios.

After four days of a combination of group and individual therapy, Faith checked herself out of the hospital and resumed treatment with her psychiatrist, who had increased her antidepressant and anti-anxiety medications while she was in the hospital. She also resumed TPT sessions on a weekly basis.

In her first TPT session following her hospitalization, she explained that she had become what would be considered "psychotic" and described how whenever she visited her husband's grave site, she felt he was pulling her into the grave with him. Her loss of appetite for food as well as life was extreme — indicating subconscious forms of suicide. She was also hearing voices.

The TP therapist discussed how Faith suffered not from a mental illness but from a mental injury — the tragic and needless death of her husband. Together, they reviewed Faith's past positives. Before her husband's death she had lived a contented life and enjoyed a deep spiritual connection with her husband and adult children. She was once a vibrant and youthful woman, and that woman still existed within her. The heartbreaking experiences she had recently endured would add to her already rich life and make her a stronger woman with a depth known by few of her age.

Faith was now ready to embrace her past positives and work on being a little present hedonistic. Since her husband's passing, Faith didn't believe she deserved to have fun or enjoy herself. Whenever she did start to have fun, she stopped herself and thought guiltily about Peter. To boost the past positives, the TP therapist suggested that Faith start by replacing negative thoughts of the past with positive memories. Then, to boost her present hedonism, each weekend Faith was to make short day trips with Belle. The TP therapist also suggested they start to plan a brighter future for Faith.

In the coming months, Faith suffered additional personal disasters: the business her husband and children owned was going bankrupt, and she was losing her own job of thirty years. The therapist worked with Faith to concentrate on a future positive, even when it seemed that everything was going wrong, and Faith tried hard to do this. Through ingenuity and finesse her children were able to save the business. And because Faith herself was an exemplary worker, she acquired a position with a local company closer to home. On the home front, she repainted the interior and exterior of her house, rearranged her bedroom, and gave away the majority of her husband's clothing and tools to friends and family.

At the TP therapist's suggestion she celebrated her husband's birthday with a cake and acknowledged him during holiday meals in celebration of the continuation of their relationship. The TP therapist explained that although her husband had passed away, their relationship continued in an even more spiritual way.

faith's brighter future

Faith had only been with one man — Peter — and the thought of being single frightened her tremendously. So during a recent TPT session the therapist was amazed when Faith shared that she had been having coffee once a week with a single man she had known for over thirty years. The TP therapist encouraged Faith's relationship with her new companion and secretly danced a jig after the session. Faith continues TPT on a monthly basis. She feels good about completing one chapter in her rich life and starting a new, exciting chapter.

faith's pre-TPT and post-TPT test results

Interpreting the Graphs: The clinical graph on the left in Figure 6.3 indicates very good improvement following time perspective therapy. Faith's depression score lowered from severe to way down in the normal range. Her greatest improvement is in anxiety, which dropped from extreme to near normal. Her trauma level also lowered from severe to mild.

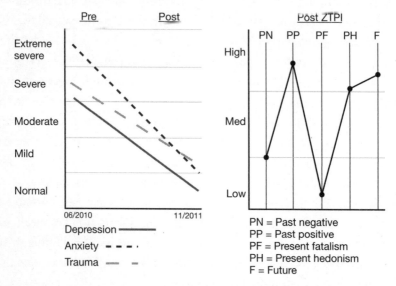

Figure 6.3   Faith—Woman with PTSD—Psychological Test Graphs

In her post ZTPI scores on the right, Faith's high past positive, high future, and borderline medium to high present hedonism scores are outstanding. Her past negative score, which rests on the borderline between low and medium, and even lower present fatalism score indicate that Faith is moving both rapidly and positively forward with her life.

"i hid in the closet for what seemed like eternity"

keiko

Like many children of divorce, Keiko divided her time between staying at her mother's house during the week and staying at her father's on the weekends. At age six, everything changed for Keiko: her mother was repeatedly assaulted by her abusive boyfriend, while a terrified Keiko hid in the closet. By the time she came to therapy as a teenager, Keiko had taken to cutting herself. Keiko's mother, the boyfriend long gone, was very concerned about her depressed child (and unaware of her cutting). She had sent Keiko to two other therapists, but Keiko dropped out of therapy with both after a few months, feeling the therapists were "old school" and could not or would not relate to her.

Psychological Diagnosis: *PTSD due to repeated childhood trauma*

I don't have many memories of life before the divorce—I was only five. My sister Shawnee was ten. She remembers "divisive," but I remember division—weekdays with Mom, weekends with Pop.

Growing up with a celebrity parent isn't all it's cracked up to be. Mom's a famous artist. We couldn't go anywhere without somebody stopping her to ask about this painting or that mural or would she donate something, anything to this charity auction or that school fundraiser. Somebody always wanted something from Mom. Pop's a super-intelligent, super-linguistic, super-musician with a bad case of "hermititis." By that I mean he is a super-loner. Pop made sure nobody wanted anything from him.

These bipolar lifestyles were each filled with art, which held great appeal for me. I enjoyed painting with Mom, learning about colors, transforming a blank canvas into candy for the eye. Nothing I made was wrong. Everything I made was "perfect." Pop would take me to poetry slams. I'd sit in a corner in the back of the room, make myself as tiny as I could, and watch him, eyes closed, recite about the difference between love and lust. Sometimes his other hermit friends would come over to his house and play everything from classical to bluegrass music until I'd fall asleep, curled up like a puppy at Pop's tapping feet.

Life was copacetic until I was six, when Mom dumped her new boyfriend. I didn't know anything about him. She explained to Shawnee and me later that she didn't want to introduce him into our lives unless she thought he was a keeper, which, being an IBTB—intimidating blowhard terroristic bully—he wasn't. One day he showed up at our doorstep—a big, scary guy with shaggy hair, yelling for Mom. Shawnee wasn't home. As he was kicking in the door, Mom told me to hide. I hid in the closet for what seemed like eternity. I could hear Mom pleading with him not to hurt her. Things were slammed around, and then I heard the bed squeaking and Mom sobbing. I was too young to know what was going on. It was nearly dark when Shawnee knocked on the closet door and told me to come out. Mom was sitting on the living room couch drinking a cup of tea. That night, Mom read children's stories to Shawnee and me for a long time. She forgot to make us dinner.

Mom's a very intelligent woman; why she fostered this sick relationship with the IBTB is beyond me. We saw him rarely, maybe every couple of months. But that's not to say Mom wasn't seeing him on the sly. I figured when she dressed up at night and said she was "going out," she was probably meeting up with the IBTB.

When he did show up at the house, I always hid in the closet. The pattern was the same: Mom would tell him it was over. He would yell obscenities. Mom would plead for him to leave. He would yell more obscenities and throw things around. Mom would plead *and* cry. He would throw her on the bed—or the couch or the floor—rape her and exit the crime scene. I'd be balled up in the closet with my fingers in my ears, silently crying until Mom knocked on the closet door to tell me it was safe to come out.

Sometimes I didn't feel like coming out. I started liking the closet. I felt safe. I made myself a little nest out of her cashmere sweaters. I kept a few of my loveys in there so I had something to hold on to while I plugged my ears. Then I snuck a flashlight, books, and some snacks and left them there—just in case I decided to stay after he left. Once in a while I'd fall sleep and wake up in the morning, all achy from basically sleeping on the floor. I really related to Harry Potter in volume one, when his "room" was the storage space under the stairs. It seems I spent years in the closet, until I couldn't fit in there anymore.

I love Mom and had thought of her as an angel up until IBTB, because that's how she looks—all sparkly white gold and beautiful. But after the second and the third and then the fourth rape, I started seeing her in this different light: she was becoming a dull, dark fallen angel. If I am one thing, it's pretty forgiving; and I had plenty of opportunities to practice it. When you're a little kid, you want to think that your parents are perfect; you want to hold them up on a pedestal and worship at their feet. You want to be just like them when you grow up. Most of the time, after an IBTB visit, I was able to get Mom back up on that pedestal. But with each rape, she fell harder and stayed there longer, until there was no way to even pick her up. No wonder I developed a fear of well-dressed, shaggy unkempt men with booming voices; no wonder hiding became second nature.

I was always a shy child, but Mom thought something more was wrong with me. She took me to a psychiatrist who diagnosed me with early childhood depression. I started to think, yeah, I guess I've always been depressed. Mom had the diagnosis she was looking for, but she didn't want me medicated. I remember adopting the "attitude" of what I thought a depressed child would be: No smiling; if people addressed me, look away. I barely talked in school. I didn't have friends. I tried to fake being sick as much as possible so I didn't have to go to school. I wanted to stay at home and read. I tried to miss the maximum number of school days permissible before Child Protective Services came to your house. I wanted nothing to do with anything outside. Outside scared me.

Shawnee earned a scholarship and went to a private arts university when I was thirteen. That's when I decided to make some changes, starting with my name. Mom named me after the street she lived on when she was a child . . . it's a nice name, but I never felt it fit me. I'm not Japanese but I've always been interested in Japanese culture, so I changed my name to Keiko. It means "Blessed Child." Next, I decided to change my appearance. I have naturally Nordic-blonde hair and hardly any eyebrows. I shaved off my eyebrows and started dying my hair different colors. If I got tired of auburn, I'd go golden blonde. When golden blonde was boring, I'd go deepest brown. When boxed colors were too norm, I started mixing my own. Jet black and teal, bleached white and shocking pink were gorgeous.

Shawnee had a knack for buying the coolest, most eclectic clothes and accessories at thrift stores. She also had an extensive makeup collection. Lucky for me, she left almost everything at home. I'd rummage through her things and come up with these eccentric outfits—every day I wore a different costume. Being a budding young artist, I had a steady hand. My face and body were my canvas.

The following year I used some money I'd saved up from Christmas and bought my first tattoos—permanent eyebrows. I had my ears pierced multiple times. I couldn't wait for Shawnee to come home. But it wasn't to be. A movie executive had gone to Shawnee's art school and liked her work so much that she was hired on the spot to design costumes and makeup for a major motion picture. Shawnee wouldn't be coming home for holidays or the summer—she had an electrifying new career and I had her old clothes.

Cutting became my new best friend. If I was faking depression before, I wasn't any longer. When I was with Dad, I stayed at his house instead of going to poetry slams. I hid in my bedroom if he had his musician friends over. At Mom's I didn't think I did anything out of the norm—at least not for me. But she said I was sleeping too late. I countered that I was a growing teenager. She'd come back with, "It's not normal to sleep until three in the afternoon." I admit I wasn't doing my chores anymore, but that's normal for teenagers, right?

Mom was worried about me again. She didn't know about my cutting when she sent me to another psychologist. I went for a few months to please her. He was a nice old man. He tried to act like he wasn't shocked by my appearance. But you can see it in the eyes—or rather the skin around the eyes—it tightens up. People can't help it. He reminded me of my grandpa—same reaction. I told him about the cutting, which threw him. He had me see another doctor, who prescribed antidepressant medications. I took them for a while but I didn't like the way they made me feel—like I wasn't in control. So I stopped taking them. I kept cutting.

I pretended I was okay so Mom felt better. I befriended another eccentric I met at my favorite place of all time—the super-bookstore. On the weekends, Dad would drop me off with some cash and pick me up six hours later. My BFF and I would roam the stacks, checking out the newest anime, classic literature, or kooky books, listening to samples of alternative or techno or world music. We'd sit and have chai and a bagel. It was my haven and my heaven. I *lived* for weekends at the bookstore.

For three years I fooled my parents into thinking I was a normal, if not odd, teenager. In all fairness, Dad came by being clueless naturally. He thought I was his Mini-Me. Mom, on the other hand, had been seeing a counselor who helped her finally, once and for all, break up with IBTB. Since her time was now free to focus on me, she noticed that I showed no interest in learning how to drive when other kids had had their licenses for at least a year. Mom started up her "You've got to see a therapist" campaign. She made me an appointment.

Mom pulled her nifty sports car into the driveway and walked me into the office. Nice office; lots of artwork. She hugged the therapist, whispered something to her, told me to "open up," and then peeled out. The therapist shook my hand and asked if I'd like a cup of tea or a snack. She made us both a cup while I perused the basket of health bars and Japanese rice crackers on display. I chose the rice crackers. We settled into the little office and I sat there, staring at my crackers.

I have a good memory and I recall that first session with clarity. I thought just because Mom trusted this woman, I didn't have to—I didn't know her. She checked out my hair and makeup. I remember I was wearing Cleopatra eyes and basic black. She said she liked my look; her eyes didn't go all squinty. I was curious about what my Mom said to her and I asked. She said, "Please help my baby." I don't cry often, and when I do it's in my room. But I felt like it then. I asked if she had children. She did, boys and girls, ages eleven to twenty-four. Maybe she knew something about kids.

She asked me to tell her about myself and I did. I told her I live a clean life—no drugs or alcohol. I have always been shy, lived in two households, have an older sister who's doing great, I didn't like to do much of anything other than go to the bookstore. She asked me what types of books I like to read and when I told her, she said she knew of an author I might like in the genre I read that I didn't know about. I thought that was nice but a little strange. Then she switched topics and told me that she knew about IBTB and how it must have been hard for me witnessing the trauma. I told her about hiding in the closet.

And then I told her about cutting. She asked if Mom knew about the cutting. No. She asked if my other therapist knew about the cutting. Yes, but he was old school and didn't seem to know how to handle it. His answer was medication. I told her I usually cut on my legs because they're easier to hide but sometimes I cut my arms. I rolled up my sleeve to show her some marks. She commented on a Japanese tribal tattoo I had just had done on my forearm—she knew what it was and said a couple of her sons have tattoos.

She asked me if it hurt when I cut. I told her it doesn't really hurt anymore. It's more of a thrill. It takes my mind off of my emotional pain...I focus on how my body is bones and muscle and blood encased in this thin layer of skin. When I see the blood from a cut, I think of how I'm letting some of my inside out. It's like exposing a little bit of my psychic pain, and it makes me feel better...sometimes I get so down or overwhelmed by everyone's expectations. I feel so hopeless about my life and see my future as a continuation of now—always hiding. The only thing that helps is cutting.

While I was telling her all this she nodded. Then she told me that I was really good at expressing myself and thanked me for being so open with her. She gave me her cell phone number and told me to text or call her if I felt like cutting. But the strangest thing was she told me that if I couldn't stop myself from cutting, then to make sure I cleaned the cut so that it wouldn't get infected. Of course that's what I was doing but I thought that was nice that she thought about it.

Mom pulled up at the end of the session. The therapist asked me if I wanted to come back for another "meeting." Mom answered for me: Yes, but we'd call. Then she asked Mom to wait a minute because she had something for me. She ran inside and came back with a book. She said it wouldn't hurt her feelings if I didn't read it but if I did, we could talk about it in the future. I thought, *This is a tricky way to get me to come back.*

The next session was two weeks later. The therapist started off by asking if I had felt like reading the book, which I did and I really liked. I pulled it out of my purse and returned it to her. We talked about the characters in the book for a while and we talked about music. She said she had plenty of books for me to read if I wanted to borrow them. Then she explained about Temporal Theory and TPT. I took some psych tests. The trauma one showed that I had suffered severe trauma; my depression was severe; and anxiety was extreme, with panic attacks; I did have PTSD. Then we reviewed my ZTPI scores and there it was: off the charts past negative and present fatalism. I didn't think about the future at all. She explained that in their work with young people, this was sort of normal—apparently, kids just don't think much about the future and most are present hedonists.

I learned the language of PTSD and time perspective therapy, and felt a little better about myself. I had started out being a quirky but normal child, but because of my early trauma, I had become super fatalistic and really fearful. Flashbacks to my early traumas were a lot less but they still happened, especially when I saw an older guy with shaggy hair. The TP therapist taught me to think past positive "happy thoughts" whenever I started to feel a flashback coming on. My favorite past positive thoughts are painting with Mom, playing dress up with Shawnee, listening to Dad play music, and anything to do with the time I spent at the super-bookstore.

Then she switched topics and said she had a bunch of maybes to tell me about. Maybe my early childhood depression was a symptom of posttraumatic stress caused by the stuff IBTB did to Mom. People who have PTSD have depression and anxiety, and when a person is very depressed, they might have thoughts of suicide. Thoughts of suicide can take different forms. Maybe my cutting was sort of a mini-suicide. Maybe my feelings of being powerless to help Mom caused me to hide. Maybe my fear of IBTB had morphed into fear of everything outside my world. This all made sense to me.

We worked on my present fatalism, which the TP therapist thought was rooted in my witnessing Mom being victimized and grew into me thinking it was normal to be a victim and adopting a victim mentality. So we talked about ways to help me grow a backbone. The therapist said one was to stop staying home and go to school. Not what I wanted to hear. She said the academic stuff was important, but even more important was the social contact. At the end of the session I told her I'd only cut once in the past two weeks. She hugged me and handed me another book.

My next session was about a month later. After we talked about the book and music, we continued with my present fatalism and feeling like a victim. I had been stuck there for so long it was hard to get out. I told her about being bullied. This was nothing new. My form of self-expression was not appreciated by a lot of students or teachers, but the teachers rarely said anything. We worked out a plan that if someone made a comment, I'd do what I always do—walk away. But if someone started to even hint at getting physical—like spitting—I'd stand up to them by reciting what our country is built on: the right to express ourselves as long as we didn't hurt others. If this didn't work then I'd report the fucktard! I was feeling pretty strong. And I hadn't felt the need to cut in a month. I was doing so well we decided to make appointments when I felt I needed to talk.

I came for sessions about every two months. The TP therapist helped me get stronger and stronger. I had a boyfriend for a while. He started using. I thought I could fix him, but in therapy I learned I could only fix myself. When I realized he was a loser, I dumped him. I did well in school and graduated.

In every session, we worked on making plans for my bright future. Like I said before, I hadn't thought much about the future—it seemed so far away—so I definitely needed an assist. She helped me decide what I wanted, which was easy and hard at the same time; easy because when I *really* thought about it, I knew what I wanted and hard because I didn't know how to get there.

One of my future plans was to legally change my name. The TP therapist helped me with the paperwork so now I am legally "Keiko." Another future plan was to be more independent—move to Los Angeles and live with Shawnee. I wanted to get a job like her. My therapist pointed out Shawnee got her job because she had been in school. But I had no interest in going to school. I'd worry about it later.

Another future plan is to marry a nice, eccentric man and have a family—that's really important to me. Mom wanted me to get my license, but I still had no interest in learning how to drive; I took the bus. My therapist said that when I moved to LA I wouldn't need a car anyway because they have a good bus system there. Once I had my plan, I started working toward making my brighter future happen. I needed money for the move so I pumped myself up and applied for a job—and got it! I moved in full time with Mom, saved my money, and bought a one-way plane ticket to Los Angeles.

For over a year now, I've lived with Shawnee and I work at a boutique in Hollywood that sells high-end vintage clothing and accessories. On a few occasions, celebrities have come in and told me they love the way I dress! Sometimes I help Shawnee with special projects for movies and television shows. It's very creative and a lot of fun.

After being away for a year, I returned home for a visit and the only person outside Mom and Pop I wanted to see was my therapist. We had an update session and I filled her in. Mom is living by herself—writing her memoir and enjoying for the first time being totally unattached. Pop continues to isolate himself but he seems content with his life. Shawnee's career is heating up. She likes me living with her, being her side-kick, and we've become very close friends.

I saved the best for last. One day, shortly after I started working in Hollywood, I was waiting at the bus stop when this incredibly tall, incredibly handsome guy with the most gorgeous long, dark hair literally bumped into me. His name is Mick. He's a college student. We talked a little and I told him where I work. I hoped, but didn't really think I'd see him again. Well, he showed up at the boutique and we've been together ever since.

I have never been around a real *Leave It to Beaver* type family. I didn't think they existed. But there is so much love in Mick's family... they all have their jobs or schooling and chores they automatically do, without being told. I have my chores too! They discuss their problems and help each other out. They eat dinner together every night. It's something I've never experienced. And I love it! We talk about getting married someday ...

In the future, I want to create a wholesome atmosphere in my own family. No fear. No hiding. Just love.

keiko's cognitive behavioral therapy

Some people are born with *endogenous depression,* a genetic predisposition to being depressed. The theory behind endogenous depression is that these folks have less than an optimum supply of neurotransmitters, causing them to depress cognitive function — which causes the blues. Psychiatrists and medical doctors treat this chemical imbalance with antidepressants, with the hope of balancing the chemistry of the brain's neurotransmitters, improving the way the brain functions by increasing its signal transmissions. Essentially, this creates more lubricant for the system so it can run more smoothly.

Keiko started therapy before the development of TPT. In the first session, Keiko described her life and personality prior to the onset of her "childhood depression." She had been an intelligent, contented, but shy child; interested in all things artistic. The therapist assisted her in pinpointing a particular incident, when Keiko was six years old, in which her mother's ex-boyfriend had terrorized her mother, causing Keiko to hide in a closet for several hours at a time. These rapes occurred repeatedly; eventually, Keiko came to prefer isolating herself in the closet. After this initial interview, the therapist determined that Keiko did not so much suffer from endogenous depression as she did from childhood PTSD brought on by continued frightening experiences and feelings of powerlessness.

The therapist employed cognitive behavioral therapy and positive psychology, as well as client education and response normalization, to help Keiko cope and deal with life situations. They addressed her cutting, and Keiko explained it as an expression of a way to take her mind off her emotional pain. The therapist asked Keiko to call her the next time she felt like cutting, and to consider the events that lead to the desire to cut and try to sort them out. But if she found she was unable to stop herself from cutting, then she was to clean and bandage the wound to avoid infection. Compassion rather than shame, understanding instead of judgment, and willingness to communicate on the part of the therapist led to an immediate reduction in Keiko's cutting incidences.

keiko's time perspective therapy

Upon the advent of TPT, the therapist helped Keiko see her experiences in a framework of time perspectives. She explained Temporal Theory, TPT, and how Keiko's past negatives could be replaced with past positives, moving beyond Keiko's present fatalism. Then Keiko and the TP therapist commenced planning Keiko's future.

By this time, Keiko had graduated from high school and was working part-time at a quaint curio shop within walking distance of her mother's house. The shop owner was a friend of her mother's and didn't mind her goth dress. But Keiko's dream was to work at the super-bookstore she continued to frequent. Unfortunately, she still had no interest in driving and was afraid to ride the bus. She had taken up with a younger high school student whose life was a shambles. Keiko, having gained coping skills through therapy, wanted to "fix" him and his life. After several months, as her boyfriend started a downward spiral into drugs, Keiko recognized that she had no control over someone else's life and started fully focusing on her own.

She became more practical in her thinking and realized that if she wanted to embrace life and her multiple talents, she needed to get away from those she depended on: namely her mother, her father, and the TP therapist. She ditched her dreams of working at the super-bookstore, didn't feel the need to take the required undergraduate courses offered by the state college, and planned instead to move to Los Angeles to be near her sister and see if she could eventually acquire a position in the entertainment field.

Now Keiko began working in earnest on her brighter future. She lived full-time with her mother so she could put in more hours at work. One of her goals was to legally change her name to "Keiko," so the TP therapist assisted in this process. She saw her father for short periods on the weekends. She lived frugally and accumulated her earnings until the day she had saved enough to pay for a plane ticket and a couple months' rent in Los Angeles.

keiko's brighter future

Keiko, now twenty-one, has not felt the need to cut herself in two years. She works at a trendy vintage clothing boutique in Hollywood where her quirky appearance is seen as a benefit rather than a disadvantage. Her flair for makeup and costume is greatly appreciated by the many celebrities who frequent the shop. She fearlessly rides the bus to and from work, as well as to other places of interest. She lives with her sister, whose career in makeup and costume design is flourishing. Keiko occasionally assists her sister on projects and is hopeful that she will soon be able to use her many talents on a full-time basis.

One day after work, while waiting at the bus stop, she met Mick, a young college student. In a relatively short amount of time, a healthy relationship developed. Mick's positive outlook on life, his ambitious character, and his spiritual background resonate with Keiko's reclaimed inquisitive, artistic spirit. Mick's solid family has accepted Keiko with open arms. Keiko and Mick have been together for a year. They discuss the idea of marriage when Mick completes his college education. "In the future, I want to create a wholesome atmosphere in my own family. No fear. No hiding. Just love."

keiko's pre-TPT and post-TPT test results

Interpreting the Graphs: The clinical graph on the left in Figure 6.4 indicates excellent improvement following time perspective therapy. Keiko's depression score lowered from severe to normal. Her anxiety score dropped from the extreme level to the normal range. And her trauma score lowered from severe to mild. She represents one of our most successful treatment outcomes, with dramatic improvements across all measures.

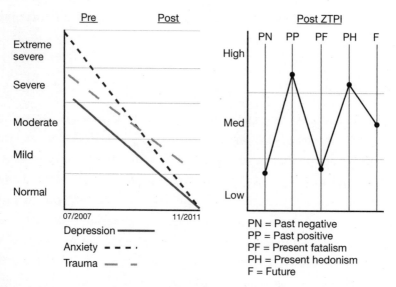

Figure 6.4   **Keiko — Woman with PTSD — Psychological Test Graphs**

In her post ZTPI results on the right, Keiko's high past positive and high present hedonism scores balance her low past negative and low present fatalism scores. Her future score is firmly in the center of the medium range, which, although a little lower than the ideal, indicates she has made good improvement. This suggests that Keiko has embraced the positives in her life and is bravely progressing into her brighter future.

> ### "it has been so hard"
> #### *betty*
>
> *Betty, now seventy-eight, got pregnant and dropped out of school at eighteen. She married Roy, the father, when her son was five months old. Despite the fact that Roy was abusive and played around, they stayed married for more than four decades and went on to have five children. Betty came to therapy with a deep depression brought on by the sudden drug-related deaths—one after the other—of two of her adult children and one of her grandchildren.*
>
> *Betty's youngest daughter, Dee, brought her to her first appointment because Betty was unfamiliar with therapy and afraid of what might happen. "My doctor said I should see the therapist because he thought I was becoming addicted to pain medications and my memory is going fast. I wanted Dee to come with me because I didn't know what to expect," she explains. "I thought people who go to therapy were crazy and had to see psychiatrists and take pills, like the ones you see in the television advertisements... I didn't feel crazy."*
>
> *Psychological Diagnosis: PTSD due to the drug-related deaths of two adult children and one grandchild*
>
> That first time with the therapist, he explained to me and Dee the difference between psychiatrists and psychologists, or therapists. He said psychiatrists are medical doctors and they see people who have mental illnesses, like being bipolar or psychotic, and they give medications. He said sometimes the psychiatrists would spend some time and talk to you, but many times the psychiatrists referred people to psychologists too. Psychologists are different because they work with people who have mental injuries and help people by talking with them and coming up with ways to help the person learn to cope.
>
> The therapist seemed nice but I didn't feel like talking, so Dee told him why I was there. She told him about all my medications and how I had pain but nobody knew what caused it and she told him how I couldn't remember things like I used to. I just thought it was old age. The therapist listened, and then he told us about Temporal Theory and explained about TPT. He showed us a way

to breathe slowly in and out and how to space the breaths, and said I should try to do that breathing every day to relax. Then I took a bunch of these psychological tests and he said next time he would tell us how I did on them.

Dee came with me to my next appointment too. The therapist told us that the tests showed I had severe PTSD [severe trauma, severe depression, and borderline moderate to severe anxiety] and that I had probably had it for a long time. He said that when someone has bad PTSD, like me, sometimes their memory isn't good—it doesn't matter how old they are; and sometimes they can have aches and pains even though there isn't anything wrong with them. He said when you are really depressed, a small pain might feel like a big pain and small things that go wrong feel like big problems.

The therapist said that one of the tests showed I had a lot of past negatives, bad memories from my past, and that made me present fatalistic. Then Dee started telling him some of the bad things that happened in my life. When she told him about all the deaths in my family, I cried. It was so painful for me to think about...I started to have an asthma attack, like I get, and I couldn't breathe. The therapist said this was a panic attack and helped me with the breathing technique, and it slowed down my beating heart until I could breathe normally. I think now that maybe my asthma attacks were really panic attacks.

When I felt better, I wanted to talk...I told him that when my granddaughter died, and next my son, who was her father, and then my daughter died—all of drug overdoses—I wanted to forget things. I was so upset about my granddaughter... My poor great-grandchildren! Then my son—I was in bed for a year and a half after he passed. I was starting to get better, but then my daughter died...it's all very traumatic.

I love my children so deeply—it has been so hard! The therapist reminded me to do my breathing and said it would help me.

I was feeling comfortable now, so I didn't ask Dee to come with me to the next appointment. This time, I talked for a long time about growing up in a big family, and taking care of my younger brothers and sisters, and then marrying and having my kids. I got pregnant when I was a junior in high school. I dropped out, and when my son was five months old his Dad and I got married. Roy was mean—he used to beat me, run around, fool around—he was a playboy. But I loved him so much!

We had two more children. I was a stay at home mom, and my husband started his own refuse collection business. I was the office manager. He did very well. Eventually, we had five children all together.

My daughter Melanie was in ninth grade when she started smoking marijuana, she got her brother Tommy to smoke too—I didn't know at the time. But as the years progressed and they were in high school, I knew something was going on. But I understood that a lot of kids smoked marijuana, so ...

All this time Roy would yell at me and hit me, and he would keep women on the side—but I loved him. He was a good provider and a good father. He took out his anger on me. But finally, after forty-four years of marriage, I was fed up with his other women. I had thought about divorcing him for a few years. Then one day I was so angry I told him not to come home—I threw his clothes out onto the lawn and told him to come pick them up.

My son Tommy got married and had three children, but he and his wife were drug users—cocaine, crystal methamphetamine, heroine and prescription medications. Melanie got married and had two children. She became addicted to prescription pain medications. And I knew that something was very wrong with my granddaughter, one of Tommy's children—she would call me at 2 or 3 a.m. Then one day, Tommy called and told me that my granddaughter had been found dead in her house with her two little children, who were crying and trying to wake their mother.

Tommy got divorced, and he ended up living on the streets. He kept in touch with me whenever he needed money. I was so worried about him—I couldn't sleep at night. So four years ago, I went and found him and brought him home to live in a studio on our property. I couldn't handle him not being cared for. But he got back into heroin. He died of an overdose. I found him in the studio. It was too late.

My daughter Melanie was living with an abusive man and got pregnant. I was there when my grandson was born, and I took the baby for a month because that man beat her and I was afraid for the baby. Melanie got back into drugs, and by the time her son was thirteen she was doing cocaine—Tommy introduced her to it. We all had our suspicions, but I couldn't tell if she was high—I didn't know enough. I just knew there was something missing in her eyes.

Later, she got into crystal meth. Her drug use caused her to have heart problems and she had open heart surgery. Then she got hooked on prescription medications. She was told not to do illegal drugs again. But a year and a half after Tommy's death, Melanie died of an overdose. The police arrived and told me that she had expired. I was in shock. I was just getting out of my depression over Tommy's dying, and my granddaughter before him, and now my daughter was dead too.

I have thought for many years: What did I do wrong? What happened? I think my children had a hard time because of the way we lived—their father was so abusive to me. He was mean and drank a lot. When he threw us out, I would pack up the kids in the car and go to my mother or to friends. We would be gone for two to three days and he would be hunting for me. I finally got enough courage to leave him, but by then the kids were grown and had their own children. The damage was already done. My husband took care of us financially but he wasn't there for us emotionally.

I told the therapist all about my children's lives, and my grandchildren and great-grandchildren. I talked about the past negatives. I told him that I didn't feel I knew who I was anymore; I was in a lot of pain and depression.

I did tell him one positive—that I had a live-in boyfriend who I knew from grade school; we've been together for twelve years. Then I told him that my boyfriend was an invalid and couldn't leave the house. The therapist asked if I had been doing the relaxation and breathing exercises, and I admitted to him that I was bad, I had only done it twice. But I told him I had a hard time remembering things.

The therapist said we were going to work on changing the way I think. He asked me to tell him some past positives. This was easy for me. I loved raising my children, spending time together on holidays with our huge family—my sisters and brothers and all their kids—I loved that time in my life … So he told me that when I start to think past negative thoughts like about how my children died from drugs or my husband cheating on me, I should right away think of past positives: think about how my children were when they were little, or about the big family feasts we had. He made me feel good about the good times. I felt so much better, like a load had been lifted from my shoulders.

The next time I saw the therapist, he explained to me about my memory. He said PTSD can make somebody's memory not so good... He told me there are little paths in the brain, and when things are working right you can travel from the past to the present and the future easily—you can remember things. But if you have bad PTSD, you get stuck on the bad things that happened in the past negative path and then you think your life now is really bad—present fatalistic—like me, or you just want to try to forget everything and maybe drink too much or take drugs so you become too much present hedonistic. When he told me this, I thought of my children who died. They were all too present hedonistic, addicted to drugs.

The therapist asked me if I liked to play games and I told him I played solitaire online. He said this was good for my memory and that I should get some crossword puzzles and Sudoku books and do those a little bit every day to improve my memory. I had told him that sometimes I watch my little four-year-old grandson, so he told me to play easy card games with him, especially Concentration. He said doing things with my grandson was good: it was pro-social and also it was present hedonistic. I told him that since our last appointment, my pain wasn't so bad and I didn't have to take so many medications. He was happy and said I should tell my doctor so he knew what was going on.

In my next session, we talked about the future. The therapist helped me plan my brighter future—which was pretty simple. I think maybe I have about a dozen or so years left and I want the rest of my life to be as stress free and happy as possible... I am happy right now, my life is wonderful. In my brighter future, I will live long enough to see my grandson grow... He is a healing gift—I lost two children and a grandchild—but I have my wonderful grandson right next door. I look forward to watching him grow into a healthy, intelligent young man... My boyfriend lives with me, and I am his main caregiver. In my brighter future I will take care of him as long as I can... The therapist helped me learn how to appreciate all the past positives in my life and not dwell on the past negatives.

I have anything and everything a woman could want. I live in a house and I have my loving daughter helping me. I see my grandson every day. I am very happy with my family and my boyfriend. Most of all I'm happy with me. I've come a long way. I finally found me—I am finally Betty.

betty's time perspective therapy

Betty's physician referred her to therapy for her deteriorating memory, as well as to learn coping skills that would help her reduce her prescription pain medication intake. Betty's youngest daughter, Dee, attended the first TPT session. Betty was introverted during this session and did little talking. Dee filled in the therapist as to the initial reason Betty was referred to him, reviewed the number of prescription medications Betty was taking, and said that her mother had no real reason to be on them. She also reviewed the deterioration of Betty's memory.

The therapist explained Temporal Theory and time perspective therapy, and demonstrated a simple breathing technique, which they practiced together. He asked Betty to practice the breathing technique every day. Psychological tests were administered, with the understanding that the results would be reviewed during the next session.

Dee also attended the second TPT session, in which the therapist explained Betty's psychological test results and her diagnosis of chronic and severe PTSD. He noted that PTSD might be responsible for her memory loss as well, and might also psychologically increase the level of physical pain she was experiencing. Her ZTPI scores indicated very high past negative and present fatalistic orientations. Dee said that her mother had indeed experienced numerous traumatic experiences in her life, including the drug-related deaths of her granddaughter, son, and daughter. Betty had a panic attack that she interpreted as asthma, and the therapist helped her use the breathing technique until she regained her composure.

For the remainder of the session Betty detailed the past negatives of the drug-related deaths—first of her granddaughter, then of her son, and more recently of her daughter. It was clear that she had been trying to work her way through extended mourning, and her coping mechanism was to "forget things." The therapist introduced Betty to a relaxation video that incorporated time perspective therapy, and suggested that she watch it every day to learn coping skills for her extreme past negative and present fatalistic tendencies.

Dee did not attend the third or any subsequent sessions. Betty explained that after the previous treatment she felt at ease with the therapist and no longer needed Dee to sit in for comfort's sake. Betty wanted to talk more about her past negatives and was allowed to do so for about half the session. She said she felt she had lost her identity in all her many past negatives and didn't know who she was anymore.

Betty was not compliant, and had only practiced relaxation and breathing twice—when she remembered, she said. The therapist explained the importance of replacing past negative thoughts with past positives. She said that she had no difficulty remembering past positives, and recalled a few: "I loved raising my children, spending time together on holidays with our huge family—my sisters and brothers and all their kids. I loved that time in my life . . . " Whenever she found herself recalling a past negative memory, she was asked to trade it for one of her many happy past positives. These positive experiences and the good feelings she effortlessly drew on were an important indication of the person she was and has always been—an optimist at heart who had endured tremendous tragedy and stress. She felt overlaying past negatives with past positives was achievable. She left the session in a much lighter mood.

In the fourth session they addressed Betty's failing memory. The therapist explained in detail how PTSD can affect a person's memory, as thoughts that travel pathways in the brain that would ordinarily be free to journey back and forth between past, present, and future become stuck in the past negative or present fatalistic time perspective, as in Betty's case, or in present hedonism. Betty grasped this concept quickly, and realized that her deceased granddaughter, son, and daughter had been stuck in extreme present hedonism and had died due to their hedonistic drug addictions.

The therapist, seeking ways for Betty to exercise her mind, asked if she enjoyed playing games. He suggested that Betty continue her habit of playing solitaire on the computer, and indicated that she might also do crossword and Sudoku puzzles. He also suggested that Betty introduce her young grandson to simple games of memory, such as Concentration. This not only would help her with her own memory issues but also would begin to address pro-social behavior and selected present hedonism.

The therapist noted that since the previous session, Betty had experienced a decrease in the level of her physical pain and had reduced her intake of prescription medications. He was pleased, and asked Betty to discuss this reduction with her medical physician.

betty's brighter future

The fifth session focused on Betty's brighter future. Together, they began to make a simple plan. Betty is very close to Dee, her son-in-law, and her young grandson, who live on the same property. Her brighter future plans include being an integral part of her grandson's life and watching him grow. She expressed her feelings about him warmly: "He is a healing gift—I lost two children and a grandchild—but I have my wonderful grandson right next door. I look forward to watching him grow into a healthy, intelligent young man."

Her significant other is a man she has known since grade school but had not seen in forty years; they have been together for the past twelve years. His poor health has left him housebound, and Betty is his main caregiver. Her future positive plans include seeing to his needs as long as she can. At age seventy-eight, she feels that she has perhaps a dozen or so years. "I want the rest of my life to be as stress free and happy as possible . . . I am happy right now, my life is wonderful."

Betty has successfully learned to replace past negatives with past positives; she has replaced her past heartache and depression with gratitude for what she has. She practices present hedonism with her grandson, and focuses on a brighter future. Through TPT, Betty rediscovered herself. She continues TPT treatment on a monthly basis.

betty's pre-TPT and post-TPT test results

Interpreting the Graphs: The clinical graph on the left in Figure 6.5 indicates improvement from time perspective therapy. Betty's most significant advance is seen in her depression score, which dropped from severe to the high-normal range. Her anxiety level lowered from the borderline between moderate and severe to the low-mild range. Her trauma lowered from severe to the borderline between moderate and mild.

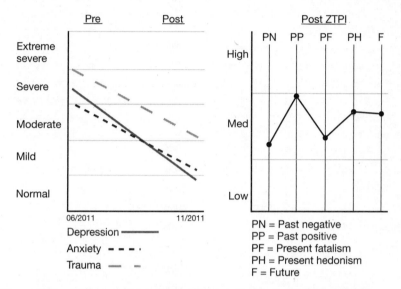

Figure 6.5   **Betty — Woman with PTSD — Psychological Test Graphs**

In her post ZTPI scores on the right, Betty's mid-range levels are understandable given her age and the severity of her trauma. Her highest score is past positive, which is in the high-medium range. Her high-medium present hedonism and future scores offset her low-medium present fatalism and past negative scores. Although she continues to struggle with the traumatic loss of her children, she is valiantly working toward her future positive.

"i got really scared"

grace

Grace, forty-seven, had been working in administration at a correctional facility for twenty-five years. She treasured her occupation and the close relationships she'd developed with her coworkers. She was known for her confidence, competence, and ability to multitask. But then her supervisor hired Helen, a union administrative assistant, without Grace's knowledge, and sat Helen at a new desk squeezed into Grace's already tiny office.

Helen was extremely religious, and it appeared that she felt her real job was to save Grace's soul—not reduce her workload. Grace tried her best to ignore Helen's proselytizing, but the work piled up. When she reported Helen to her supervisor, Helen somehow found out and started making death threats, saying she would burn Grace's house down and kill everyone in it. Grace was freaked out. She couldn't sleep at night and couldn't eat. She became hyper-vigilant and terrified, and had what she describes as a "breakdown." Finally, she went on leave from work and entered therapy.

Psychological Diagnosis: PTSD due to extreme bullying by a co worker

I have always thought of myself as a strong, capable person. It takes these qualities to work in a correctional facility, which I have for twenty-five years. I had really good relationships with my co-workers, and never had any problems. We were like family.

I loved raising my kids, but I didn't realize how much of my time was spent meeting their needs and worrying about them. Once they were grown, the energy and thought I put out for them went right into my relationship with my husband and work. We love rodeo and have horses. We would spend the weekend camping, go on vacations ...

I had a new supervisor at work and he saw I was capable, so he kept giving me more work. This was fine with me but after a while he saw I needed help. One day I came to work and a woman named Helen was sitting at a desk that had been squeezed into my little office. I was shocked. I knew that my supervisor's intentions were good, but I really should have had a say in who I'd be working with.

I am a religious person and go to church every Sunday. But because I didn't believe exactly as Helen believed, she tried to convert me. At first I listened, and then I tried to ignore her preaching. Helen was easily distracted at work and wasn't very fast; I always had to finish her jobs. Her sermons took up a lot of her time, and she started coming in late to work and late after lunch, and taking personal phone calls all the time, and having to leave work early because of some emergency.

I was falling further and further behind. Helen was supposed to be my assistant but she wasn't working out. I had to come to work on the weekends to make up for all the things she didn't do. I didn't have time to spend with my husband anymore. I started writing down all the things that Helen was supposed to accomplish and all the things she didn't do so my supervisor wouldn't hire her permanently. When I gave him the list, he said basically he couldn't let her go because she was a union hire.

I don't know how it happened, but Helen found out about my list and she was very, very angry with me. She tried to convert me even more. She'd pray all day long. She told me she was God's messenger and that if I didn't think she was doing a great job then I must be possessed by the devil. She would talk to herself out loud and say that the world would be better if I wasn't in it. Then she started making death threats—she'd tell me that she was going to burn my house down with me and everyone in it.

I got really scared. I couldn't sleep at night because I was afraid Helen was going to follow through on her threats. Every time a car drove by our house I'd run to the window to see if it was Helen. I was nutty about keeping all the doors and windows locked—at home and in my car. I stopped working on the weekends because I was afraid Helen might follow me or be waiting for me at work. I talked to my supervisor about Helen, but he said I was overreacting. He sort of threatened me too—said I had to catch up on my work.

I talked to my husband, and he went to speak with my supervisor. He told my husband that Helen and I had a personality conflict and I had better work it out with Helen. I had a mental breakdown. There was no way Helen would work anything out with me. I went to work one day and my supervisor took me aside and told me to take some time off.

I took two weeks off and started to feel like my old self, so I went back to work. I walked into my office and there was Helen sitting at my desk. She gave me a weird smile and started praying out loud, saying the Lord should damn me to hell...she said she had a knife and when I turned my back, she was going to stab me. I had another breakdown. My supervisor told me that Helen was going to replace me temporarily... He took me off work and put me on workers comp leave for psychological therapy.

In the beginning of my TPT, I saw the therapist twice a week for two months because I was such a wreck. I remember my first session was twice as long as it should have been...all I could do was cry. When I told him about Helen and how she made death threats, I couldn't stop shaking. I told him I felt like I was back in school being bullied and I didn't know how to stop the bully. I told him that my supervisor didn't believe me and was backing up Helen. I told him how I didn't feel safe anywhere, and all the strange things I was doing, like running to the window to see if she was outside my house. I told him my mental breakdown was ruining my marriage. He asked me if I was on any medications. I told him that my physician prescribed them for me but I wouldn't take them because I was afraid of them turning me into a zombie.

The therapist took my blood pressure and it was high. Then he did guided breathing with me, and that taught me how to slow down my breathing so my heart would slow down. Then he took my blood pressure again and it was down twenty points. I was amazed at how breathing for a few minutes can do that—lower your blood pressure!

Then he gave me some psychological tests and told me that I had extreme PTSD [extreme trauma, severe to extreme depression, and extreme anxiety and panic attacks]. He explained Temporal Theory and TPT to me and said my ZTPI scores showed I was very high in present fatalism and past negative. He was concerned because my present hedonistic and future time perspectives were very low. Then we watched a relaxation video that incorporated time therapy. He gave me a DVD of it to watch at home, and also some relaxation CDs to listen to. When I left I felt much calmer.

In my next session, and for weeks after, I could not let go of my past negative flashbacks to Helen or my present fatalistic behavior. It's all I wanted to talk about. He tried to get me to focus on past positives but I wasn't ready. It was like I had drunk poison and it had to work its way out of my system.

Every time the therapist asked me to think of a past positive, I would start talking about past negative Helen and how scared I was and how she was ruining my life. I only left the house to come for appointments. My husband and kids did everything for me. I couldn't sleep and I wasn't eating. I didn't think I'd ever be able to work again, so I gave all my good work clothes away—they didn't fit anymore anyway because I had lost so much weight. I had lots of makeup and I threw it all away. I was consumed by fear—by my present fatalism. I was very emotional. The therapist would tell me to close my eyes and talk me through a guided visualization; or we would practice the breathing technique. It would calm me down.

After a couple of months into TPT, instead of waking up scared I woke up mad—at myself! Something snapped into place in my brain and I realized I had been letting Helen get to me. I was *not* going to be a victim! I was so ready when the therapist asked me to replace my past negatives with past positives. I told him about how I felt good when I accomplished things at work, about how I took pride in looking professional, about the wonderful times I spent with my kids, and how much I love my husband. I talked about all my great past positives for the whole session—I felt like I had a real breakthrough!

Then it was time to change my present fatalism into selected present hedonism. The therapist knew that I had been holing up at home and only leaving to come to our sessions. He reminded me my husband had been really patient with me and I should reconnect with him. He suggested I start by going with my husband every morning to take care of our horses. I missed our horses—they used to be such a big part of my life. I went along every morning and fed and groomed them. Then my husband and I started going for drives and then we went on little dates. All this took time, but I was feeling closer to my husband and closer to being fearless.

I was doing well with past positives and selected present hedonism, and then I had a little setback. I thought I was mad before, but in a following TPT session I told the therapist I was livid! Since Helen had replaced me she had a new assistant. Her new assistant called me to say that Helen was bullying her! When I spoke to the poor girl, she was so scared. I thought, *That's me!* Why are we allowing Helen to threaten us? Why are we living in fear? No more! Helen's assistant had to go on workers comp leave. Together, we decided to file criminal charges against Helen for threatening us—public safety officers.

My goal in TPT was always to return to work once the case was closed. In my sessions, after we reviewed how I was replacing my past negatives with past positives and practicing selected

present hedonism, the therapist worked with me on my future positive. We didn't know what type of job I might go back to, but I knew
I had to stand up for my rights and not be bullied.

When the case closed, I stopped seeing my therapist.
The court found Helen guilty of terroristic threatening, but she
plea-bargained and her charges were reduced from a felony
to a misdemeanor with a no-contact order. She was allowed to
continue to work! Helen's assistant decided to join the military
instead of return to work.

Legally, Helen couldn't be anywhere near me, so she was
reassigned to a different office and I returned to my old job. But
I didn't last a week...Helen and I started work at the same time
each day. We parked in the same parking lot and walked through
the same security checkpoint and had to share the same break
room...I could run into Helen anywhere at any time. I was afraid
that she was angrier with me than ever, and would follow through
with her threat and stab me in the back! I started to fall apart
again. I went to my physician, and to my therapist, and they both
said I could not be allowed to work in such a toxic environment. I
was back on workers comp for a few more months.

Now I attend biweekly TPT appointments. Every session we
review how I'm doing. I am keeping up my pro-social selected
present hedonism with my husband and family and friends—and
my horses. One of my future positive plans is to return to the
rodeo circuit. My husband and I started socializing with a couple
we've known for many years. The husband is a veteran that
was treated for PTSD a long time ago. It's really good to have
someone else with PTSD to talk to.

I finally reached my brighter future plans to return to work in a
different department. I was hired as a temp, but I'm doing so well
that my new supervisor is talking about hiring me permanently.

I have a grandson now, and he's the light of my life! I love
spending time with him. I can laugh again. I see the beauty
around me. Life is good. I'm building new relationships with my
co-workers. I know how to balance my time perspectives and feel
very positive about the future. I have a new pro-social selected
present hedonistic activity—Zumba! I go three times a week. The
gals there are so much fun! We laugh the whole time!

I don't know what I would have done if I wasn't mentally prepared each week to deal with the negative possibilities. TPT sessions saved my life.

grace's time perspective therapy

During Grace's first TPT session she cried profusely and shook uncontrollably. When she spoke about her past negative traumatic history with Helen, it was apparent that she was having flashbacks, gasping for breath as her face and eyes turned red. It was difficult to even bring up her work conditions, as she would break down.

Her description of Helen was that of an extreme schoolyard bully. She hadn't encountered this type of behavior since grade school and was at a loss as to how to handle the situation. Her supervisor, for unknown reasons, was unsupportive to the point of taking the bully's side. It seemed her supervisor thought only men could be bullies, and this belief system blinded him to the situation.

Her extreme past negative and present fatalistic orientations caused her blood pressure to spike as she explained how her ideal marriage was falling apart due to her PTSD symptoms—especially her present fatalistic hyper-vigilance, her estrangement from others, and a generalized fear of social contact. She didn't even feel safe in her own home, fearing that Helen would come and burn her house down. Her past positive previous love of horses was no longer on her radar, much less any of the other present hedonistic fun things she used to do with her husband.

Her medical doctor had prescribed medications for her, but Grace refused to take them because she was afraid they would turn her "into a zombie." The therapist used a guided breathing program with her, which brought her blood pressure down twenty points. Psychological tests were administered, and these indicated extreme trauma, severe to extreme depression, and extreme anxiety and panic attacks. The diagnosis was extreme PTSD.

Grace's ZTPI results indicated extremely high present fatalism, high past negative, and very low future scores. The therapist reviewed Temporal Theory and time perspective therapy with her, and asked Grace to watch a TPT relaxation video every day.

Grace's extreme PTSD symptoms caused her to be an exceptionally tough case. She attended TPT sessions twice a week for two months. In that time, she was incapable of letting go of her past negative and present fatalistic tendencies. She was unable to change her focus from past negative to past positive during this period. She was stuck in the mire of the past, which prevented her from being able even to contemplate the future. During these sessions, her need to recount her past negatives overrode the TPT process. She was highly emotional, and much of each session was spent on calming her with guided visualization and relaxation breathing techniques.

Attempts to replace past negatives with past positives appeared impossible at this time, so the therapist determined that it was best to allow Grace to unload her numerous accounts of living in present fatalism: she experienced constant fear, isolating herself at home with the curtains drawn, only leaving the house for doctors' appointments and therapy sessions. Her husband and adult children handled the shopping and errands. She suffered from sleep deprivation and had no appetite. In the past, before Helen's threats, Grace took pride in her appearance. But present fatalistically she now no longer cared about what she looked like. She threw away all of her business clothes and makeup and took to wearing oversized T-shirts, baggy jeans, and boots.

After the first two months of twice-weekly TPT, Grace attended weekly TPT sessions for the subsequent year. The therapist's goal was to get Grace back to work. After two months of past negative and present fatalistic expelling, Grace arrived at her session ready to move forward with her TPT. Her victim mentality had been replaced with anger directed toward herself; she questioned how she could have allowed fear to control her actions. When she was asked to replace her past negative flashbacks of Helen's extreme bullying tactics, Grace found that she had plenty of past positive memories of good times at work—of being complimented on her work capacity, capabilities, and neat appearance. For the remainder of the session she recalled not only her past positive work experiences but past positives from her personal life as well.

In the following session, the therapist suggested that Grace work on replacing her present fatalism with pro-social selected present hedonism by reconnecting with her husband and doing activities she had once enjoyed. Slowly, she started getting out of the house and refocusing from her fears to something she previously had cared about: her horses. The therapist suggested she go with her husband each morning to feed and groom them. Once Grace had established this routine, she started going for drives with her husband, followed by short dates. Grace was gradually expanding her interests and leaving the fear behind.

The next session was devoted to proactive behavior and planning Grace's future positive. Recently, Helen's new assistant had called Grace and told her in a fearful voice that Helen was now bullying *her*. Instead of reverting back to present fatalistic isolation and fear, Grace became incensed. She had truly had enough of bullying. Taking a proactive stance, she and Helen's assistant filed criminal charges against Helen for threatening public safety officers. Helen was eventually found guilty of terroristic threatening in a court of law. However, during plea bargaining Helen's charges were reduced from a felony to a misdemeanor with a no-contact order, which allowed her to maintain her job with the state.

TPT was back on track in succeeding sessions, which involved making plans for Grace's future positive. Her major future positive plan was to return to work in some capacity once the case was closed. She had also begun to expand her pro-social selected present hedonism by increasing her social circle to include other family members and old friends. Grace felt she was sufficiently equipped to stop therapy at the completion of the case.

When the case closed, instead of returning to work, Helen's assistant decided to join the military. The no-contact order meant Helen could not be in the same vicinity or be in contact with Grace in any way, shape, or form. Grace returned to work at her old position, and Helen was placed in another office. The possibility of running into Helen proved too stressful for Grace, however, and she went back on workers' comp leave. Furthermore, Grace's physician agreed that she could not be allowed to return to work in such a toxic psychosocial environment; both the physician and therapist felt returning to such conditions was against the judge's court order. This was proving to be a *very* tough case.

At this point, Grace returned to TPT. Working with the correctional facility and Grace's workers' comp adjuster, the therapist was able to assist with Grace's placement in a different government office. While waiting for her start date, Grace continued working on selected present hedonism and recommenced spending quality time with her husband, horses, and family. She also started practicing pro-social present hedonism by getting together with old friends she had been too depressed to talk to before that point. One couple has been particularly helpful in Grace's recovery — the husband, a former PTSD veteran client of ours who served in Vietnam, has been supportive in assisting Grace in overcoming her PTSD symptoms. With this new attitude and the ability to balance her time perspective, Grace returned to a new temporary job.

grace's brighter future

Grace is currently living her brighter future. When she came to her TPT session at the end of her first week at her new job, she was glowing: tanned, toned, and wearing a smart business outfit. She shared that she was told by her new boss after the second day that she was already performing at a level she wasn't expected to reach for three months. Happy with her supervisor and new coworkers, she felt her abilities were respected and appreciated. It's important to note that Grace's recovery from PTSD and her successful reintegration into the workforce were accomplished without medications.

Grace's brighter future includes doing the very best she can at her job. Given her outstanding performance, there is discussion about making it a permanent position. Her selected present hedonistic and future positive plans include returning to the rodeo circuit in the coming months. She and her husband are actively working on expanding their social circle, and Grace finds joy and laughter in the selected present hedonistic aerobics classes she attends three times a week. Grace plans on laughing a lot in her brighter future.

grace's pre-TPT and post-TPT test results

Interpreting the Graphs: The clinical graph on the left in Figure 6.6 indicates improvement from time perspective therapy. Grace's severe to extreme depression and extreme anxiety scores dropped significantly to the mild range, whereas her extreme trauma score lowered to the moderate range.

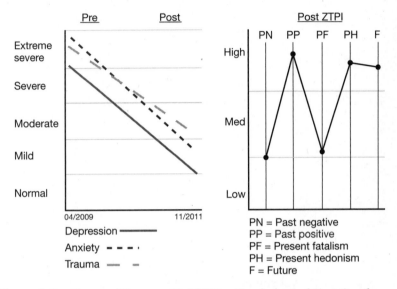

Figure 6.6   Grace — Woman with PTSD — Psychological Test Graphs

Grace's post ZTPI scores on the right indicate great improvement. Her high past positive is followed closely by her high present hedonism and future scores. These elevated positive scores counteract her borderline low-medium past negative and present fatalism scores, indicating Grace understands how to balance her time perspective.

o to sum up

- Women who have suffered from a trauma are more than twice as likely as men to develop PTSD.
- The foremost cause of PTSD for women is sexual assault.
- According to recent scientific studies, estrogen, the primary female sex hormone, may amplify the effects of stress.

epilogue

In late 2009 Larry Borins, a young mental health professional based in Toronto, attended a one-day time perspective therapy (TPT) work-shop held at our office facilities in Maui. Larry is a marriage and family therapist who specializes in cognitive behavioral therapy (CBT) and mindfulness-based approaches for treating anxiety and depression and for relapse prevention. He trained in mindfulness-based cogni-tive therapy (MBCT) with Zindel Segal and in mindfulness-based stress reduction (MBSR) with Jon Kabat-Zinn. He has been running MBCT and MBSR groups in Toronto since 2008.

Larry began using what he learned in the workshop immediately upon returning to his practice in Toronto. Soon after, he shared the fol-lowing story:

> I had a really powerful breakthrough with a client yesterday and wanted to share my experience with you. I have been working with a young woman in her late twenties for the past six months. She presented with serious panic attacks. In Toronto she was having trouble making new friends, was not pursuing her passion of the arts, writing, acting, or singing, and was too anxious to even pick up the telephone to inquire about volunteer work.
>
> I had introduced her to CBT, exposure therapy, and a mindfulness practice, but I found that we kept getting stuck. Some weeks her anxiety improved, and other weeks she would regress and have multiple panic attacks. It was driving her husband bonkers.

Three weeks ago, when I came back from Maui, I introduced her to time perspectives, and we had an interesting discussion about it. For homework, I suggested that she watch Dr. Zimbardo's and John Boyd's lectures at their website [www.thetimeparadox.com], and assess her time perspective using the ZTPI [Zimbardo Time Perspective Inventory]. Yesterday, when I saw her for the first time in a few weeks, she shared that her panic attacks have gone away. Pleased, I asked her why she thought this had happened.

She explained that her perspective had shifted as a result of simply becoming aware of the time paradox she was in. Whereas CBT helped her identify her automatic thoughts, mindfulness supported her in becoming more present with difficult physical and emotional sensations, and helped her respond to them instead of simply reacting to them. When TPT was added as a therapeutic modality, it helped her to identify when she was having "in the moment" past negative experiences. Being able to label them in this way was one more tool that helped her come back into the moment and refocus on the future. This new skill helped improve her mood and also gave her a feeling of more agency. Not only did she start identifying her strengths and competencies, but she also started scheduling them into her daily routine and activities. As for her future positive, I asked her the crystal ball question: "Let's say that we had a crystal ball and you were able to look into the future a year from now, what would you see?" It generated an interesting discussion about wanting to have a job and have more friends and a better relationship with her husband . . .

Over the past few years since we have been using time perspective therapy in our practice, we have begun to see other therapists, like Larry Borins, put it into practice with their own clients. Through their good results and ours, we are encouraged that TPT will gain acceptance by the psychological community at large, truly becoming the next evolutionary step after cognitive behavioral therapy. We want to emphasize here that all of our thinking and treatment applications, though novel in one sense, are solidly grounded both in cognitive science as well as in proven social reinforcement theory.

Psychology today is at a turning point. The mental illness and traditional doctor-patient models established by Sigmund Freud in the nineteenth century have made up the core theoretical basis and delivery system for mental health services for more than one hundred years. Yet despite undeniable successes, some of these methods—particularly in the treatment of PTSD—are simply not working.

If we want to extend psychology's reach to the growing number of people currently suffering from mental distress, we will seriously need to consider new, effective, and more user-friendly ways to help those in need. As this book makes clear, TPT has proven highly effective in the treatment of PTSD. But we encourage the study and exploration of other psychotherapeutic uses for this modality: prison rehabilitation, anger management, industrial and organizational development, family therapy, cross-cultural psychology, child psychology, and sports psychology are just a few of the possible applications of TPT.

Time perspective therapy is in its infancy, but it heralds a paradigm shift in the field of psychology, leaving the narrow, medical metaphor of mental illness and working in the human context of personal time perspectives to achieve practical solutions and improved functioning. In a very real way, this means replacing our field's collective past negatives with more positive conceptions, and working together for a brighter future for our clients, for their families, and for ourselves as treatment providers.

glossary

Balanced time perspective   Having free emotional and mental mobility between thoughts of the past, present, and future; the optimum psychological state. See **Time perspective(s).**

Brighter future   A future time perspective free of the emotional and mental suffering from untreated PTSD; the goal of time perspective therapy. It is the hope that the future will be better than the past.

Cognitive behavioral therapy (CBT)   A systematic, goal-oriented psychotherapeutic approach merging two established talk therapies: cognitive therapy (aimed at changing unconstructive emotional responses and dysfunctional thinking) and behavioral therapy (reinforcing wanted behaviors and eliminating undesired behaviors).

Future   See **Time perspective(s).**

Past negative   See **Time perspective(s).**

Past positive   See **Time perspective(s).**

Post-traumatic stress disorder (PTSD)   A severe anxiety disorder that can develop after exposure to a physically or psychologically traumatic event. This event may involve the threat of death to oneself or to someone else, or a threat to one's own or someone else's physical, sexual, or psychological integrity, overwhelming the individual's ability to cope. As an effect of psychological trauma, PTSD is less frequent and more enduring than the more commonly seen acute stress disorder.

Diagnostic symptoms for PTSD include reexperiencing the original trauma(s) through flashbacks, recurrent thoughts, or nightmares; avoidance of stimuli associated with the trauma; and increased arousal, such as difficulty falling or staying asleep, anger, hyper-vigilance, and emotional overreactivity. Formal diagnostic criteria (both the fourth edition of the *Diagnostic and Statistical Manual of Mental Disorders* and the International Classification of Diseases, ninth edition) require that the symptoms last more than one month and cause significant impairment in social, occupational, or other important areas of functioning.

Present hedonism   See **Time perspective(s).**

Present fatalism   See **Time perspective(s).**

Suicidal and homicidal ideations with or without plan(s)
Thoughts of taking one's own life or the life of another, either including thoughts of how to proceed (such as by the use of a weapon, vehicle, drugs, and so on) or without such a thought (for example, wishing one would simply die).

Symptom minimizer   An individual suffering from depression, anxiety, trauma, and related symptoms (such as avoidance, isolation, irritability, increased anger, suicidal thoughts, and so on) who downplays the severity of his or her symptoms. Repression, denial, and displacement are the favorite coping strategies.

Temporal Theory (TT)   The theory that one's time perspective(s) affect one's view of one's life and the choices one makes. Temporal Theory, as posited by Philip Zimbardo, stresses the importance of one's individual time perspective and its impact on one's sense of mental distress or well-being. Being stuck in one or two negative time perspectives of the six possible time perspectives seems to be a critical factor in emotional distress; a balanced time perspective is the cornerstone of emotional well-being.

Time Paradox   The idea that one can be "stuck" in a particular time perspective, such as the past, even though time is considered linear and progressive. According to Philip Zimbardo, there are two Time Paradoxes. First, our attitudes toward time have profound impacts on our lives and our world, yet we seldom recognize this. Second, moderate attitudes toward the past, the present, and the future are indicative of health; extreme attitudes are indicative of biases that lead predictably to unhealthy patterns of living.

Time perspective(s) (TP)   The psychological term for the process by which each of us sorts out our personal experiences into temporal categories. Each of the three primary subjective time zones—past, present, and future—is divided into two parts, yielding six main time perspectives:

- **Past positive (PP)** A positive focus on the memories of the good old days, family, and tradition. Balancing past positive and future positive orientations creates the following:

  - **Expanded or holistic present** A focus on the here and now, a belief that all things are connected.

- **Past negative (PN)** A negative focus that recalls past abuse, failures, and regrets over missed opportunities.
- **Present hedonism (PH)** A focus on pleasure, risk taking, and sensation seeking. Also of note is

  - **Selected present hedonism (SPH)** A focus on a moderate amount of pleasure and sensation seeking; frequently as a reward for accomplishments

- **Present fatalism (PF)** A focus on not taking control of situations that is driven by a belief that life is fated to play out in a certain way, no matter what one does.
- **Future (F)** A focus on working for goals, meeting deadlines, and achieving objectives. In the development of time perspective therapy, the future time perspective was split into

- **Future positive** A focus on a brighter future
- **Future negative** A focus on a fatalistic future

- **Transcendental future** A focus that places spiritual life after the death of the body above all else (religious); a focus that places the long-term future of many generations, or the life of the planet, above all else (secular).

Time perspective therapy (TPT)   The implementation of Zimbardo's Temporal Theory into clinical practice, using a context of time perspectives; an evolution of cognitive behavioral therapy. Developed by Richard and Rosemary Sword in 2008–2009, it has been used successfully to treat PTSD, depression, and anxiety. It has been employed in the field with disaster workers, in hospitals with cardiac patients, and in cardiac rehabilitation.

Transcendental future   See **Time perspective(s).**

resources

○ temporal theory and the time paradox

"Are You Future Focused or Present Focused? The Marshmallow Experiment."
http://sivers.org/time

Derek Sivers writes about the Time Paradox and time perspectives in
an interesting take on Temporal Theory, and even explains how Ghana
almost won the 2006 World Cup.

"Make Time Work for You." www.5min.com/Video/Make-Time-Work-For-
You-with-Philip-Zimbardo-499991408

In this five-minute video, Philip Zimbardo describes the classic Marshmallow Experiment by Stanford psychologist Walter Mischel, and discusses how the results of the study can be attributed to each child's time
perspective.

"Philip Zimbardo Prescribes a Healthy Take on Time." www.ted.com/talks/
philip_zimbardo_prescribes_a_healthy_take_on_time.html

Phil details how our choices play into our time perspective and, consequently, into our everyday life. He explains that happiness and success are
rooted in a trait most of us disregard: the way we orient toward the past,
present, and future.

"Professor Philip Zimbardo on the Secret Powers of Time." www.intelligence
squared.com/talks/professor-philip-zimbardo-on-the-secret-powers-of-
time

In a forty-five-minute lecture at London's Royal Society of Arts, Phil conveys that most people tend to be past, present, or future oriented, and that this makes a big difference in terms of their behavioral style, decision making, and outlook on life. His talk touches on the need for the U.S. education system to start to use virtual worlds in the classroom, on how an Italian political party is trying to divide Italy into North and South due to what amounts to regional differences in their time orientation, and on how cultural and religious differences also affect one's outlook on time.

"The Secret Powers of Time." www.thersa.org/events/video/animate/rsa-animate-the-secret-powers-of-time

This ten-minute video was created from a 2010 lecture that Phil gave at London's Royal Society of Arts (RSA). It is a detailed summary of the six time orientations brought to life through a remarkably creative RSA animation. It has been viewed on YouTube by more than 2.5 million people worldwide.

"Time from A to Z—Zimbardo, That Is." http://blogs.law.harvard.edu/yulelog/2010/05/22/time-from-a-to-z-zimbardo-that-is/

This is a further look at Phil's lecture to the Commonwealth Club and how the Time Paradox explains the current financial crisis, overfishing, and even drug use.

"The Time Paradox." http://fora.tv/2008/11/12/Philip_Zimbardo_The_Time_Paradox

Phil gives a lecture about punctuality, chronic lateness, the psychology of time, and the subprime crisis to the Commonwealth Club in San Francisco. He discusses how our internal time perspective determines our thoughts, feelings, and actions, and can even influence national destinies.

"The Time Paradox." www.marieclaire.com/career-money/jobs/time-paradox-zimbardo

In this interview with *Marie Claire* magazine, Phil talks about time perspectives in layman's terms and gives advice about how to employ them in everyday life.

The Time Paradox: The New Psychology of Time That Will Change Your Life, Philip Zimbardo and John Boyd (New York: Free Press, 2008).

Read about the new psychology of time that is the basis for time perspective therapy. This book includes the Zimbardo Time Perspective Inventory (ZTPI) and scoring instructions.

The Time Paradox Web site: www.thetimeparadox.com

Phil's Web site includes recent news, blogs, and the ZTPI online.

"The Time Paradox with Phil Zimbardo." www.insidepersonalgrowth.com/ 2010/08/podcasts/podcast-212-the-time-paradox-with-philip-zimbardo

In this 2010 podcast with host L. Greg Voisen, Phil talks about how our internal perception of time dictates who we are and how we see the world — specifically, how we view death and how it determines how we live our lives.

Zimbardo Time Perspective Inventory (ZTPI). www.thetimeparadox.com

Take the ZTPI online.

o time perspective therapy

The Time Cure Web sites: http://timecure.com and http://lifehut.com

Richard and Rosemary Sword's Web sites are a rich source of information and soothing videos for use in conjunction with time perspective therapy.

o relaxation and breathing

The River of Time. http://lifehut.com/rivervid.html

This soothing video leads you through a powerful yet relaxing experience, offering and reinforcing the opportunity to let go of past negatives, enjoy the present, and embrace a positive future. Watch it daily for maximum effect. This video includes breathing exercises.

o post-traumatic stress disorder

American Psychological Association, Help Center. www.apa.org/helpcenter/ wellness/index.aspx

Search for articles on dealing with traumatic stress; get help finding psychological assistance.

County of San Mateo Network of Care for Service Members, Veterans, & Their Families, Library. www.sanmateo.networkofcare.org/veterans/ library/index.cfm

This library "contains more than 35,000 articles, fact sheets and reports produced by the leading experts and organizations in the health field. Articles provide straightforward explanations and guidance on combat-related stress, traumatic brain injury (TBI), depression, and substance use issues. You'll also find helpful, fresh information on health conditions, medications, medical tests and procedures, and everyday health and wellness issues."

"Guide on PTSD," Vietnam Veterans of America. www.vva.org/benefits/ptsd .htm

This guide aims to assist veterans and their survivors in presenting claims for benefits based on exposure to psychologically traumatic events during military service resulting in PTSD.

"A Guide to Post-Traumatic Stress Disorder" (plus resources). www.remilitary .com/article-ptsd.html

This is a guide to online PTSD facts, symptoms, support, and more.

Military Veterans PTSD Reference Manual. www.ptsdmanual.com

This frequently updated manual includes valuable information about PTSD, traditional and nontraditional treatment, as well as how to file service-connected PTSD disability claims.

Posttraumatic Stress Disorder, Joel Kupersmith.

This is a brochure series on PTSD by Joel Kupersmith, chief research and development officer for the Department of Veterans Affairs. Contact R&D Communications (12)103 South Gay Street, Ste. 517, Baltimore, MD 21202; call 410-962-1800, ext. 223; or e-mail research.publications@va.gov.

"Post-Traumatic Stress Disorder." www.apa.org/topics/ptsd/index.aspx

The American Psychological Association Web site contains information, options for finding help, articles, and research.

"Posttraumatic Stress Disorder (PTSD)," National Institute of Mental Health.

This booklet on PTSD explains what it is, treatment options, and how to get help. Contact National Institute of Mental Health (NIMH), Science

Writing, Press, and Dissemination Branch, 6001 Executive Boulevard, Rm. 8184, MSC 9663, Bethesda,MD208929663; call 866-615-6464(toll free); or e-mail nimhinfo@nih.gov.

PTSD Alliance. www.ptsdalliance.org/home2.html

This Web site contains resources and information concerning PTSD, drug rehab, and more.

"Soldiers Learn to Deal with PTSD," ABC News Nightline report (December 16, 2004). http://abcnews.go.com/Nightline/story?id=334445&page=1#.TujvJ1ajOuI

This is an ABC News special report on returning active duty military personnel learning to cope with PTSD.

o stress, depression, and anxiety

National Institute of Mental Health.

Download or send for any of the following booklets and fact sheets. Contact National Institute of Mental Health, Science Writing, Press, and Dissemination Branch, 6001 Executive Boulevard, Rm. 8184, MSC 9663, Bethesda, MD 20892-9663; call 866-615-6464 (toll free); e-mail nimhinfo@nih.gov; or visit www.nlm.nih.gov/.

- "Generalized Anxiety Disorder (GAD): When Worry Gets Out of Control" explains the signs, symptoms, and treatment of generalized anxiety disorder.
- "Panic Disorder: When Fear Overwhelms" explains the signs, symptoms, and treatment of panic disorder.
- "Anxiety Disorders in Children and Adolescents" describes the development in our understanding of how anxiety disorders affect children and adolescents and the direction of future research.
- "Depression" is a detailed booklet that describes depression symptoms, causes, and treatments, with information on getting help and coping.
- "Women and Depression: Discovering New Hope" describes the symptoms and treatment of and factors contributing to depression that are unique to women.

- "Depression in Children and Adolescents" describes the development in our understanding of how depression affects children and adolescents and the direction of future research.

Yahoo Anxiety Center. http://health.yahoo.net/channel/panic-disorders.html

This Web site is a gateway to information and resources on anxiety.

how TPT compares with other approaches

Since 1980 the clinical field has been searching for the best approach to treat post-traumatic stress disorder. Over the past thirty years, numerous theories and therapies have emerged into the practice and have been shown to help. The following is a comparison of the effectiveness of three of these therapeutic modalities: time perspective therapy, cognitive behavioral therapy, and prolonged exposure therapy.

o cognitive behavioral therapy

Cognitive behavioral therapy (CBT) is a talk therapy that aims to solve problems concerning dysfunctional emotions, behaviors, and cognitions through a goal-oriented, systematic procedure in the present. It is a widely used and accepted form of treatment for numerous psychiatric disorders (for example, anxiety, mood, insomnia, and depression disorders), including PTSD.

In the limited controlled trials published, CBT has been shown to be quite successful in comparison to its counterparts. A recent meta-analysis (combined results of several studies) of CBT for all anxiety disorders found that CBT was more effective than no treatment or "expectancy control" conditions (pill placebo, attentional placebo, or nonspecific therapy) across all anxiety disorders.[1] However, it is to be expected that any intervention will have more significant results in comparison to a placebo.

For clients diagnosed with PTSD, a meta-analysis of CBT results found that by post-treatment follow-up, 67 percent of clients who completed treatment no longer met criteria for PTSD, and 56 percent of clients who entered treatment (that is, including dropouts) no longer met criteria for PTSD. CBT was found to be more effective than the wait-list control or supportive therapy.[2] Sherman examined seventeen controlled trials in a meta-analysis to find that 43 percent of CBT clients improved and no longer met the criteria for PTSD post-treatment.[3] Nevertheless, one of the largest faults of the psychology community is the lack of longitudinal research to understand the long-term effectiveness of these treatments.

Although most therapies are shown to be successful in the short term, long-term results still seem to be unknown, and few CBT studies follow up beyond a two-year period.[4] However, one study found that CBT cannot sustain the post-treatment outcomes. Durham et al. followed the long-term effects of CBT on anxiety disorders.[5] It was found that the differences between the CBT and non-CBT groups were obvious immediately after treatment; however, they were much smaller over time, indicating an erosion of the positive effects. Two to fourteen years after receiving CBT treatment, 34 percent of clients treated for generalized anxiety disorder (GAD) and 55 percent of clients treated for PTSD met the *Diagnostic and Statistical Manual of Mental Disorders* (fourth edition) criteria for their treated disorder. In addition, 52 percent of the GAD and 74 percent of the PTSD clients were diagnosed with comorbid psychiatric disorders (adding one or more disorders; for example, PTSD plus addiction), with almost two-thirds requesting additional treatment during the follow-up. The therapy is a fast fix for current problems, not addressing or preparing the client for long-term problems associated with PTSD.

○ prolonged exposure therapy

Prolonged exposure therapy (PE) is a form of CBT. It uses a method called "in vivo exposure" that seeks to desensitize the client to the client's triggers, causing the client to reexperience the traumatic event by remembering and engaging with the trauma repeatedly rather than avoiding it. This has not been shown to solve the underlying issues—the traumatic experiences at the root of the "psychiatric disorder"—nor does it prepare the client for possible relapses and flashbacks.

○ comparisons

In contrast to PE and CBT, time perspective therapy (TPT) addresses the whole picture by acknowledging the past negative trauma, understanding how it affects one's present hedonism and fatalism, then working toward identifying and making plans for achievable goals to empower the client and create a future positive time perspective. By readjusting and balancing clients' time perspective, TPT helps clients gain vital tools that they can implement in their daily lives for both the short term and the long term.

CBT had significantly lower dropout rates (9 percent) than pharmacotherapy (involving prescription medication) (25 percent), suggesting it was better tolerated.[6] Although there is no established pharmacotherapy for PTSD, studies have shown that there are multiple medications (for example, amitriptyline, nefazodone, and anticonvulsant carbamazepine)[7] that seem to be successful in reducing symptoms. Previous research indicates that an estimated 70 percent of clients benefit from some form of pharmacotherapy.[8]

Unlike TPT, CBT has extensive recommended prerequisites for the client for the therapy to be successful. In *Acute Stress Disorder: A Handbook of Theory, Assessment, and Treatment,* Bryant and Harvey list the situations in which an intervention may be inappropriate for a client suffering from PTSD. In other words, CBT may not be effective if the client is experiencing any of the following: excessive avoidance; dissociation; anger; grief; extreme anxiety; catastrophic beliefs; prior trauma; comorbidity; substance abuse; depression and suicide risk; poor motivation; ongoing stressors; cultural issues; failure to distinguish between appropriate versus inappropriate avoidance (for instance, "appropriate avoidance" means avoiding harmful or life-threatening situations, and "inappropriate avoidance" may mean avoiding family gatherings or paying taxes); or being one of multiple survivors of the same trauma (for instance, numerous people injured in a natural disaster or transportation accident).[9] It should be noted that this information is endorsed and published on the National Center for PTSD Web site.[10] In a meta-analysis by Bradley and colleagues,[11] researchers noted that most studies excluded participants due to psychosis (85 percent), organic disorders (77 percent), alcohol or drug abuse or dependence (62 percent), unspecified concerns of serious comorbidity (62 percent), and suicidality (46 percent). The list of constraints for CBT limits both therapists and clients in their ability to be successful.

In comparison, TPT's post-treatment outcomes are proven in our pilot study results as well as client follow-up, indicating promise that it can be a long-lasting solution. TPT can be used to treat PTSD and, we believe, the majority of the listed disqualifying criteria for CBT as well, with the exception of psychosis and organic disorders. TPT pilot study results (see Appendix B) indicate improvements between pre- and post-treatment over the three-and-a-half-year pilot study. Overall, 87 percent of clients reported decreased trauma and PTSD symptoms; astonishingly, 100 percent decreased their depression rating. These positive results indicate that TPT is proving to be an effective and long-lasting treatment for PTSD.

appendix B

clinical trial: TPT pilot study research data

In June 2009 the Z Team set up and executed a clinical trial to test the significance of time perspective therapy (TPT) to determine if TPT was helping clients. Figure A.1 shows the results of this study.

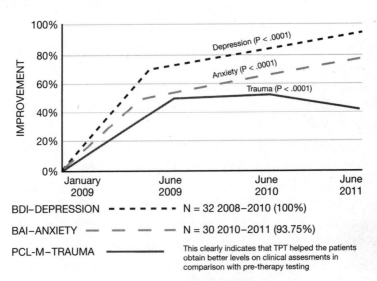

Figure B.1   TPT Pilot Study Results, 2008–2011

o method

This is an ongoing clinical trial, in which data are collected annually in June. The present study details results from June 2009, when the trial started, until June 2011, the last data collection. The participants and procedure are detailed in the following subsections.

participants

Variables Key

m—The mean or the mathematical average of all the numbers.

n—The number of participants or sample size in a research study.

p—Probability; the probability of obtaining a test statistic at least as extreme as the one that was actually observed; also provides a quantitative description of the chance that something will happen. The probability scale is from 0 to 1; a rare event has a probability close to 0, and a very common event has a probability close to 1.

r—A statistical technique that measures whether and how strongly pairs of variables relate; a correlation coefficient. The most widely used type of correlation coefficient is *Pearson r*.

SD—standard deviation; indicates variation of the numbers or how spread out the numbers are.

t—The statistical notation for a t-test. A t-test is used to evaluate the differences between two groups using their means.

Our sample was composed of thirty male veterans of mixed ethnicities; ages ($m = 64.77$, $SD = 10.35$); marital status; and military combat history. All had been in the military during one U.S. war (World War II, Korean War, Vietnam War, Gulf War, and Iraq War; the war in Afghanistan is not represented because no client currently receiving therapy in the clinic has served in that country). All live in Maui and are clients of the Swords. In 2011 two veterans dropped out (for the purpose of this study, their reports were not included).

procedure

Prior to starting the TPT program, all clients took an intact clinical assessment comprising at least three of the following: the Burns Anxiety Inventory (BAI), Burns Depression Checklist (BDC), Post-trauma Diagnostic Scale (PDS), Post-trauma Checklist for military (PCL-M), Trauma Symptom Inventory (TSI), Hamilton Anxiety Rating Scale (HARS), and Beck Depression Inventory II (BDI-II). The time of intake determined which tests they were given. Because the tests had changed over the years, during this trial researchers chose to employ the more recently used tests to ensure that all clients from this point forward would have the same baseline clinical assessment tests (that is, the BAI, BDC, and PCL-M), in addition to the Zimbardo Time Perspective Inventory (ZTPI), to understand each client's perception of time. To be able to compare them to the results of previous pre-assessments, all scores were converted to the standard Likert scale. (Note: The Likert scale is a rating device that employs questionnaires specifying levels of agreement or disagreement.)

There were four waves of this longitudinal clinical trial, and clients were measured every June in Maui: Time 0 — pre-test (scores before January 2009, prior to receiving therapy, and with no ZTPI); Time 1 — June 2009; Time 2 — June 2010; and Time 3 — June 2011. The average number of TPT sessions is broken down as follows: Time 1, $m = 44.00$, $SD = 31.12$; Time 2, $m = 8.67$, $SD = 6.92$; and Time 3, $m = 6.03$, $SD = 6.35$, with an overall average of $m = 58.70$, $SD = 39.11$. All thirty clients were receiving TPT at Time 1. At Time 2 (average TPT sessions, $m = 11.30$, $SD = 5.72$), only twenty-three clients were actively receiving therapy. At Time 3 (average TPT sessions, $m = 9.53$, $SD = 5.51$), nineteen clients were still enrolled in TPT, with an overall clinical trial average of $m = 7.35$, $SD = 6.83$. Due to the severity of PTSD suffered by these nineteen PTSD vets, they have chosen to continue TPT.[1]

o results and discussion

There was a significant difference between pre- and post-data PTSD ($t = 4.19, p = .001$), depression ($t = 7.08, p < .0001$), and anxiety ($t = 5.29, p < .0001$) levels. This clearly indicates that something helped the clients obtain better levels on the clinical assessments in comparison to pre-TPT testing.

Present hedonism is negatively associated with the number of TPT sessions the clients attended ($r = -.43, p = .02$). The more TPT sessions the client had attended, the less likely he was to "live in the present by seeking pleasure activities."

Future orientation is negatively associated with post-data PTSD levels ($r = -.36, p = .04$). The stronger the client's conception or grasp of his future, the lower the levels of PTSD the client had in the present.

central role of present fatalism and a past negative orientation

Present fatalism is negatively associated with age ($r = -.45, p = .01$). The older the client, the more the client understands that his present is within his control.

Present fatalism is positively associated with pre-data PTSD levels ($r = -.56, p = .013$). The more the client understands that his present is in his control and not part of uncontrollable fate, the lower his level of PTSD when he *entered* the program.

Present fatalism is positively associated with post-data anxiety levels ($r = .54, p = .002$). The more the client feels as though his present is out of his control and is a part of an uncontrollable fate, the more anxiety the client has *now*.

Present fatalism is positively associated with post-data depression levels ($r = .70, p < .000$). The more the client feels as though his present is out of his control and is a part of an uncontrollable fate, the higher the reported level of depression.

Present fatalism is positively associated with post-data PTSD levels ($r = .36, p = .046$). The more the client feels as though his present is out of his control and is a part of an uncontrollable fate, the higher the level of PTSD.

A past negative orientation was found to be positively associated with post-data PTSD, depression, and anxiety levels ($r = .47, p = .006$). This indicates that the more past negative the client's outlook is now, in the present, the higher his levels of PTSD, depression, and anxiety.

future testing

The authors hope to continue this project annually, and have changed the intact clinical assessments to permanently include the ZTPI for a stable baseline. The goal is to administer the tests each summer over a number of years to collect systematic longitudinal data of clients' progress. This also allows for monitoring any setbacks, such as higher past negative, present fatalism, and future negative scores, or lower past positive, present hedonism, and future positive scores, in comparison to earlier results.

pro-social behavior

Following their military career, many veterans suffering from PTSD seek to recreate their intense pro-social military experiences through their involvement with the Veterans Administration and nongovernment (veterans') organizations. Others avoid it altogether, as an expression of their symptoms.[2]

Social avoidance by PTSD vets is a common symptom of their PTSD. Conversely, social acceptance and the encouragement of peers whom they respect and with whom they identify are the solutions. Group therapy has been shown to be helpful in reducing isolation and social stigma.[3] Previous studies in which clients have shown signs of withdrawal, traumatic stress symptoms, or both have shown improvements (that is, enhanced relationships with family and medical personnel, improved symptom control, fewer mood disturbances, and an increase in social support) when placed in this therapy method.

We've found it best to work first with the PTSD vets individually, in a client education mode wherein they identify, understand, and balance their time perspective. The next step is to introduce them through socialization to other PTSD vets, who understand the value of a future positive time perspective. The outcome is momentum toward a positively reinforced and energized future time perspective.

A sense of belonging and community is a central part of reducing negative, violent, and self-destructive coping responses to adversity and increasing pro-social civic engagement.[4] Identifying, making sense out of, and responding to injustice are also important. According to research by DuRant et al. and Grover,[5] a sense of purpose and an avenue of action in response to injustice are important factors in promoting social resilience and reducing psychological symptoms and engagement in violent behaviors among youth.

In the military, more experienced GIs show less experienced ones the ropes. The same is true of veterans. Due to the intensity of their social network, it is much easier for PTSD vets to trust other PTSD vets who have achieved success using this method.[6]

Pro-social attitudes and behaviors evolve from actual pro-social involvement, perceived rewards from involvement, attachment to others, and belief in pro-social values, according to DaSilva and colleagues.[7] For PTSD vets, this positive reinforcement becomes self-reinforcing when activated and operational. The PTSD vets who have found a brighter future (and improved their present and thoughts of their past) promote this approach for fellow PTSD vets. PTSD vets appear to be happiest when they are establishing a brighter future for themselves and assisting their fellow vets to follow them to that brighter future.

For these reasons, the social aspects of the TPT model for PTSD vets should not be ignored—rather they should certainly be used because the social influence of peers on the PTSD vets' behavior is extremely powerful.[8] They easily recall times when their lives depended on trusting their fellow GIs, now veterans, who were more experienced and knew how to stay alive. This intense and powerful social alliance has proven to be one of the most useful tools in the implementation of a successful TPT program. Initial individual therapy is complemented with group therapy as the individuals start to move toward a balanced time perspective and can then share positive images and strategies in a supportive group structure.[9]

appendix C

client psychological test scores

The following test scores correspond to the clients whose stories are told in Part Two. Testing reflects their scores before time perspective therapy (pre-TPT) and after time perspective therapy (post-TPT).

Abbreviations used are as follows:

BAI: Burns Anxiety Inventory

BDC: Burns Depression Checklist

BDI-II: Beck Depression Inventory II

F: Future

HARS: Hamilton Anxiety Rating Scale

N/A: Not applicable (client did not take test; usually in regard to pre-TPT Zimbardo Time Perspective Inventory)

PCL-C: Post-trauma Checklist for civilians

PCL-M: Post-trauma Checklist for military

PDS: Post-trauma Diagnostic Scale

PF = Present fatalism

PH = Present hedonism

PN = Past negative

PP = Past positive

SPH: Selected present hedonism

TSI: Trauma Symptom Inventory

ZTPI: Zimbardo Time Perspective Inventory

In each of the following client psychological test results sections, the client's highest ZTPI score (if one particular time perspective stood out above others on the ZTPI graph), two highest scores (the norm — usually two time perspectives are higher than the others), or three highest scores are listed, as these were the client's predominant time perspectives at the time the test was taken.

o chapter 4: war veterans, PTSD, and time perspective therapy

aki's (world war II) pre- and post-TPT psychological test results

Pre-TPT	Post-TPT
HARS — 52 (severe)	BAI — 12 (mild)
BDI-II — 46 (severe)	BDC — 7 (normal but unhappy)
TSI — 74 (severe)	PDS — 18 (moderate)
ZTPI — N/A	ZTPI — F/PP

Aki's Therapy Sessions:

Total therapy visits: 66

Total TPT visits: 8

Group sessions: 100+

mike's (korean war) pre- and post-TPT psychological test results

Pre-TPT	Post-TPT
HARS — 54 (severe)	BAI — 8 (borderline)
BDI-II — 34 (severe)	BDC — 1 (none)
TSI — 95 (severe)	PCL-M — 28 (minimal to none)
ZTPI — N/A	ZTPI — PP/F

Mike's Therapy Sessions:

Total therapy visits: 95

Total TPT visits: 19

Group sessions: 36

ed's (vietnam war) pre- and post-TPT psychological test results

Pre-TPT	Post-TPT
BAI — 61 (extreme/panic)[1]	BAI — 27 (moderate)
BDC — 37 (severe)	BDC — 3 (minimal to none)
PDS — 47 (severe)	PDS — 9 (mild)
ZTPI — N/A	ZTPI — PN/SPH

Ed's Therapy Sessions:

Total therapy visits: 15
Total TPT visits: 6
Group sessions: 19

sean's (gulf war) pre- and post-TPT psychological test results

Pre-TPT	Post-TPT
HARS — 45 (severe)	BAI — 24 (moderate)
BDI-II — 39 (severe)	BDC — 16 (borderline to mild)
TSI — 130 (severe)	PDS — 34 (moderate to severe)
ZTPI — N/A	ZTPI — F/SPH

Sean's Therapy Sessions:

Total therapy visits: 59
Total TPT visits: 17
Group sessions: 12

everest's (iraq war) pre- and post-TPT psychological test results

Pre-TPT	Post-TPT
HARS — 55 (severe)	BAI — 4 (minimal to none)
BDI-II — 47 (severe)	BDC — 4 (minimal to none)
TSI — 185 (severe)	PDS — 3 (normal)
ZTPI — N/A	ZTPI — N/A

Everest's Therapy Sessions:

Total therapy visits: 13
Total TPT visits: 9
Group sessions: 7

○ chapter 5: everyday trauma, PTSD, and time perspective therapy

mary's pre- and post-tpt psychological test results

Pre-TPT	Post-TPT
BAI—48 (severe)	BAI—19 (mild)
BDC—42 (severe)	BDC—15 (borderline to mild)
PCL-C—63 (severe)	PCL-C—30 (borderline to mild)
ZTPI—PN/PF	ZTPI—PP/F

Mary's Therapy Sessions:

Total TPT visits: 14

jenny's pre- and post-TPT psychological test results

Pre-TPT	Post-TPT
BAI—83 (extreme/panic)	BAI—14 (mild)
BDC—31 (severe)	BDC—6 (normal but unhappy)
PCL-C—68 (severe)	PCL-C—26 (minimal)
ZTPI—PN/PF	ZTPI—PP/PH/F

Jenny's Therapy Sessions:

Total TPT visits: 10

sherman's pre- and post-TPT psychological test results

Pre-TPT	Post-TPT
BAI — 64 (extreme/panic)	BAI — 53 (severe)
BDC — 24 (moderate)	BDC — 19 (mild to moderate)
PDS — 35 (severe)	PCL-C — 37 (moderate)
ZTPI — PN/F	ZTPI — F/SPH

Sherman's Therapy Sessions:

Total therapy visits: 32

Total TPT visits: 14

randall's pre- and post-TPT psychological test results

Pre-TPT (estimated)[2]	Post-TPT
BAI — severe	BAI — 27 (moderate)
BDC — severe	BDC – 22 (moderate)
PDS — extreme	PCL-C — 57 (moderate to severe)
ZTPI — N/A	ZTPI — F/PF

Randall's Therapy Sessions:

Total therapy visits: 132

Total TPT visits: 26

❍ chapter 6: women, PTSD, and time perspective therapy

iris's pre- and post-TPT psychological test results

Pre-TPT	Post-TPT
BAI — 45 (severe)	BAI — 21 (low moderate)
BDC — 40 (severe)	BDC — 17 (borderline to mild)
PCL-C — 53 (severe)	PCL-C — 18 (borderline to mild)
ZTPI — PN/PH	ZTPI — SPH/PP/F

Iris's Therapy Sessions:

Total TPT visits: 7

eve's pre- and post-TPT psychological test results

Pre–TPT	Post-TPT
BAI—62 (extreme) BDC—32 (severe) PCL-C—73 (extreme) ZTPI—PN/PF	BAI—29 (moderate) BDC—19 (borderline to mild) PCL-C—24 (mild) ZTPI—PP/SPH

Eve's Therapy Sessions:

Total TPT visits: 10

faith's pre- and post-TPT psychological test results

Pre-TPT	Post-TPT
BAI—69 (extreme) BDC—5 (severe) PCL-C—55 (severe) ZTPI—PN/PF	BAI—19 (mild) BDC—10 (normal but unhappy) PCL-C—22 (borderline to mild) ZTPI—PP/F

Faith's Therapy Sessions:

Total TPT visits: 13

keiko's pre- and post-TPT psychological test results

Pre-TPT	Post-TPT
BAI—78 (extreme) BDC—35 (severe) PCL-C—60 (severe) ZTPI—PN/PF	BAI—4 (minimal to none) BDC—4 (minimal to none) PCL-C—18 (borderline to mild) ZTPI—PP/SPH

Keiko's Therapy Sessions:

Total TPT visits: 8

betty's pre- and post-TPT psychological test results

Pre-TPT	Post-TPT
BAI—31 (moderate to severe)	BAI—15 (mild)
BDC—41 (severe)	BDC—12 (borderline to mild)
PCL-C—58 (severe)	PCL-C—34 (borderline to mild)
ZTPI—PN/PF	ZTPI—PP/SPH/F

Betty's Therapy Sessions:

Total TPT visits: 10

grace's pre- and post-TPT psychological test results

Pre-TPT	Post-TPT
BAI—89 (extreme)	BAI—23 (low moderate)
BDC—45 (extreme)	BDC—14 (mild)
PCL-C—83 (extreme)	PCL-C—35 (low moderate)
ZTPI—PN/PF	ZTPI—PP/SPH

Grace's Therapy Sessions:

Total TPT visits: 32

acknowledgments

In the course of the last few years, we have created an outstanding research and clinical team of young and more mature colleagues dubbed the Z Team. They work collaboratively and tirelessly pro bono in collecting and analyzing data that continually assess treatment effectiveness, as well as conducting literature searches. We'd like to thank Sarah Brunskill, MA; Mel Borins, MD; Ryan Daley; Tiffany Dawson, MS; Brian Denney; Nikita Duncan; Kathy Fernandez; Anthony Ferreras, MS; Marjan Haghighatgoo, MA; Harold Hall, PhD; Robert Hollis, PhD; Paul Janes-Brown; Robert Masters; Moira Ogata; Martha Sword Ray, MEd; Judith Rocap, PhD; Elizabeth Sword; and Michael Yannell. Special thanks to Noah Milich for illustrations and graphs.

We'd like to thank the following organizations for their assistance in the development and promotion of time perspective therapy: the 100th Battalion and 442nd Regimental Combat Team; Disabled American Veterans—Maui; Vietnam Veterans and Korean War Veterans of Maui; the Hawaii Psychological Association; Roger Weiss, PhD; and the Hawaii Island Psychological Association. We thank the Maui Memorial Medical Center Cardiac Rehabilitation Unit—Integrative Medicine Team; Harold Hall, PhD; and the Pacific Institute for the Study of Conflict and Aggression. We also thank state and federal disaster response teams and the U.S. Department of Defense.

We express our gratitude to the dedicated doctors and staff of the Veterans Administration, especially Maurice Springer, MD; Don Kopf,

PhD; Kathleen MacNamara, PhD; and Rob Torigoe, MD, of the Hawaii VA, as well as Cheryl and Don Beck of the Portland, Oregon, VA.

Many thanks to those veterans who continue to serve their fellow veterans in the trenches: Tamickco Jackson of Maui Veterans Services; John Condello of Oahu Veterans Services; Ipo Messmore of the Maui Vet Center; and Judith Rocap, PsyD, Schofield Barracks–Tripler Army Hospital.

Thanks to Congressman Bob Filner, former chairman of the House VA Committee; Admiral Mike Mullens, former chairman of the Joint Chiefs of Staff; General Douglas Robb, MD, Joint Staff surgeon; and Lieutenant Colonel Tammy Savoie, PhD. Special thanks to Brian Widdowson and congressional aide Lee Hernandez.

Domo arigato to Junichi Suzuki, Rumi Suzuki, Minako Tsuda, and Erica Jones of Universal Television Broadcasting for including time perspective therapy in the documentary film *442: Live with Honor, Die with Dignity.*

Mahalo nui loa to all our clients over the past few years who so willingly participated in time perspective therapy, especially those who consented to share their stories. You are our inspiration and our heroes.

Our heartfelt gratitude and deep appreciation go to Paul Janes Brown for his insight and help in formulating the seeds of this book.

Our sincere thanks must also go out to those few who directly made this book possible, who shared our vision that such a novel approach could be presented in an inviting yet scholarly fashion to the general public as well as to relevant professionals. Our thanks to Marjorie McAneny, Tracy Gallagher, Lesley Iura, Jennifer Wenzel, and Justin Frahm from Wiley Publishers.

But most of all, we are indebted to Naomi Lucks, who magically transformed our original story, case studies, and empirical data into what we have found to be a compelling narrative well beyond what any of us could have done alone or even in our trio. This book is a celebration of her sensitive and caring midwifery for time perspective therapy.

about the authors

Philip Zimbardo is internationally recognized as the "voice and face of contemporary psychology" through his widely viewed PBS TV series, *Discovering Psychology;* his media appearances; his bestselling trade books, including *The Time Paradox: Reconstructing the Past, Enjoying the Present, Mastering the Future* (with John Boyd, Free Press, 2008), and *The Lucifer Effect: Understanding How Good People Turn Evil* (Random House, 2007, paperback, 2008); and his classic research, the Stanford Prison Experiment.

Zimbardo has been a Stanford University professor since 1968 (now emeritus), having taught previously at Yale, NYU, and Columbia University. He also continues to teach at the Naval Post Graduate School in Monterey, California (courses on the psychology of terrorism), and is a professor at the Palo Alto University in Palo Alto, California (teaching social psychology to clinical graduate students). Zimbardo has been president of the American Psychological Association (2002), president of the Western Psychological Association (twice), and chair of the Council of Scientific Society Presidents, and is now chair of the Western Psychological Foundation as well as the director of the Center for Interdisciplinary Policy, Education, and Research on Terrorism.

Zimbardo has been given numerous awards and honors as an educator, researcher, writer, and media contributor, and for service to the profession of psychology. He has been awarded the Vaclav Havel Foundation Prize for his lifetime of research on the human condition. Among his more than four hundred professional publications, including fifty trade books and textbooks, are two of the oldest current textbooks in psychology, *Psychology and Life* (with Richard Gerig, Allyn & Bacon, 2009), in its nineteenth edition, and Core Concepts in Psychology (with Robert L. Johnson and Vivian McCann, Prentice Hall, 2004), now in its seventh edition.

Richard Sword is a private practice clinical psychologist on the island of Maui. A graduate of the University of Florida and Saybrook Institute, San Francisco, he has taught at the University of Florida and the University of Hawaii. His work in behavioral medicine has helped people heal from traumatic events, accidents, physical injuries, depression, anxiety, and addiction. He played a lead role in developing a model for psychology in disaster stress response with the National Disaster Medical System and FEMA. Over the years he has assisted in dozens of plane crashes and ten presidentially declared disasters. He is a member of Maui Memorial Medical Center Cardiac Care Rehabilitation Unit – Integrative Medicine Team.

Sword's major clinical focus has been on treating veterans and civilians suffering from post-traumatic stress disorder. His work with veterans of many wars caused him to search for a more effective treatment of PTSD, and that led him to the development of time perspective therapy.

Sword has made numerous presentations to professionals as well as to laypeople concerning stress management, cardiac rehabilitation, and Zimbardo's Temporal Theory and time perspective therapy.

Rosemary Sword is a counselor and time perspective therapist in private practice on the island of Maui. As part of her Hawaiian heritage, she was schooled in the Hawaiian psychology based on forgiveness known as *ho'oponopono* (literally "to make right"). She has practiced this art form for over two decades. In recent years, along with her husband, Rick, she developed time perspective therapy.

endnotes

introduction

1. Zimbardo, P., & Boyd, J. (2008). *The Time Paradox: The new psychology of time that will change your life.* New York: Free Press.

chapter 1

1. McNally, R. J., Bryant, R. A., & Ehlers, A. (2003). Does early psychological intervention promote recovery from posttraumatic stress? *Psychological Science in the Public Interest, 4*(2), 47.
2. Reprinted from United States Department of Veterans Affairs, National Center for PTSD. (n.d.). DSM criteria for PTSD. Retrieved from www.ptsd.va.gov/professional/pages/dsm-iv-tr-ptsd.asp
3. Beigel, A., & Berren, M. R. (1985). Human-induced disasters. *Psychiatric Annals, 15*(2), 143–150; Horowitz, M. J. (1997). *Stress response syndromes: PTSD, grief, and adjustment disorders.* Lanham, MD: Jason Aronson.
4. Cohen, R. E., & Ahearn, F. L. (1980). *Handbook for mental health care of disaster victims.* Baltimore: Johns Hopkins University Press.
5. Adapted from Zimbardo, P. G., Johnson, R. L., & McCann, V. (2012). *Psychology: Core concepts* (7th ed.). Boston: Allyn & Bacon.

6. Eagleman, D. (2011). *Incognito: The secret lives of the brain.* New York: Pantheon, 1–2.

7. Bremner, J. D., Randall, P., Scott, T. M., Bronen, R. A., Seibyl, J. P., Southwick, S. M., . . . Innis, R. B. (1995). MRI-based measurement of hippocampal volume in patients with combat-related posttraumatic stress disorder. *American Journal of Psychiatry, 152,* 973–981; Fennema-Notestine, C., Stein, M. B., Kennedy, C. M., Archibald, S. L., & Jemigan, T. L. (2002). Brain morphometry in female victims of intimate partner violence with and without posttraumatic stress disorder. *Biological Psychiatry, 52,* 1089–1101; Gerber, D. J., Weintraub, A. H., Cusick, P. C., Ricci, P. E., & Whiteneck, G. G. (2004). Magnetic resonance imaging of traumatic brain injury: Relationship of T2*SE and T2GE to clinical severity and outcome. *Brain Injury, 18,* 1083–1097.

8. Kennedy, K. (2009, December 8). 2 studies: PTSD is chemical change in brain. *Air Force Times.* Retrieved from www.airforcetimes.com/news/2009/12/military_ptsd_diagnosis_120809w/

9. Pitman, R. K., Gilbertson, M. W., Gurvits, T. V., May, F. S., Lasko, N. B., Metzger, L. J., . . . Orr, S. P. (2006). Clarifying the origin of biological abnormalities in PTSD through the study of identical twins discordant for combat exposure. *Annals of the New York Academy of Sciences, 1071,* 242–254.

10. Kennedy, 2 studies; see also American College of Neuropsychopharmacology. (2009, December 8). Researchers use new techniques to assess PTSD: Findings from two studies with newly returning veterans presented. Press release. Available from www.acnp.org/; Murrough, J. W., Czermak, C., Henry, S., Nabulsi, N., Gallezot, J. D., Gueorguieva, R., . . . Neumaier, J. F. (2011). The effect of early trauma exposure on serotonin type 1b receptor expression revealed by reduced selective radioligand binding. *Archives of General Psychiatry, 68,* 892–900.

11. Blanco, C., Heimberg, R. G., Schneier, F. R., Fresco, D. M., Chen, H., Turk, C. L., . . . Liebowitz, M. R. (2010). A placebo-controlled

trial of phenelzine, cognitive behavioral group therapy and their combination for social anxiety disorder. *Archives of General Psychiatry, 67,* 286–295; Blanco, C., Schneier, F. R., Schmidt, A., Blanco-Jerez, C.-R., Marshall, R. D., Sanchez-Lacay, A., & Liebowitz, M. R. (2003). Pharmacological treatment of social anxiety disorder: A meta-analysis. *Depression and Anxiety, 18,* 29–40; Brent, D., Emslie, G., Clarke, G., Wagner, K. D., Asarnow, J. R., Keller, M., . . . Zelazny, J. (2008). Switching to another SSRI or to venlafaxine with or without cognitive behavioral therapy for adolescents with SSRI-resistant depression: The TORDIA randomized controlled trial. *Journal of the American Medical Association, 299,* 901–913; Fava, G. A., Rafanelli, C., Grandi, S., Conti, S., & Belluardo, P. (1998). Prevention of recurrent depression with cognitive behavioral therapy. *Archives of General Psychiatry, 55,* 816–820.

12. Society for Neuroscience. (2007, November 7). Biomarker for PTSD and why PTSD is so difficult to treat. *ScienceDaily.* Retrieved from www.sciencedaily.com /releases/2007/11/071107211450.htm

13. National Center for PTSD. (n.d.). Women, trauma and PTSD. Retrieved from www.ptsd.va.gov/public/pages/women-trauma-and-ptsd.asp

14. Our review of the cognitive processing therapy studies shows that a significant number of veterans drop out or fail to complete their study. No reason is given for why they failed to complete the study or why they dropped out. Statistical analyses were produced only on the program completers, which positively skewed the results. It would be instructive and responsible for these researchers to follow up with the "dropouts" to determine whether they were harmed by the process and the reason for their leaving the study.

15. Many studies have a large dropout rate of 20 percent up to 60 percent or greater. These dropouts are often not included in the final analysis, yielding unrealistically favorable results. A case in point in regard to dropout rates: Vietnam veteran Ed in Chapter Four

recently revealed that following his time perspective therapy treatment, he participated in a cognitive processing therapy (CPT) class with the VA. He reported that twelve veterans started his CPT class, but only four completed the class. This indicates a problem with either acceptability, compliance, or perceived efficacy.

16. Flora, S. R. (2007). *Taking America off of drugs: Why behavioral therapy is more effective for treating ADHD, OCD, depression and other psychological problems.* New York: State University of New York Press, 2.

17. Ibid., 4.

18. Barlow, D. H., Gorman, J. M., Shear, M. K., & Woods, S. W. (2000). Cognitive-behavioral therapy, imipramine, or their combination for panic disorder: A randomized controlled trial. *Journal of the American Medical Association, 283,* 2529–2536; Davidson, J. R., Foa, E. B., Huppert, J. D., Keefe, F. J., Franklin, M. E., Compton, J. S., . . . Gadde, K. M. (2004). Fluoxetine, comprehensive cognitive behavioral therapy, and placebo in generalized social phobia. *Archives of General Psychiatry, 61,* 1005–1013; Otto, M. W., McHugh, R. K., & Kantak, K. M. (2010). Combined pharmacotherapy and cognitive-behavioral therapy for anxiety disorders: Medication effects, glucocorticoids, and attenuated treatment outcomes. *Clinical Psychology: Science and Practice, 17*(2), 91–103.

19. Mitchell, J. T. (1983). When disaster strikes . . . the Critical Incident Stress Debriefing process. *Journal of Emergency Medical Services, 8*(1), 36–39.

20. Rose et al. (2001) concluded that psychological debriefing is not a useful treatment for PTSD prevention after traumatic incidents. Further, they suggest that compulsory debriefing of victims of trauma should not be conducted. Another meta-analysis revealed that trauma-exposed individuals who had not received such debriefing experienced reductions in PTSD symptoms, whereas those who had received this debriefing did not (van Emmerik, Kamphuis, Hulsbosch, & Emmelkamp, 2002). Cited in McNally

et al., Does early psychological intervention promote recovery from posttraumatic stress?

21. McNally et al., Does early psychological intervention promote recovery from posttraumatic stress? 45.

22. Holtzworth-Munroe, A., & Jacobson, N. S. (1985). Causal attributions of married couples: When do they search for causes? What do they conclude when they do? *Journal of Personality and Social Psychology, 48,* 1398–1412.

23. Zimbardo, P. G., & Boyd, J. N. (1999). Putting time in perspective: A valid, reliable individual-differences metric. *Journal of Personality and Social Psychology, 77,* 1271–1288.

24. National Japanese American Historical Society. (n.d.). Research on 100th/442nd Regimental Combat Team. Retrieved from www.nikkeiheritage.org/research/442.html

o chapter 2

1. Abridged from Zimbardo, P., & Boyd, J. (2008). *The Time Paradox: The new psychology of time that will change your life.* New York: Free Press, pp. 109–111.

2. Ibid.

3. Although the Swords find the transcendental future orientation fascinating, it is not discussed further in this book because they do not administer the Transcendental-future Time Perspective Inventory in their clinical practice. However, both the spiritual and secular aspects of the transcendental future time perspective are talked about during individual time perspective therapy sessions—especially when working with the older population or when dealing with the passing of a loved one.

4. Zimbardo & Boyd, *The Time Paradox.*

5. Lyons, O. (1980). An Iroquois perspective. In, & Vecsey, C., & Venables, R.W. (Eds.). American Indian Environments: Ecological Issues in Native American History (pp. 171–174). Syracuse, New York: Syracuse University Press, 173–174.

6. Zimbardo, P. G., & Boyd, J. N. (1999). Putting time in perspective: A valid, reliable individual-differences metric. *Journal of Personality and Social Psychology, 77,* 1271–1288; Zimbardo & Boyd, *The Time Paradox.*

7. Gonzalez, A., & Zimbardo, P. G. (1985). Time in perspective: The sense we learn early affects how we do our jobs and enjoy our pleasures. *Psychology Today, 19,* 21–26.

8. As of this writing, over thirty nations are participating in a cross-cultural sample that is being written for publication. All have scientifically validated the Zimbardo Time Perspective Inventory as a viable and useful psychological test. Additional translations are being added each year.

9. Due to the different measures in various scales, we've taken into account the dispersion of scores so that a 4.4 on the past negative is the 98th percentile, whereas it takes a 4.9 on the past positive to reach the 98th percentile.

10. Adapted from Zimbardo & Boyd, *The Time Paradox.*

● chapter 3

1. The Z Team is made up of Philip Zimbardo, PhD; Richard Sword, PhD; Rosemary Sword; Robert Masters; Mary Jo Masters; Brian Denney; Robert Hollis, PhD; Harold Hall, PhD; Judith Rocap, PhD; Mel Borins, MD; Larry Borins, MSW; Sarah Brunskill, MA; Marjan Haghighatgoo, MA; Martha Sword Ray, MEd; Anthony Ferreras, MS; Tiffany Dawson, MS; Michael Yannell; Elizabeth Sword; Ryan Daley; Noah Milich; and Paul Janes-Brown.

2. The 'halo effect' refers to the idea that global personality traits about a person (for example, she is friendly) influence judgments by others about that person's specific traits (therefore she is intelligent). Dean, J. (2007, October 31). The halo effect: When your own mind is a mystery. *PsyBlog.* Retrieved from www.spring.org.uk/2007/10/halo-effect-when-your-own-mind-is.php

3. The "placebo effect" refers to the subliminal expectation of getting well even if there is no medical basis. Niemi, M. (2009, February 25). Placebo effect: A cure in the mind. *Scientific American.* Available from www.scientificamerican.com/article.cfm?id=placebo-effect-a-cure-in-the-mind

4. Unrealistically favorable results are produced in many studies due to a large dropout rate (20 percent up to 60 percent) of participants; these dropouts are not included in the final analysis.

○ chapter 4

1. Epstein, J., & Miller, J. (2005). U.S. wars and post-traumatic stress disorder. *San Francisco Chronicle.* Retrieved from http://articles.sfgate.com/2005–06–22/news/17378506_1_ptsd-post-traumatic-stress-disorder-gulf-war-veterans; Gradus, J. L. (2011, December 20). Epidemiology of PTSD. Retrieved from www.ptsd.va.gov/professional/pages/epidemiological-facts-ptsd.asp

2. Daily Mail Reporter. (2011, November 3). One U.S. veteran attempts suicide every 80 minutes: Hidden tragedy of Afghanistan and Iraq wars. *Daily Mail.* Retrieved from www.dailymail.co.uk/news/article-2057061/One-U-S-veteran-attempts-suicide-80-minutes-Hidden-tragedy-Afghanistan-Iraq-wars.html#ixzz1h3TKI0Xv%20%20Accessed%20December%2020,%202011; Donnelly, J. (2011, January 24). More troops lost to suicide. *Congressional Quarterly.* Retrieved from www.congress.org/news/2011/01/24/more_troops_lost_to_suicide. According to Donnelly, "For the second year in a row, the U.S. military has lost more troops to suicide than it has to combat in Iraq and Afghanistan . . . Overall, the services reported 434 suicides by personnel on active duty, significantly more than the 381 suicides by active-duty personnel reported in 2009. The 2010 total is below the 462 deaths in combat, excluding accidents and illness. In 2009, active-duty suicides exceeded deaths in battle."

3. Classen, C., Butler, L. D., Koopman, C., Miller, E., DiMiceli, S., Giese-Davis, J., ... Spiegel, D. (2001). Supportive-expressive group therapy and distress in patients with metastatic breast cancer: A randomized clinical intervention trial. *Archives of General Psychiatry, 58,* 494–501.

4. DuRant, R. H., Cadenhead, C., Pendergrast, R. A., & Slavens, G. (1994). Factors associated with the use of violence among urban black adolescents. *American Journal of Public Health, 84,* 612–617; Glover, H. (1984). Themes of mistrust and the posttraumatic stress disorder in Vietnam veterans. *American Journal of Psychotherapy, 38*(3), 445– 452.

5. Lewis, R., personal communication, 2003–2009.

6. DaSilva, L., Sanson, A., Smart, D., & Toumbourou, J. (2004). Civic responsibility among Australian adolescents: Testing two competing models. *Journal of Community Psychology, 32,* 229–255.

7. Laffaye, C., Cavella, S., Drescher, K., & Rosen, C. (2008). Relationships among PTSD symptoms, social support, and support source in veterans with chronic PTSD. *Journal of Traumatic Stress, 21,* 394–401.

8. DaSilva et al., Civic responsibility among Australian adolescents.

9. Spiegel, A. (2010, December 4). Study: Female vets especially vulnerable to suicide. Retrieved from www.npr.org/2010/12/04/131797071/study-female-vets-especially-vulnerable-to-suicide

10. McFarland, B. H., Kaplan, M. S., & Huguet, N. (2010). Datapoints: Self-inflicted deaths among women with U.S. military service: A hidden epidemic? *Psychiatric Services, 61,* 1177.

11. Spiegel, Study.

12. Zimbardo, P. G. (2007). *The Lucifer effect: Understanding how good people turn evil.* New York: Random House. The Stanford Prison Experiment (SPE) was conducted at Stanford University in August 1971 by Philip Zimbardo, with graduate research assistants Craig Haney and Curtis Banks, in the basement of the Psychology Department in Jordan Hall. It has become one of the most cited studies in all social sciences, and even in the arts — there have been

several movies made about its theme, as well as a recent museum exhibit at DOX, Contemporary Arts Museum in Prague, Czech Republic. The study is often paired with Stanly Milgram's research on obedience to authority in the 1960s as evidence of situational power over individual behavior.

The SPE, funded by the U.S. Office of Naval Research, addressed the issue of situational and systemic power over individual behavior by randomly assigning twenty-four normal, healthy young college students to the roles of either prisoner or guard. They were chosen from among seventy-five men who answered an ad in the Palo Alto city newspaper based on psychological assessments and clinical interviews. Although it was planned to last for two weeks, the study was terminated after only six days because a number of the "prisoners" were suffering extreme emotional distress and had to be released early. Their unexpectedly severe negative reactions were in response to the brutal, even sadistic behavior of many of the "guards." Even though all the participants knew it was just an experiment, that reality faded in face of the relentless power of the "guards," who quickly helped create a prison run by psychologists.

For more information on the SPE, see the remarkably comprehensive Web site developed by Scott Plous, www.prisonexp.org, and also the detailed day-by-day analysis of the descent into hell recounted in Zimbardo's book *The Lucifer Effect: Understanding How Good People Turn Evil,* with its associated Web site: www.lucifereffect.com.

Although this experiment was performed more than forty years ago, evidence of its continuing relevance and fascination for the public abounds: as of this writing there are seventy-three thousand Google citations about it. Of twenty-five million hits for the word "experiment," the SPE is the second-most-visited site after Kids Science Experiments. It is also in the number four and number seven positions for Wikipedia and Movie links, respectively. Ordinary people can be seduced or corrupted into doing evil deeds, usually starting small and then increasing in severity when immersed in social situations that encourage or make possible crossing the fine line between good and evil. Many institutional settings, such as nursing departments in hospitals, clinics, or residential care facilities, have the potential to transform what should be good service to clients and patients into indifferent or even abusive treatment when any or all of the following situational forces are operating: obedience to authority (doctors, administrators); dehumanization (of patients, clients); group pressures to conform; anonymity of staff and patients; diffusion of personal responsibility; and other processes identified in *The Lucifer Effect* and at www.lucifereffect.com. We are all vulnerable to those insidious influences — the power of the situation — unless the system that creates, maintains, and justifies them is willing to change and challenge these influences' operation. For more on the power of the situation, visit this forum: www.thesituationist.wordpress.com.

13. 100th Battalion, 442nd Infantry. (n.d.). Retrieved from www.globalsecurity.org/military/agency/army/100 – 442in.htm. The 442nd Regimental Combat Team was deactivated in 1946 but reactivated in 1947 as the U.S. Army Reserve. It was deployed in 1968 during the Vietnam War and again in 2004 for duty in Iraq, where soldiers came from across the United States, including Hawaii, the Philippines, Samoa, and Palau. Battalion headquarters is at Fort Shafter, Hawaii, with subordinate units based in Hilo, Hawaii; American Samoa; Saipan; and Guam.

14. Epstein & Miller, U.S. wars and post-traumatic stress disorder; Gradus, Epidemiology of PTSD.

○ chapter 5

1. Blanchard, E. B., & Hickling, E. J. (1997). *After the crash: Psychological assessment and treatment of survivors of motor vehicle accidents.* Washington, DC: American Psychological Association.

2. Sexual Trauma & Counseling Center. (n.d.). Statistics. Retrieved from www.sexualtraumacenter.org/statistics.html

3. Elias, M. (2008, October 28). Post-traumatic stress is a war within for military and civilians. *USA Today,* 1. Retrieved from www.usatoday.com/news/health/2008–10–26-PTSD-main_N.htm. "About 20% of those in car accidents that caused injuries have PTSD a year after the accident, suggests a long-term study in Albany, N.Y. There were 2.5 million people injured in car crashes last year, according to the National Highway Traffic Safety Administration, so many are at risk."

4. National Institute of Mental Health. (2010, August 31). Post-traumatic stress disorder (PTSD). Retrieved from http://nimh.nih.gov/health/publications/post-traumatic-stress-disorder-ptsd/complete-index.shtml

5. Federal regulations prevent Disaster Medical Assistance Team–Hawaii and Disaster Mortuary Operational Response Team–Region IX team members from disclosing the location of their deployments. Further, they do not permit sharing specific details of disaster response missions to protect confidentiality. This being the case, specific information about the incident described here cannot be divulged.

6. Salazar, B., personal communication, 2011. Barbara Salazar is the administrative officer, Disaster Mortuary Operational Response Team–Region IX, National Disaster Medical System.

o chapter 6

1. Eastman, Q. (2011, February 24). Study: Stress hormone linked to PTSD found in women only. *Emory Report.* Retrieved from www.emory.edu/EMORY_REPORT/stories/2011/02/research_study_stress_hormone_ptsd_women.html?utm_source=; National Center for PTSD. (n.d.). Women, trauma and PTSD. Retrieved from www.ptsd.va.gov/public/pages/women-trauma-and-ptsd.asp

2. Melnick, M. (2011, February 25). Why are women more vulnerable to PTSD than men? *Time: Health-land.* Retrieved from http://healthland.time.com/2011/02/25/are-women-more-vulnerable-to-ptsd-than-men/?xid=huffpo-direct

3. Miller, G. (2011, February 23). A marker for PTSD in women? *Science.* Retrieved from http://news.sciencemag.org/sciencenow/2011/02/a-marker-for-ptsd-in-women.html

4. Melnick, Why are women more vulnerable to PTSD than men?

⊙ appendix A

1. Norton, P. J., & Price, E. C. (2007). A meta-analytic review of adult cognitive-behavioral treatment outcome across the anxiety disorders. *Journal of Nervous and Mental Disease, 195,* 521–531.

2. Bradley, R., Greene, J., Russ, E., Dutra, L., & Westen, D. (2005). A multidimensional meta-analysis of psychotherapy for PTSD. *American Journal of Psychiatry, 162,* 214–227.

3. Sherman, J. J. (1998). Effects of psychotherapeutic treatments for PTSD: A meta-analysis of controlled clinical trials. *Journal of Traumatic Stress, 11,* 413–435.

4. Arch, J. J., & Craske, M. G. (2009). First line treatment: A critical appraisal of cognitive behavioral therapy developments and alternatives. *Psychiatric Clinics of North America, 32,* 525–547.

5. Durham, R. C., Chambers, J. A., Power, K. G., Sharp, D. M., Macdonald, R. R., Major, K. A., ... Gumley, A. I. (2005). Long-term outcome of cognitive behaviour therapy clinical trials in central Scotland. *Health Technology Assessment, 9*(42), 1–174. Retrieved from www.hta.ac.uk/fullmono/mon942.pdf

6. Gould, R. A., Safren, S. A., O'Neill Washington, D., & Otto, M. W. (2004). A meta-analytic review of cognitive-behavioral treatments. In R. G. Heimberg, C. L. Turk, & D. S. Mennin (Eds.), *Generalized anxiety disorder: Advances in research and practice* (pp. 248–264). New York: Guilford Press.

7. Davidson, J. R. (1992). Drug therapy of post-traumatic stress disorder. *British Journal of Psychiatry, 160,* 309–314; Davidson, J. R., Kudler, H. S., Saunders, W. B., Erickson, L., Smith, R. D., Stein, R. M., ... Cavenar, J.O., Jr. (1993). Predicting response to amitriptyline in post-traumatic stress disorder. *American Journal of Psychiatry, 150,* 1024–1029; Davidson, J. R., Weisler, R. H., Malik, M. L., & Connor, K. M. (1998). Treatment of posttraumatic stress disorder with nefazodone. *International Clinical Psychopharmacology, 13*(3), 111–113.

8. Bleich, A., Siegel, B., Garb, R., & Lerer, B. (1986). Post-traumatic stress disorder following combat exposure: Clinical features and psychopharmacological treatment. *British Journal of Psychiatry, 149,* 365–369.

9. Bryant, R. A., & Harvey, A. G. (2000). *Acute stress disorder: A handbook of theory, assessment, and treatment.* Washington, DC: American Psychological Association.

10. National Center for PTSD. (n.d.). Cautions regarding cognitive-behavioral interventions provided within a month of trauma. Retrieved from www.ptsd.va.gov/professional/pages/cbi-after-trauma.asp

11. Bradley, Greene, Russ, Dutra, & Westen, A multidimensional meta-analysis of psychotherapy for PTSD.

○ appendix B

1. Sword, R. M., Sword, R.K.M., Brunskill, S. R., Ferreras, A. C., & Zimbardo, P. G. (2012). Time perspective therapy: A new time-based metaphor therapy for PTSD. Unpublished raw data and journal article.

2. American Psychiatric Association. (2000). *Diagnostic and statistical manual of mental disorders* (4th ed, Text rev.). Washington, DC: Author, 467–468.

3. Classen, C., Butler, L. D., Koopman, C., Miller, E., DiMiceli, S., Giese-Davis, J., ... Spiegel, D. (2001). Supportive-expressive

group therapy and distress in patients with metastatic breast cancer: A randomized clinical intervention trial. *Archives of General Psychiatry, 58,* 494–501; Foy, D. W., Glynn, S. M., Shnurr, P. P., Jankowski, M. K., Wattenberg, M. S., Weiss, D. S., et al. (2004). Group therapy. In E. B. Foa, T. M. Keane, & M. J. Friedman (Eds.), *Effective treatments for PTSD* (pp. 155–175). New York: Guilford Press.

4. Brunskill, S. R., Ferreras, A. C., & Zimbardo, P. G. (2010, April). They don't understand: Social intensity desire phenomenon and military families. Poster presented at the 90th Annual Convention of the Western Psychological Association, Cancun, Mexico; Zimbardo, P. G., Ferreras, A. C., & Brunskill, S. R. (2011). Social Intensity Syndrome Phenomenon Theory and its effects on the individual: Standardization of a theory. Unpublished raw data and journal article.

5. DuRant, R. H., Cadenhead, C., Pendergrast, R. A., & Slavens, G. (1994). Factors associated with the use of violence among urban black adolescents. *American Journal of Public Health, 84,* 612–617; Grover, S. (2005). Advocacy by children as a causal factor in promoting resilience. *Childhood, 12,* 527–538.

6. Brunskill et al., They don't understand; Zimbardo et al., Social Intensity Syndrome Phenomenon Theory and its effects on the individual.

7. Da Silva, L., Sanson, A., Smart, D., & Toumbourou, J. (2004). Civic responsibility among Australian adolescents: Testing two causal models. *Journal of Community Psychology, 32,* 229–255.

8. Laffaye, C., Cavella, S., Drescher, K., & Rosen, C. (2008, August). Relationships among PTSD symptoms, social support, and support source in veterans with chronic PTSD. *Journal of Traumatic Stress, 21,* 394–401.

9. Brunskill et al., They don't understand; Da Silva et al., Civic responsibility among Australian adolescents; Sword et al., Time perspective therapy; Zimbardo et al., Social Intensity Syndrome Phenomenon Theory and its effects on the individual.

o appendix C

1. The "extreme/panic" designation indicates that the client's anxiety was so severe as to cause panic or anxiety attacks.
2. Randall was not given psychological tests during his first round of therapy, which commenced in 2003, as it was not the standard practice of this office until 2006.

index

C